Management by Seclusion

Management by Seclusion

A Critique of World Bank Promises to End Global Poverty

GLYNN COCHRANE

berghahn
NEW YORK · OXFORD
www.berghahnbooks.com

First published in 2019 by
Berghahn Books
www.berghahnbooks.com

Library of Congress Cataloging-in-Publication Data

Names: Cochrane, Glynn, author.
Title: Management by Seclusion: A Critique of World Bank Promises to End Global
   Poverty / Glynn Cochrane.
Description: New York: Berghahn Books, 2019. | Includes bibliographical references and
   index.
Identifiers: LCCN 2018053522 (print) | LCCN 2018057230 (ebook) |
   ISBN 9781789201321 (ebook) | ISBN 9781789201314 (hardback: alk. paper) |
   ISBN 9781789201338 (pbk.: alk. paper)
Subjects: LCSH: World Bank—Developing countries. | Economic assistance—
   Developing countries. | Poverty—Developing countries.
Classification: LCC HG3881.5.W57 (ebook) | LCC HG3881.5.W57 C64 2019 (print) |
   DDC 332.1/532091724—dc23
LC record available at https://lccn.loc.gov/2018053522

British Library Cataloguing in Publication Data

A catalogue record for this book is available from the British Library.

ISBN 978-1-78920-131-4 hardback
ISBN 978-1-78920-133-8 paperback
ISBN 978-1-78920-132-1 ebook

For Alison

CONTENTS

ACKNOWLEDGMENTS

Without my wife Alison's help and encouragement, I doubt there would be a book. I am also grateful to Barbara Miller of The George Washington University and Deanna Kemp of the University of Queensland for advice and encouragement and to Richard Perry of St Lawrence University who has helped me better understand Indigenous peoples. I also want to acknowledge the help of an old friend who should remain anonymous since he still works at the World Bank.

Over the period covered by the book I have had the privilege of knowing public servants who did unforgettable things: Donald Dunham, author of *Envoy Extraordinary*, who resigned his post in the US Foreign Service because, having lived overseas for many years, he no longer felt he knew enough about the country he represented; junior civil servants from the Olduvai Gorge Museum, in the Ngorongoro Conservation Area of Tanzania, who, on their own initiative, made the journey to Dar-es-Salaam to ask if there was any way the civil service reform program I was working with could provide funds to run the museum's air conditioning because they feared for their collection of priceless skulls and artefacts (shortly afterward the J. Paul Getty Museum came to their rescue).

I am grateful to an anonymous reviewer for a useful suggestion about the book's title.

INTRODUCTION

Will more money and better policies produce the massive social change that global poverty alleviation by 2030 would require? Highly unlikely. Poverty has not been eliminated in the rich countries and the elimination of global poverty would require nothing short of a worldwide revolution: something very large like the impact of socialism would surely be needed. Global change would need, on a global level, the inspiration and leadership of a Gandhi or a Kemal Atatürk. The cultural change associated with the rise of Islam yielded the logic of mathematics, advances in medical knowledge, and splendid architecture. Islamic expansion in the sixth and seventh centuries, Scandinavian expansion in the ninth and tenth centuries, the rise of capitalism, and the rise of socialism all testify to the importance of cultural and belief factors that cannot easily be harnessed by the World Bank's burgeoning bureaucracy.

This book looks at World Bank poverty alleviation over a fifty-year period in order to try to gain a deeper level of understanding about the factors that have influenced the approach and the results. The International Bank for Reconstruction and Development (IBRD), as the World Bank is formally known, was established in 1944 at the Bretton Woods Conference at the end of World War II by the victorious allies and it is an organ of the United Nations. The World Bank now has 180 member countries; under the Articles of Agreement, which have undergone remarkably little amendment, the business of the World Bank is the making of sound loans for economic development. When it began in 1947 its immediate task was to help overcome the impact of war in Europe. The first loans of the new institution were made to Britain, France, and other European countries; loans to the Republic of Ireland were made until the early 1970s.[1] The Board of Governors of the World Bank comprises civil servants who represent member countries. Decisions about lending and new policies are made using a weighted voting system, one that favors France, the UK, and the US in a manner not unlike that used by the UN Security Council.

In 1973, at the same time that the fight against global poverty began, Ireland started to get money for underdeveloped areas of the country from the European Union (EU). Ireland was at that time also a recipient of World Bank lending. Since 1973 the Irish have received $28 billion (all dollars are US dollars unless indicated otherwise) from the EU. During that same period the 2 billion poor of the world have received around $280 billion from the World Bank. This means that the world's 2 billion poor were allocated around $140 per capita (of course neither World Bank nor EU money is evenly spread) from the World Bank and the Irish were allocated around $9,000 per capita from the EU. However, Ireland still has poverty in its cities and in the countryside.

By looking at what seem to have been the institution's major intellectual, organizational, and management challenges I hope to show how the World Bank has made use of the relationship skills of anthropology and other disciplines over the course of the past fifty years. Finding a way to explain what has shaped the treatment of social factors in an economic institution such as the World Bank is not easy.[2] This massive bureaucracy has now completed over 13,000 development projects. In 1968 the World Bank had just under 800 staff in Washington; in September 2017 there were 9,150 US-based staff and 6,900 in country offices of 180 country members. Although this book mentions my early attempt to introduce anthropology to the World Bank my main concern is with the much broader field of poverty alleviation.[3] (See appendix A "Engagement Issues for Anthropology.") This includes the idea of social development, the use of social science and technical expertise, and public administration. I also draw on my work in the private sector on the introduction of a systematic approach to social relationships in the community.[4]

World Bank Presidents, from Robert McNamara to the present incumbent, Jim Yong Kim, have all shared a keen interest in expanding the institution's loan portfolio in order to achieve the elimination of global poverty.[5] In the 1980s World Bank economists concluded that, given enough money, the institution could defeat impoverishment in the poor countries because poverty was a fairly homogenous category for which objective quantifiable cash income/material consumption standards could be developed. Those with incomes below $1.90 a day were below the poverty line and labeled the poorest on the planet.[6] The economists saw poverty as the material deprivation of the individual, arising from poor utilization of capital and technology that resulted in low labor productivity; they believed that cash or material consumption standards could be developed and assessed by means of household surveys.[7] Of course, economic development can raise incomes but not always in any direct and predictable way and as a result there was, and still is, no certainty of ending poverty.

Moreover, those calculating poverty reduction in their Washington offices on the basis of global statistical probabilities based on possibly statistically unreliable household surveys cannot assume what a poor person in some distant society feels about his or her poverty.

The most important source of data on living standards has been household surveys but these have not been regularly or reliably carried out in countries with poor communications and difficult terrain such as Papua New Guinea, the Amazon, or central Africa.[8] Expenditure data would have been much more useful than income data but it is difficult to collect such data if the poor do not use money. The global enumerators of the World Bank did not pay much attention to these realities—and to be honest it is not something that they pay much attention to in most poor countries—because, as in other poor countries, they assumed that what would be best would be the loans and projects they were dishing out in other countries.

Global assumptions made about income and poverty made little sense in Papua New Guinea or other countries where it was difficult to run around with a clipboard and a handheld calculator. The most common aid agency approach—and it is awesomely complicated and cumbersome—to defining absolute poverty lines is to estimate the cost in each region or at each date of a certain bundle of goods necessary to attain basic consumption needs (this is called the basic needs approach). This might be fine in Michigan or Biarritz but when there was no shop and no market what did one measure? How was one to know who was eating small jungle animals called cus or crocodile or fruit bats or grubs from a rotting sago palm? To measure food energy requirements, agencies needed to make an assumption about food energy levels that could maintain the body's metabolic rate at rest. Once the energy intake had been determined and its cost calculated, an allowance for nonfood spending could be added by finding the total expenditure level at which a person typically reached the level of the poverty line. In the highlands a man might work in his gardens for a while, then he might sit and think for a day or two. He might go to war at the weekend with his neighbors or go walkabout covering long distances and traversing mountain ranges.[9]

The only obvious example of global measurement may be greenhouse gas emissions, as their effects are felt throughout the planet. Looked at closely, homogenized global poverty may make no more sense than would global weather. It is clear when one examines different societies and different cultural contexts that not all poverty is the same; this makes it difficult to compare all poverty as an unbounded set.

The World Bank's economists saw the evolution of social security in three stages: The first stage was the provision of relief for the poor by private voluntary groups. Stage two saw the evolution of social insurance schemes designed to provide compulsory benefits for the poor, the sick, and individuals who are out of work. More recently the aim has been to prevent poverty or to cushion the impact of poverty on target groups. The major nineteenth-century systems of poor relief in Western Europe and North America took a hard line with poverty. They only provided help as a last resort. This policy was intended to discourage idleness. Although many changes in welfare have taken place in response to social and economic changes in the industrialized societies, there is little or no agreement in the industrialized countries that the state should automatically provide relief funds to all who are impoverished.

Trickle Down

Many development professionals had assumed that top-down solutions for poverty had gone out of style when, in 1973, the US Congress adopted the New Directions in Foreign Aid as a result of a realization that constructing dams and building roads helped the economy but the benefits of this growth did not necessarily trickle down to those at the bottom of society.[10] Social scientists such as David Leonard produced books with titles like *Reaching the Peasant Farmer*.[11] Had one looked carefully at World Bank lending a few years after global poverty alleviation became popular, it would have become obvious that the World Bank had not given up on infrastructural development and was instead regularly doubling and quadrupling its lending for dams and railways, while telling us that these contributions to economic development were lifting millions out of poverty.

The World Bank's global poverty strategy envisaged that a massive project bombardment would improve health, education, and welfare. In the past, some bombardment has worked and, when there was a failure to properly consider the importance of human factors in technological change, some has not. Early on, the introduction of agricultural practices in Africa resulted in a massive need for resettlement because the change in farming practices caused massive soil erosion in the fragile ecosystems of Africa. Even the introduction of cash cropping, which seemed a good idea at the time, fostered the break-up of traditional forms of agriculture and the breakdown of traditional social organization.[12] While it is true that a rising economic tide can, in theory, raise all ships, that is not the reality for many of the very poorest who remain stuck in the mud of despair because they are unable, or do not wish, to take advantage of uplifting opportunities. For example, some homeless people in big cities would rather face a terribly cold night than take advantage of a shelter provided by city government or a charity.

Nevertheless, Robert McNamara and later World Bank CEOs were persuaded that the homogenous poverty paradigm could drive global poverty elimination in which World Bank economic development could play a major role.[13] Thereafter, the poverty numbers and their reduction goal were repeated so often it looked as if the World Bank was engaged, and believed, in statistical evangelism. However, the connection between economic growth and ending poverty remains an unproven assumption, one lacking authoritative empirical verification.[14] The World Bank has continued to say that, by doing more of what the institution has been doing, hard-core poverty can be ended. However, using the same economic development approaches that have had an impact on easy-to-reach poverty will not necessarily work with hard-core poverty unless the World Bank has discovered how to ensure that economic growth does not produce increasing inequality in society. Therefore, the promise to eliminate poverty rests on shaky ground though the idea that economic growth could sometimes, and did have, an impact on individual incomes and poverty was essentially correct.

With the use of homogenized poverty and statistical evangelism the World Bank's poverty business boomed. The dreams and aspirations of poor people all over the world could apparently be centralized, understood, and responded to with money and economic advice from Washington. Global poverty elimination became part of the World Bank's DNA, an article of faith encouraging the institution to behave like an "organized charity, scrimped and iced and all in the name of a cautious statistical Christ."[15] The promise to be able to eliminate poverty enabled the World Bank to collect and spend larger and larger amounts of money.

Management by Seclusion

Use of the poverty paradigm generated what one very senior staff member called management by seclusion, because in order to raise and spend more and more money World Bank staff had to spend more and more time in their offices.[16] Homogenized poverty made it look as if the problems of the world's poorest could indeed be addressed by World Bank employees in their offices without the need for close contact with the poorest: If a person has a low income he or she must earn more money. If a person is illiterate he or she needs to learn to read and write in primary schooling. If a person is malnourished he or she needs food. If a person has too many children, then birth control is necessary. The same approach can be seen with poor educationalists who believe you can wrap a whole child up in a test score. The result of describing the problems of the very poor in this manner is that solutions then become a matter of supply without any encouragement to learn about the poor. The global programs promised progress whose benefits were thought to be so obvious that only corrupt or incompetent or lazy leadership in the poor countries could frustrate their adoption.

The poverty data that were then collected by the World Bank UN agencies reduced poor countries to a series of tables and materialistic progress targets based on the idea that the way of life that was best was that of the industrialized countries.[17] Like the Victorians who used to wonder why savages had not made it to civilization, World Bank economists wondered why the socioeconomic performance of poor countries is so far behind their own. Every country in the world had more or less the same goals and more or less the same problems. If they did not see that, then they had to be helped to see things the right way. Wean them away from separateness! Forward the day when they followed their own progress up and down the paper world! Countries that were unique were statistically unique. They had phenomenal high or low growth rates, high or low capital output ratios, high or low rates of privatization, high or low inflows of foreign investment, high or low debt service ratios. Poor countries do not advance by means of coffee-table league tables, nor does our understanding of those countries' problems.[18]

Working for the United Nations Development Programme (UNDP) and posted as an adviser to the Prime Minister of the Cook Islands, Sir Geoffrey Henry, in Rarotonga in the 1990s I took a special interest in the remote islands of the northern Cook Islands. I found it amazing that the Cook Islands were ranked by UNDP's Human Development Index as number 101 in the world with a 0.829 score similar to that of the US Virgin Islands and American Samoa. This was a tremendous distortion because the northern Cook Islands were like the poor south in Italy, way below the national average that reflected the rich north of Italy. The main islands in the southern Cooks, including Rarotonga, had high income from tourism and even a flourishing offshore banking industry not unlike like that of the Cayman Islands.

The northern group of small islands, which have fewer than 1,000 residents, are located 1,000 miles from the capital, Rarotonga. Having lived and worked in Africa and Asia I knew that remote islands had some of the world's poorest people whose lives illustrate some of the misunderstandings that can occur when national statistics are used as an indication of poverty.[19] Incomes in the northern group are about half the national average. Educational and health statistics for the nation are also of little help in understanding low local standards, and quick missions by UN agencies to assess poverty seldom get it right. In the Northern Cook Islands, poverty is not low income: it is the absence of family members through migration, premature death from illness, or accident at sea.[20] Aid can't do much about that, but neighbors can. The wealth of the area is not its beauty or the strength of its people: it is the strength of the community. The local community is solid. It has strong religious beliefs, low rates of crime or deviance, and a limited ambition to join the outside world. In such small communities, poverty has a very local meaning: it depends on local perception, history, personalities, epidemics, and cyclones.[21]

Everything in the Northern Group is below the national average: education is weak, the diet is inadequate, moneymaking opportunities don't exist, and freedom of expression is constrained by kinship ties. Islanders don't seem interested in preserving the environment—they eat any birds they can trap including rare birds, overfish the lagoons, dump rubbish in the lagoons, leave old refrigerators lying around, and heave old batteries into streams. There is not much interest in exploiting solar energy potential, hydroponic gardening, microfinance, or mainstreaming women.

The Social and Cultural Meanings of Poverty

What was missing from World Bank poverty alleviation was information showing what monetary incomes meant to local people in different cultural contexts.[22] A hundred years ago Seebohm Rowntree discovered that in Britain to be without shoes in one community in the north of England was to be regarded as poor while in another community only those with no money were considered poor.[23] In Colombo, Sri Lanka, I found poverty associated with the ability to buy female sanitary napkins; in Latin America poorly nourished dogs can be an indication of poverty; in Asia poverty can be gauged by looking at the sizing of goods offered for sale in stores—not a large bag of rice but a small bag, not a packet of cigarettes but a few or even a single cigarette. In other areas poverty can be measured by a downturn in sales of cement or roofing iron, the sale of electrical spares, or motor car spare parts. (See appendix B "The Culture of Poverty Debate.")[24]

Is the Salvation Army wrong, and are faith organizations and social workers wrong, when they suppose that it is necessary to establish and maintain a relationship with a poor person in order to provide help that works? Poor people suffer from relationship poverty, the very poorest even more so, and this is also a missing element in the quantitative approach to global poverty alleviation. The more severe the poverty, the greater the degree of social disconnectedness for the individual involved. Social atrophy, which accompanies poverty, can affect speech, food preparation, personal hygiene, and other kinds of behavior whose form and content are derived from social interaction. Poverty occurs in society, but it is often not of society. As with HIV/AIDS, its growth cuts the individual off from society.[25] It has many forms, some controllable, some not, some completely debilitating, some not. In poor communities the social relationships that exist may be strained, fractured, or broken; we need to know what is required for their repair and strengthening.[26]

Relationships are essential to bring about an active process of give and take between aid personnel and the very poorest so that those in need become fellow workers and are considered to be part of the solution rather than continuing to be seen as the obstacle to progress. The most basic need is for materialism. Though of course materialism is important it is often, as many wars have demonstrated, less of a priority than self-assertion and self-expression within a familiar social and cultural context. The poorest people may want some of the advantages of technology, such as better health and education but, inevitably, they will wish to make use of them in a rhythm of their life and in the society that they have inherited, even if it is a modified society.[27]

To affect poverty the World Bank has to use the relationships and connections between the well-off as well as relationships between the well-off and the poor. The poor are embedded in society and in its relationships. Some of these relationships involve old people, some involve young people, and some involve those who cannot communicate or who are in institutions. Hoping that a portion of the gains from economic development will reach the very poorest may be optimistic. The successful redistribution of wealth relies on a redistribution of skills and knowledge. The rich are rich because they have the most skills and knowledge and, in most cases, they have little or no intention of passing those advantages on to the poorest people.

Ten years after writing a report on the use of anthropology in World Bank project operations in 1973 I spent a sabbatical year at the World Bank in 1983 looking at the potential use of development administration.[28] I remember there was a person who was homeless living on the hot air grate in front of the old "A" building and another who lived on another hot air grill on 23rd Street, right next to the State Department building, which housed US Agency for International Development (USAID).[29] Inside these two agencies officials were trying to reach the poor all over the world, while outside was a homeless person we all walked past each day. What was happening in offices inside the building helped poor countries and potential contributors to believe that the aid agencies had cracked the poverty problem and that their World League tables showed the winners and the losers.

The UN Children's Fund (UNICEF) has to use relationships to reach needy children since needy children are not all neatly assembled and waiting in a school playground for help to arrive. It is necessary to first reach families, social groups, faith and political organizations, as well as government ministries in order to be able to gain contact with children. In the case of the World Bank, the poor are no easier to identify and reach than children; the poor of the world are not a discrete, distinct, and visible category. They are not fruit on the lower branches of a tree nor are they ripe fruit lying on the ground, easy to pick up.

The India Famine Commission of 1880 faced this problem of identifying who should be helped and how they could be identified, saying

> We have to consider the manner in which the proper recipients of the public charity can be most effectually ascertained. The problem to be solved is how to avoid the risk of indiscriminate and demoralising profusion on the one hand, and of insufficient and niggardly assistance on the other—how to relieve all who really need relief, and to waste as little public money as possible in the process. Where limited numbers have to be dealt with, and there is a numerous and efficient staff of officials, it may be possible to ascertain by personal inquiry the circumstances of every applicant for relief sufficiently for the purpose of admitting or rejecting his claim. But in an Indian famine the Government has to deal, not with limited numbers, but with millions of people, and the official machinery at its command, however strengthened for the occasion, will inevitably be inadequate to the task of accurately testing the individual necessities of so great a multitude. Nor again is it possible to entrust the administration of public charity to a subordinate agency without providing sufficient checks against dishonesty and neglect on the part of its members. Some safeguards then are essential in the interests of the destitute people no less than of the public treasury, and they are best found in laying down certain broad self-acting tests by which necessity may be proved, and which may, irrespective of any other rule of selection, entitle to relief the person who submits to them. . . . The chief of these tests, and the only one which in our opinion it is ordinarily desirable to enforce, is the demand of labour commensurate in each case with the labourer's powers, in return for a wage sufficient for the purposes of maintenance but not more. This system is applicable, of course, only to those from whom labour can reasonably be required. The great bulk of the applicants for relief being thus provided for, we believe that it will be possible for an efficient staff of officers to control with success the grant of relief, on the basis of personal injury and knowledge of the individual circumstances of each applicant, among the comparatively small numbers of destitute persons to whom the test of labour cannot be applied.[30]

The $1.90 per day definition of poverty ignores the role of subsistence and kinship, and has little utility for an anthropologist. Some individuals are poor because they are mentally ill, some are poor because they are lazy, some are poor because they are physically handicapped. The more severe the poverty, the greater the likelihood of social isolation. Extreme poverty can affect the ability to speak, to prepare food, or to look after basic hygiene. Many of the things that poor people do not have, besides purchasing power, are those things the rest of society takes completely for granted.

Many matters that affect the well-being of very poor people are not in the market, such as cultural integrity and social or community solidarity, parent–child relationships, or religious attitudes. The performance of traditional rituals can be thought of as income. Similarly, health, nutrition, and education benefits are not materialistic or quantifiable. Individual money incomes may be high or low, a fact not easily or obviously related to the availability of and satisfaction with health, education, or nutrition services. These group sentiments are characteristic of many traditional societies and, once eroded, cannot easily be replaced. Income distribution figures do not usually show how income is distributed with respect to variables such as ethnicity, social class, education, aptitude, geographical location, and so on.

Anthropological fieldwork confirmed the fact that culture provided the essential glue that bound members of society together. Culture animated the social relationships between members of society that persisted through time. Anthropologists celebrated cultural difference—the unique cultural heritage of each society—by showing how each society had unique features. They were able to show that, far from being pre-scientific, magic and witchcraft, and taboos and sacrifices, had their uses. Culture was no longer seen as a constraint, but instead provided an explanation as to how the world started and mankind developed. Culture provided the basis for law and order and governance, hope that danger and threats could be managed, that crops would grow, and that disaster could be kept at bay.

The homogenous poverty paradigm treated social and cultural features as if they were extrinsic variables, something that could be added to the design of a project after the important technical decisions had been made. Anthropologists saw social factors as intrinsic variables that should be a part of the basic analysis. That led them to collect as many facts as possible and to have those facts suggest the appropriateness of any theory. This was a quite different approach to that of the environmentalist or the economist who started with a good hunch that they hoped could quickly be supported by data.[31]

The failure to account for cultural difference was also a defect in Victorian thinking about traditional societies. The fundamental error made by Victorian anthropology, and now World Bank thinking, was the failure to ensure that behavior was first understood in the social and cultural context of which it formed a part.[32] In 1890 the anthropologist Sir James Frazer published the first two volumes of his epic book, *The Golden Bough*. When he learned that individuals all over the world jumped over bonfires, Sir James assumed that all bonfire jumping had the same meaning. However, even within continental Europe, the meanings attached to bonfire jumping varied. In Russia, bonfire jumping might signify a man's wish for spiritual cleansing and good health; in Portugal, it is a woman's wish to find a marriage partner. The Victorian approach could be amusing as, for example, when practitioners went looking for accounts of cures for jaundice that used gold or when they tried to confirm stories of Greek women who ate ravens' eggs as a way of begetting black-haired children.[33]

Sir James is known as an armchair anthropologist because he designed questionnaires on the basis of reflection in his study and sent them to reliable travelers and businesses in the hope that, once completed, they would confirm what his original thinking supposed to be the case. When asked by a visitor if he had ever met any of the "savages" he had described so convincingly, Sir James replied, "Good heavens, no!" The discipline improved after anthropologists ventured out of their offices and began to visit and get to know local people. Fieldwork and participant observation methods were developed that required living in a community for several years, and learning the language and customs of the community they were trying to understand.

Like the Victorians, World Bank staff do not think it necessary to establish contact with communities or to leave their offices in Washington, DC, to meet and get to know communities. Like the Victorians, World Bank staff lack knowledge of local languages and cultures and so are forced to construct their survey questionnaires on the basis of armchair reflection without necessarily knowing whether they are taking reports of this or that behavior quite out of their social context. Questionnaire responses are used to produce league tables whose numbers and rankings convey an impression that they have captured community reality. In these league tables, it is assumed that every company (and every community) in the world should have more or less the same goals and should address more or less the same problems. Debate has been influenced by the World Bank's domination of economic thinking and the continued implication that poverty needs a quantitative approach.[34]

Why Believe in Poverty Elimination?

How is it that sensible citizens in rich countries, citizens who know that poverty has not ended in their own countries, have come to believe that poverty in the poor countries can be ended? There has always seemed to me to be something slightly millenarian about claims to be able to eliminate global poverty, and the pursuit of this dream has not always had the intended results.[35] Ending poverty has become an emotion that is lived by its supporters rather than an experience that can be squared with the views of those with hands-on experience of alleviating grassroots poverty in either poor or rich countries. Economists claim their ambitions are science-based. The industrialized country belief in the omnipotence of science, including the science of economics, has been presented as the antidote to the evils of colonialism and the slow pace of change in the poor countries.

Ask a sensible citizen in any society how many poor people they can help to escape poverty and what resources will be necessary and they will think of poor people in terms of the severity of their affliction. Some of this poverty they will see as God's will, something that neither they nor the suffering can alter. Others they will consider beyond help because of infirmity or addiction to drugs or alcohol. They will see these poor people in terms of their social situation: Are they individuals? in families? heads of households? and so on. They will identify people they know and believe could be helped as well as those who are beyond help. They will see the faces of the poor, remember who they are, be able to judge whether they are physically incapacitated, deranged from some terrible grief, jobless, homeless, prone to fits of anger, landless, idle, untouchable, strong, or mentally retarded. Armed with this information these citizens will know what they as community members, in such and such social positions, with such and such energy and funds, and having such and such neighbors in the community, can actually do to assist. They would know the possibility of making arrangements for individuals to be included within family situations; poor families might need the help of clans or other such bigger groupings. That is to say, the answer will be practical, modest, and based on personal experience with the poor.

Ask World Bank officials in Washington what global poverty alleviation needs and they will not talk about social and cultural factors affecting who is and who is not poor; instead they will speak about the required data infrastructure not yet in place, the effects of wars and natural disasters, the good governance and policy framework, the income or food subsidy safety net that must be put in place and the challenge of combating aid fatigue and raising more money in the rich countries.

The idea that science could solve society's problems and challenges has a long history. The Great Exhibition of 1851, brainchild of Prince Albert, was intended as a celebration of the British Empire and advances in technology. The major transformation that occurred across the Victorian period—with Charles Darwin, Aldous Huxley, and so on—saw a shift from gentlemen amateurs to professional scientists that involved the development and dissemination of natural laws and ongoing progress. Neil Armstrong walked on the moon in 1969. Public investments in research had helped to split the atom, splice the gene, invent the microchip, create the laser, and build the internet. Wasn't smallpox eliminated from the world with the aid of a global effort, just as piracy and slavery had been eliminated a century before?

Common sense suggests that those who are passionate about aid ending poverty are just as likely to see a flying saucer as have their dream realized. Carl Jung, the Swiss psychoanalyst, did not say that flying saucers did not exist: he said they were there because people wanted them to be there.[36] Obviously, the public wants to believe that poverty, just like disease, can be eliminated. In a world beset by natural and human-made disasters it can be comforting to believe that there are extraterrestrial beings out there who want to help solve the planet's problems.

Why do so many of those who work in the aid business put on Seven League boots when they go overseas? Is there something in the air, or in the water, that we did not know about? So many professionals up their game. This is a more serious affliction than that of the man who can understand all that he needs to know on the taxi ride from the airport to his hotel. What encourages travelers who have neither lived nor worked in the tropics for long periods to say that they can improve the lives of millions of people? How else are we to understand rock stars who, after a few days in the tropics, announce that they know how to make poverty history? Stranger still is the fact that when these good ideas have failed their authors do not seem any the wiser. Agronomists, who find it challenging to take care of a small garden at home, say they can solve the food problems of the tropics; medical people, who have spent their lives with curative medicine, say they can banish disease; engineers, who have never managed to build anything that worked well, say they can give people in the back of beyond in the tropics clean water; credit experts say they can install more accessible rural credit than you find in Europe or the US; economists say they can run entire countries; road engineers promise to build highways and bridges to higher standards than they have used at home; plant quarantine experts wish to impose more rigid safeguards than they have known at home; computer experts prepare to install better systems than they have known at home; charities say "No more crying children if you send money every month."[37]

We could look to cult thinking for an explanation as to why sensible people believe poverty can be ended. Cargo cults provide an example of the fantasy wish-fulfilment that poverty elimination is all about. Cargo cult adherents believe that a fabulous cargo—whatever you dream of, really—will arrive in the near future by ship, plane, or other heavenly means. Of course, yes, you have guessed it and many do, the cargo does not come and anthropologists are then provided with a chance to come up with new explanations. Having said that, belief in the imminent arrival of cargo did not deter believers of the Jon Frum movement in the New Hebrides (now

Vanuatu). When missionaries warned the people that their belief was silly because their cargo would not come, locals laughed and reminded them that they had waited 2,000 years for the return of Jesus Christ.[38]

Expansion and Institutional Change

Development assistance has shifted too far away from the modest objectives of faith organizations and non-governmental organizations (NGOs), to routinely embracing the millenarian poverty vision. Development assistance has begun to rely more and more on the popular support from the public that aid agencies gained by implying that they could help to build a world overseas that could deliver what the citizens of the industrialized countries hoped for, but did not yet have, at home. Silver bullet solutions in the health field that wipe out scourges to humanity through inoculation have provided a model that many would like to extend to curing poverty. Silver bullet solutions will help if a disease like malaria can be eradicated by the application of determined campaigns to deliver better science and technology, as was the case with polio and smallpox.

Nimal, my Sri Lankan friend and colleague, kept a list of aid agency silver bullet solutions to poverty that were never implemented—land for the landless, jobs for the jobless, homes for the homeless. He predicted the clever men and women in the World Bank would develop a wit for the witless initiative. If we had more historians of aid, but we do not, they could point out, in less amusing fashion than my friend, the other silver bullet solutions that have sunk without a trace. The World Bank's Integrated Rural Development Project was supposed to provide a complete way of gaining a living for rural people. To work it needed hands-on skills and knowledge that the World Bank did not have, and a significant intrusion into local lives that local people did not want. It was succeeded by the Sustainable Livelihoods Project that has raised more or less the same skills and knowledge difficulties. Enthusiasts, usually with limited local knowledge and experience, spend a great deal of time discussing what they think is involved and what their own interpretation is rather than getting down to work.

Intriguingly, when I revisited my early experiences with the World Bank, I found that many of the social challenges experienced by the institution were similar to those faced by a global mining company with 60,000 employees and operations in more than sixty countries.[39] In the past twenty years mining companies have, like the World Bank, had to deal with issues that attracted NGO campaigns such as dams, land acquisition, and resettlement in developing countries, as well as the claims and rights of indigenous peoples, human rights, environmental protection, labor issues, and the alleviation of poverty. Mining companies had to listen and learn before engaging with issues where NGOs had made it clear that they had strong views. The same process can be seen at the World Bank.

By relying on management by seclusion and fighting poverty in the office, the World Bank has failed to make the best use of economics or anthropology, or of sociology, political science, social psychology, and public administration. Max Weber, who pointed to the inevitability and the limitations of bureaucracy in large-scale organizations like the World Bank, told us that "the modern higher-ranking [German] officer fights battles from the office."[40] Today, despite the energetic efforts to increase the numbers working overseas, somewhere between 70 to 90 percent of the World Bank's staff can expect to spend their working careers toiling away in large office buildings in Washington raising money, generating public support, and processing projects and loans to eliminate homogenized poverty.[41] Consequently, the World Bank's war on global poverty cannot be expected to do any better than the 1964 US war on poverty that Ronald Reagan said poverty had won.

The book concludes that the World Bank is ill-suited to eliminate poverty or address extreme poverty elimination, though of course all the spending can help improve health, education, and economic opportunities. The World Bank became too large to succeed with poverty at the grassroots level where much may depend on the local ensemble of beliefs, values, and attitudes as well as the creativity and nimbleness of the individual aid worker. If it was a war it was a war that could be won only by hand-to-hand combat rather than with missiles and long-range artillery. Of course, the top-down benefits of economic growth could help, but all too often its effects were dissipated before the really poor experienced the benefits. Despite good intentions, a great deal of money was, and still is, being wasted as it may be in any top-down solution because the wealth created by World Bank–financed economic development flows down a very leaky pipe to the poorest and often fails to address what the poor consider to be their high-priority issues.

Eliminating the poverty of the very poor is a much sterner test than improving the lot of poor people. If we look at those organizations that work with very poor people, then their experience suggests that neither social science disciplines nor money can claim a pivotal role in poverty alleviation for the very poorest; it is the thought that they could that has contributed greatly to the World Bank's inability to lead this work. I yield to none in my admiration for the ability of anthropologists to help policymakers understand what is important in situations of distress affecting remote peoples in remote areas or the homeless on the next block. But not all anthropologists or social scientists have the qualities of compassion, the desire to engage, the interpersonal skills, and the stomach required to work in close and continuous contact with very poor people. I know that I did not have what this work needed and I suspect that many aid workers who thought they had may not have had their resolve tested.

In the early 1970s it seemed to me that the World Bank had quite a large number of staff members who had the local hands-on skills and knowledge that reaching the very poorest needed, and that the institution could make good use of anthropologists. Today, and although the institution has recruited upward of a hundred anthropologists, it would be hard to say that they have been deployed in ways that made good use of the discipline's unique fieldwork tradition and ability to throw light on the social and cultural factors linked to extreme poverty. Hands-on local skills and knowledge are in short supply and local government has not been seen to be critically important for poverty alleviation.

Aid has done, and still does, vitally important things in poor countries, but mostly when helpers have had local knowledge and experience as well as relationships with those to be helped, and when small sums of money are involved. The ending poverty movement's overselling threatens to completely distort that performance and also threatens to discredit the entire development assistance enterprise.

Chapters

Chapter 1: Money-Moving

Robert McNamara started the World Bank's war on poverty and an alms race in the industrialized countries to support his vision. He made the case for more money for global poverty alleviation. Client countries were encouraged to take loans, and in Papua New Guinea this earned them a reputation as loan salesmen. We do not yet know if the growing pressure from the US, the World Bank's largest shareholder, for graduation from aid will result in BRIC countries (Brazil, Russia, India, and China) no longer qualifying for World Bank money. That would encourage a focus on smaller countries and new opportunities for hands-on policy alleviation.

Chapter 2: Reputation Management

In order to accelerate lending the World Bank turned away from social science, technical expertise, and grassroots skills. Staff who were articulate in meetings and good on paper were needed to turn out more loans. As expansion proceeded, technical specialization in areas such as agriculture and health were abandoned and more and more of the new staff who were hired had limited overseas experience. Over the past forty years Washington's reputational management skills have become more and more important in terms of their contribution to the World Bank's public profile and to money-moving.

Chapter 3: Disciplines

The use of social science disciplines, expertise, and skills has been determined by the contribution they have been able to make to the World Bank's capacity to raise and spend money. In the 1980s NGO campaigns posed a serious threat to the World Bank's reputation and safeguards policies and procedures for resettlement, Indigenous peoples and cultural heritage protection were introduced to ensure that World Bank projects did no harm. But safeguards work was not popular among World Bank staff because it slowed down lending. One result was that anthropology, which had a significant role in safeguards work, was marginalized. What does often seem to be significant is the fact that, as time has passed, the skills of the economist and others working in similar disciplines have become less influential in the World Bank than the skills of the journalist.

Chapter 4: Public Service

Although Max Weber's "Ideal-Type" bureaucracy was not supposed to be found in empirical reality, the World Bank provides a near-perfect example. Today the World Bank behaves like a global corporation that pursues its own self-interest rather than like a publicly accountable institution. As time has passed, the burgeoning World Bank bureaucracy in Washington has become more concerned with its own internal issues such as expansion and market share than with the provision of public service in client countries.

Chapter 5: Social Soundness Analysis

The very poorest people—who were often unwell, uneducated, and on the margins of society—could not necessarily be expected to be able to take advantage of the opportunities for advancement that were presented by development projects. For fifty years the project has been thought to be the most efficient and effective way of getting the right assistance to the poorest. But projects have required above-average resources while the poorest are below-average people. More attention should now be paid to alternative ways of delivering help such as campaign organizations and social movements.

Conclusions

It is highly unlikely that the hands-on field skills and human attributes required for building relationships and rapport with the poorest, and the quantitative office skills required for lending and commercialized economic development, could ever prosper within a single institution like the World Bank. Massive publicity campaigns to persuade the public to support poverty alleviation have produced the global poor who increasingly resemble George Orwell's unpeople. It is time to part the poverty curtain provided by all the statistics to show that the global poor have a country, a culture, a language, and social relationships.[42]

Notes

1. See Ascher and Mason, *World Bank Since Bretton Woods*; Baum and Tolbert, *Investing in Development*; Please, *Hobbled Giant*. Negative accounts of the World Bank have included Hancock, *Lords of Poverty*; Rich, *Mortgaging the Earth*; Meren, *Road to Hell*; Sharma, *Robert McNamara's Other War*; Halberstam, *The Best and the Brightest*.

2. See Cochrane, *Anthropology in the Mining Industry*; Cochrane, "What Can Anthropology Do?," 20.

3. Goodenough, "Anthropology in the 20th Century and Beyond"; Heyman, "The Anthropology"; Cochrane, *Max Weber's Vision*.

4. Goodland, "Social & Environmental Assessment to Promote Sustainability"; Cochrane, *Cultural Appraisal of Development Projects*.

5. My book *Festival Elephants* argues that there was no such thing as global poverty for which there is a one-size-fits-all solution.

6. Stern, "Beyond the Transition," gives the history of UN thinking on poverty; UNDP, *Poverty Alleviation in Asia and the Pacific*, gives UNDP's view. I am indebted to Len Joy, an old friend, for discussions around the idea of homogeneity. See also Streeten et al., *First Things First*.

7. This was the moment when qualitative analysis and social development was put in the back seat of the development vehicle. Economists decided the World Bank was an economic institution run by economists; while it might gesture in the direction of social factors or sociological variables, the future thrust of the institution and the measures it would take to implement these ideas would inevitably reflect an economic bias. Nevertheless, the anthropologists continued to hope and continued to write publicly about their hope. See Davis, "Bringing Culture."

8. In the Solomon Islands unemployed young men who had come to town to see the bright lights were regarded with suspicion by expatriates. The visitors learned to avoid difficulties by saying, when asked where they worked, that they were with "Mr. Liu." He was a mythical Chinese trader. The domestic arrangements of Chinese traders were unknown and nobody was much interested in them.

9. For a very readable account see Strathern, *The Rope of Moka*.

10. See Cochrane, *Development Anthropology*; Wilbur, *Political Economy of Underdevelopment*; Aghion and Bolton, "A Theory of Trickle-Down Growth and Development"; Meier and Stiglitz, *Frontiers of Development Economics*, 422.

11. Leonard, *Reaching the Peasant Farmer*.

12. Masefield, *A Short History*. Informative and gives details of how farmyard manure was transported to the West Indies in the seventeenth century.

13. The well-known economist Thomas Balogh doubted that a single solution would suffice. See Balogh, "Failures in the Strategy against Poverty."

14. Vetterlein, "Seeing Like the World Bank on Poverty."

15. O'Reilly, "In Bohemia."

16. Bernard Chadenet suggested this term to me when I was about to talk to a group of his staff. He asked me to try to shake them up and said that they were becoming too office-bound and set in their ways, and that they practiced management by seclusion.

17. The World Bank sees poverty as related to well-being and command over commodities: "The poor are those who do not have enough income or consumption to put them above some adequate minimum threshold. This view sees poverty largely in monetary terms. Poverty may also be tied to a specific type of consumption; thus, someone might be house-poor or food-poor or health-poor. These dimensions of poverty can often be measured directly, for instance by measuring malnutrition or literacy. The broadest approach to well-being (and poverty) focuses on the 'capability' of the individual to function in society. The poor lack key capabilities, and may have inadequate income or education, or be in poor health, or feel powerless, or lack political freedoms. There are four reasons to measure poverty. First, to keep the poor on the agenda; if poverty were not measured, it would be easy to forget the poor. Second, one needs to be able to identify the poor if one is to be able to target interventions that aim to reduce or alleviate poverty. Third, to monitor and evaluate projects and policy interventions that are geared towards the poor. And finally, to evaluate the effectiveness of institutions whose goal is to help the poor." World Bank Institute, "Introduction to Poverty Analysis."

18. The 1993 UNDP *Human Development Report* gives the number of book titles published per 1,000 of population as well as the number of annual cinema outings. It is hard to see the point of this sort of data unless UNDP intends that countries with low scores be sent copies of Jurassic Park.

19. World Health Organization (WHO) and Cook Islands Ministry of Health, *Health Sector Delivery Performance*.

20. The population of the Cook Islands has dropped to 15,000. However, 61,000 in New Zealand and 30,000 in Australia identify themselves as Cook Islanders and maintain family connections. The problem of how to take the views and feelings of these overseas residents into account is not easy to solve. It is a common problem in Oceania. While living in the Solomon Islands and working as the administrator directly responsible for Tikopia, and just before voter registration and a whispering ballot was introduced, I discovered that there were far more Tikopia living overseas than on the island.

21. Scott, *Years of the Pooh-Bah*; Kücher and Eimke, *Tivaivai*; Hamilton, *Pages from Paradise*.

22. The World Bank accepted that the local meanings of poverty were important but dismissed their use on grounds that they could not be aggregated. Anthropology was said to be too subjective and not suitable for national-level assessment. World Bank Institute, "Introduction to Poverty Analysis," 27. See also appendix B.

23. Rowntree and Lavers, *Poverty and the Welfare State*.

24. For Africa see Castro, Hakansson, and Brokensha, "Indicators of Rural Inequality."

25. See also the significant contributions by Paul Farmer: *AIDS and Accusation*; *Pathologies of Power*; *Infections and Inequalities*. Farmer's work has echoes of Albert Camus's *La Peste*, the story of a plague in Oran, and Franz Fanon's *The Wretched of the Earth*.

26. On relationships see Strathern, *The Relation*.

27. Thurnwald, "Price of White Man's Peace."

28. On this work see Goodland, "Social & Environmental Assessment to Promote Sustainability."

29. I was supposed to be working pro bono publico in return for $1 and I never got the dollar.

30. Quoted in Drèze and Sen, *Hunger and Public Action*, 31–32. See Raymond Firth's remarks on famine on Tikopia in *The Elements of Social Organization*; and in Horowitz and Salem-Murdock, "Development-induced Food Insecurity."

31. See the classic exchange between an economist and an anthropologist, Knight, "Anthropology and Economics" and Herskovits, "Economics and Anthropology, A rejoinder."

32. Armchair anthropology is covered in Stocking, *After Tylor*, 15–24.

33. Lienhardt, *"Frazer's Anthropology."*

34. The World Bank now consults, but does not really listen to, NGOs on a range of issues that do not affect the institution's ability to move more and more money. In the safeguards area the most sensitive issues are usually related to the environment. Seeking to keep the critics onside, more and more former campaigners against the World Bank's environmental practices are now flown business class around the world to look at biodiversity issues. Big NGOs like Oxfam have been eager to be seen and to be treated as major players in the aid business.

35. Economist Jeffrey Sachs raised $120 million for his Millennium Villages idea in Africa that he thought would eliminate poverty. See Clemens and Demonbynas, "When Does Rigorous Impact Evaluation Make a Difference?"

36. Jung, *Flying Saucers*.

37. Clean water and other silver bullet solutions are not just a matter of engineering and handing out kits. Using wells, pumps, and water holes in sustainable ways requires appropriate behavior if results are to be maintained. Getting people to take medicine on a regular basis presents similar challenges.

38. Details are provided by Worsley, *The Trumpet Shall Sound*. See also Cochrane, *Big Men and Cargo Cults*.

39. Strictly speaking there is no such thing as a World Bank project; the investment is owned by and is the responsibility of the borrower.

40. Weber, *The Theory of Economic and Social Organization*, 1393.

41. "National programs to manage economy-wide shocks and effective mechanisms to reduce the risks faced by poor people, as well as helping them cope with adverse shocks when they occur, are necessary: formulating programs to helping poor people managing risk. Micro-insurance programs, public work programs, and food transfer programs may be mixed with other mechanisms to deliver more effective risk management: Developing national programs to prevent and respond to macro shocks, financial or natural. Design national systems of social risk management that are also pro-growth. Supporting minority rights and providing the institutional basis for peaceful conflict resolution can help prevent civil conflict and mobilize more resources into productive activities. Tackling health problems including widespread illnesses such as malaria and tuberculosis, as well as moderately common but serious conditions such as HIV/AIDS. There is no simple, universal blueprint for implementing this strategy. Each developing country needs to prepare its own mix of policies to reduce poverty, reflecting national priorities and local realities. Given the important complementarities among these three dimensions, an effective poverty reduction strategy will require action on all three fronts, by all stakeholders in society, government, civil society, the private sector and poor people themselves." World Bank Institute, "Introduction to Poverty Analysis," 95.

42. ul Haq, *Poverty Curtain*.

Chapter 1

MONEY-MOVING

Robert McNamara, President of the World Bank from 1968 to 1981, began the war against global poverty in 1968.[1] McNamara established money-moving targets to win the war on poverty. These were seen by World Bank staff members as not so different from his famous body-count fallacy in Vietnam, which assumed that if large numbers of the enemy were killed, the war would be won. When Robert McNamara was President, and since then, the job of a vice president of the World Bank has been to move more money in the current year to the region he or she is responsible for than the past year. And it is that office-bound concentration on money-moving and the concept of global poverty elimination that has maintained management by seclusion and continued to drive and characterize the development of the institution over the course of the past fifty years.[2] Raising and spending larger and larger sums of money encouraged a passion for paper rather than for poor people, encouraged the substitution of paper relations for social relations, and encouraged officials to enter into enduring relationships with tables of statistics in which they had an abiding interest. Officials believed that better numbers and figures, and better policies, would do the job. The war on poverty became something waged on paper in the rich countries.

The new poverty initiative was announced at the Annual Meetings of the Governors of the World Bank and the International Monetary Fund in Nairobi. There Robert McNamara first set out his ideas about how to eliminate global poverty. He was a man who believed that a problem that could not be quantified was a problem that had not been properly thought through; he was obsessed with growth. When Robert McNamara was questioned as to whether the World Bank's approach to ending poverty was too optimistic, he quoted George Bernard Shaw: "You see things and you say, 'why?' But I dream things that never were, and I say, 'Why not?'"[3]

His approach to poverty alleviation was maintained by World Bank CEOs, most recently the incumbent President Jim Yong Kim.

Periodic high-profile fundraising has contributed substantially to the World Bank's ability to increase lending in the past fifty years. These fundraisings have followed the same steps, beginning with the President of the World Bank providing a compelling vision, a picture of global human suffering—a situation that the average citizen can immediately grasp and recognize as something that should and must be changed. These images were calculated to suggest that this state of affairs could be addressed and overcome if sufficient funds were provided. Insufficient mention was often made of the human factors that may well be highly influential in determining outcomes. For example, appeals for funds for clean water often ignore critical human factors such as failure to maintain equipment, arguments over access and use, and failure to improve personal hygiene.[4] The so-called green revolution had a number of failures related to human factors—the same factors that now affect genetically modified crops.[5]

The logic was not much different from that of the Marshall Plan at the end of World War II: give money to war-torn Europe and those countries would, and did, recover. However, Europeans had the skills and the experience to know what to do. The use of the same approach in underdeveloped areas of Africa or Asia could not always be expected to produce the same outcome, even though the vision for which funds were sought should appear to be using tried and tested technology with boldness and imagination.

In a speech at Notre Dame University in 1969 McNamara talked about the importance of population control; he believed that rapid population increase posed a threat to his growth ambitions. So did poor nutrition. McNamara had something of the missionary about him and a real concern for poor people, though at the same time he wanted to be sure that whatever was done could be attached to numbers. On this basis he was not keen to get involved with education during the early years of his presidency because he thought hard numbers would be difficult to come by:[6]

> McNamara addressed the Board of Governors at the annual meetings in Washington, stating that the basic issues of global development reached far beyond the statistics of gross national product in the poorer countries of the world and said: "Adequate nutrition, the availability of employment, a more equitable distribution of income, and an improvement in the quality of life itself are the goals the more than two billion people of the developing world are seeking. . . . Unless we deal with these fundamental issues, development will fail. The lesson of the last decade has been that we cannot simply depend on economic growth alone. . . . Future plans of the World Bank, as well as of other bilateral and multilateral development finance agencies, and most importantly, of the developing countries themselves, must give far greater attention to the basic

problems affecting the lives of the developing peoples. . . ." McNamara pointed out that a "major barrier to human development" was malnutrition, saying that it was widespread, and was a major cause of high mortality among children. "We are not speaking here of dietetic nuances, or the fancies of food faddists. We are speaking of basic nutritional deficiencies which affect the minds and bodies of human beings."[7]

From the 1970s onward the World Bank accelerated its involvement with "basic human needs."[8] In 2015 a World Bank press release claimed:

> Jim Yong Kim, World Bank Group President, said that the continued major reductions in poverty were due to strong growth rates in developing countries in recent years, investments in people's education, health, and social safety nets that helped keep people from falling back into poverty. He cautioned, however, that with slowing global economic growth, and with many of the world's remaining poor people living in fragile and conflict-affected states, and the considerable depth and breadth of remaining poverty, the goal to end extreme poverty remained a highly ambitious target. "This is the best story in the world today—these projections show us that we are the first generation in human history that can end extreme poverty," Kim said.[9]

What the World Bank has managed to do is to convince the public to believe that raising the money is the major part of implementation. Successful charities often manage to persuade us that the challenge is not whether they will perform, but whether we will let them perform by giving them enough money. When I was living in the US there was an annual appeal from something called the Community Chest. The campaign was presented in a way that suggested that the index of success for Community Chest was not what they did with the money but the fact that we gave more than we had given in the previous year.

The President of the World Bank has considerable freedom to move the institution in a direction of his choice and, because of the internationalist nature of the World Bank and the fact that it is backed by the full faith and credit of the industrialized countries, he has more power to maneuver than the CEO of a large company in the private sector. McNamara wanted his officials to use cost benefit analysis, a rational approach that called for the development of modes and patterns of action that relate means to ends with minimum waste and maximum efficiency.[10]

Robert McNamara and his successors assumed that if funds could be raised then administrative and cross-cultural performance and the enthusiastic support of the World Bank staff would follow. However, it was not the humanitarian vision that failed to achieve the ending of poverty, or the lack of funds, or the lack of smart people, but rather an institutional inability to adjust global thinking to local circumstances and a failure to build and use the hands-on grassroots skills and the administrative performance that implementation required. Perhaps this reflected McNamara's lack of implementation experience because, when he was president of the Ford Motor Company, Ford already had an organization that had been successfully making cars for a long time and when he was secretary of defense the US had long-standing military capacity. Not a good manager, said Warren Baum, a top official in the World Bank, who saw him as someone who was interested only in "information up and decisions down."[11]

The way Presidents of the World Bank have been chosen and the nature of the job probably need substantial rethinking. International economists have wanted one of their own with strong intellectual qualifications.[12] But as chief economists at the World Bank have already shown, being a good economist is not necessarily the same as being a good manager in a world where helping the poorest needs more than economic expertise.

Organizing to Move Money

Over the past fifty years hands-on community skills and local knowledge and the ability to create rapport with the poorest people overseas have been squeezed out of the World Bank and the other aid agencies who follow its example. World Bank staff ended up working with the better-off people in poor countries. These were the people who shared their point of view, the people with whom they could communicate and on whom they could rely.

In 1971 McNamara announced that McKinsey & Company had been selected to design a reorganization of the World Bank, which at the time had basically the same structure as in 1952. The results of the study were issued in August 1972, and reorganization was implemented shortly afterward. There was some concern at the time that projects work was receiving too much attention and as a result regional vice presidents were finding it hard to gain traction for their country policy advisory functions. The complaint seemed to be that the projects division was de facto intruding into country policy and strategy decisions that properly should rest with the area people.

The 1972 reorganization resulted in a decentralization of projects work that had been concentrated in a single department of the World Bank. Instead of the World Bank continuing to have a Central Projects Department responsible for all project investments headed by Bernard Chadenet, with Warren Baum as his deputy, transportation and agricultural and other projects staff were allocated to the regional vice presidencies for the World Bank: Africa, East Asia and Pacific, Europe and Central Asia, Latin America and the Caribbean, Middle East and North Africa, and South Asia.

During the early years of the World Bank the nationalities with the largest representation were those of the former colonial powers—Britain, France, and the Netherlands. Bernard Chadenet, who had been a French railways engineer, was in charge of the powerful Central Projects Division (he personally made it possible for me to talk to all 300 staff in his division); Roger Chaufournier, another French, former civil servant, managed francophone West Africa; and Ian Cargill, who had been in the Indian Civil Service, handled India.

A number of senior staff had started their World Bank careers as loan officers. Loan officers had broad, deep technical experience in fields such as tropical agriculture and hands-on experience. The loan officer who was the on-the-ground workhorse for the World Bank was the person who had local relationships with civil servants and who knew the country. The loan officer position was gradually phased out, disappearing almost completely in the reorganization of 1987. In 1973, when I suggested that the World Bank should hire anthropologists, many of their staff, who had colonial experience, were sympathetic to the idea because so much of what an anthropologist does was already familiar to them.[13]

In the 1960s the World Bank had begun its own career development program, the Young Professionals Program, and this emphasized academic qualifications. The program took the best and the brightest young (mostly) economics graduates from the best universities in the industrialized countries. Early on they had six Rhodes Scholars.[14] Many had never lived or worked overseas. These junior professionals did the grunt work in the field. They attended meetings and negotiations, they drafted communications. But, above all, they learned from their seniors how to win on paper. After a few years of being moved around the World Bank so that they gained exposure to a broad spectrum of World Bank work they were ready for the accelerated promotion that membership in the program brought.

Meanwhile, fewer and fewer of the World Bank staff that were hired had substantial overseas experience working with very poor people before they joined the World Bank. Those who, prior to their World Bank service, lived in privileged circumstances and had often been to elite educational institutions in the industrialized countries would find living and working in Washington a less than ideal way to learn about poor people in developing countries.

In the 1980s the balance of power within the World Bank began to shift away from those with a detailed knowledge of technical subjects. Prior to the 1972 reorganization, the World Bank had on staff experienced transportation engineers and a wide variety of agricultural experts. These men and women had broad, deep technical knowledge and years of hands-on implementation in developing countries.[15] Living and working in a country for a number of years did provide an invaluable basis for judging quick-fix solutions from visitors.[16] This is knowledge that enables aid agency personnel to look at a proposal and then be able to say why it may or may not work or what needs to be changed. If President of the World Bank Robert McNamara or his staff had lived for some time in the highlands of Papua New Guinea he would have been familiar with the way locals regarded pigs and cows. When flying in a helicopter over the highlands of Papua New Guinea McNamara saw vast grasslands and concluded that the World Bank should engage in lending for cattle and pigs. The highlanders were scared of cattle and hunted them with bows and arrows, and the pigs were unpopular because they produced lean bacon rather than the fat locals loved and the animals suffered from sunstroke.

In the 1960s and 1970s, and before the arrival of homogenized poverty, the World Bank did very useful work in ways that accommodated the local cultural context. Both the World Bank and USAID said they were turning away from specialization because it was believed that it was not possible to keep genuine up-to-date expertise on staff. After the 1972 and the 1987 reorganizations the World Bank member was seen as a manager holding the ring, mediating between competing interests and by briefing and supervision, orchestrating the work of expert consultants recruited from outside the organization to deal with projects work. These new generalists were expected to work through others to secure their influence as a result of their ability to provide an integrity to the system as a whole. Much of their influence rested on their understanding of that institution and those related to it.

Specialists were recruited because they were thought to have skills that were relatively unique and exercised by them personally; these skills formed the base of their influence within the organization. Generally speaking, the contributions of specialists were not bound by institutional constraints and were limited typically by their own competence and capacity to influence others as to their quality. For those who really did practice a specialty, opportunities for development lay primarily in the professional discipline and in working with peers. For specialists, the ability to work closely and effectively with nonspecialists was less important; specialists tended to disregard interdisciplinary initiatives; specialists had fewer contacts with the doers and more with planners and policymakers. As a result, wherever there were groups of specialists there was a narrowing of working relationships within the organization itself.

Martin Paijmans, vice president for personnel in 1973, told me of an incident that showed the continuing strength of the colonial influence at the World Bank. In the late 1960s the World Bank had a vacancy for a staff member to deal with power, a vacancy that went unfilled for a long time.

Paijmans pointed to this incident as a sign that the supply of old colonials had begun to dry up. The old colonials in charge of power in the World Bank would have expected one person to do the job. However, due to the specialization that had occurred in rich countries it was becoming normal for one professional to handle power generation while another handled power distribution.

Presentation Skills

When Robert McNamara found that economists alone could not move the money as quickly as wanted he recruited staff who could do better. He looked for those who were nimble, articulate and persuasive on paper, and energetic. Veeraswamy Rajagopalan, the former head of the World Bank's Council for International Agricultural Research and an environmental engineer, said, "Increased emphasis was placed on presentation, on fine report writing [and] technical people [engineers] are not very good at writing reports."[17] As lending expanded, more and more of the World Bank's business has depended not on social science but on what Rajagopalan called presentation skills. These are the persuasive skills of the sales rep, the skills the institution relies on to do the paperwork, to develop and put in place administrative support that is required to raise and spend the vast sums now involved in poverty alleviation. Staff with presentation skills are nimble and articulate people with considerable creative capacity. They do well on paper and in meetings and they have what it takes to move to, or from, the World Bank to other global corporations. Their talents are similar to those demonstrated by staffers working for members of the US Congress. Schools of public policy and public affairs turn out hundreds of hopeful graduates with presentation skills each year. Many have not mastered a discipline but they have an easy familiarity with how things work in big organizations, and they have a hatbox full of theories and well-known research. Like a car sales rep in a showroom they can argue in favor of or against this or that model; they understand that project investments are not scientific documents but rather are documents of advocacy written in carefully judged ways to attract approval.

Staff with presentation skills have replaced the loan officers who had the skills and knowledge related to working with the poor in remote areas. In order to win more and more of the private and public money that might otherwise go to civil society organizations or bilateral aid agencies, World Bank staff have to spend more and more time at their desks in Washington processing loans. Fewer and fewer World Bank staff with personal hands-on experience of working with farmers, teaching in a classroom, or living and working in public institutions in a poor country have been hired by the World Bank. Though the new World Bank recruits are better at processing paper, they lack the wisdom and hands-on developing-country experience of the former colonial officials. In effect, McNamara moved the World Bank from a situation where its major store of capital was in the skills and experience of its seasoned staff to a situation where the institution's competitive advantage was thought to lie in its policy positions and very deep pockets.

World Bank staff earned a reputation as "loan salesmen" in Papua New Guinea for the enthusiasm they showed over getting the country to sign up to new loans despite the poor performance of previous lending. Picking the winners was never easy in investment work and there was a long history of bad calls going all the way back to when the World Bank economists advised the Australian administrators of Papua New Guinea in 1963 to abandon the interior and concentrate on the coastal areas of the island (later, in the interior, coffee and mining began to make a major contribution to government revenues). In the 1980s a loan for integrated rural development and another for livestock development were both abject failures that cost the government a considerable sum of money.

Staff with presentation skills were able to speed up the processing of big, expensive infrastructural projects that required a great deal of money, used tried and tested technology, and usually achieved their predicted outcomes. These projects had a limited number of tricky social factors and if contractor labor relations were competently handled all would be well. Aid monies could be quickly disbursed by big infrastructural projects, which was a great advantage. Today the World Bank's loans for urban mass transit systems, airports, ports, railways, hospitals, schools, universities, and roads routinely carry a poverty reduction label even though they may well widen the gap between those who have and those who have not. Poor countries need to remember that the articulate, hard-working young staff members are not trained to work themselves out of a job so that someone else can take over. They have been trained to succeed personally and if they have to get the better of someone or some country in order to do that then that is what they will do.

As the work expanded and as more and more lending decisions were influenced by the new staff, the quality of the project and program work began to decline. Loans were made for tree crops or medical research without the World Bank having any staff member with substantial qualifications and experience in tropical agriculture or tropical medicine. Loans were made for the reform of civil services without the World Bank having a staff member who had worked in a civil service.[18] The same pattern was found with respect to lending for power, transport, and communications. Management believed that specialist knowledge could be brought in on a consultancy basis. But this did not always work well and the number of nonperforming projects began to increase. Member countries did not complain because they wanted World Bank money.[19]

Statistical Evangelism

Poverty alleviation was all about individual incomes and the development assistance narrative put out and about by the World Bank was all about those low incomes and what was being done to get them to a higher level. A World Bank press release in 2015 explained that, due to the effects of war, Somalia's data infrastructure had been destroyed, leaving policy-makers and the World Bank powerless to develop measures to help the poorest people in that country. The press release went on to say that as part of a $300 million project to repair infrastructural data coverage around the world normal statistical services would be restored in Somalia.

A 2015 World Bank blog said,

> The availability of poverty data has increased over the last 20 years but large gaps remain. About half the countries we studied in our recent paper, "Data Deprivation, Another Deprivation to End Poverty," are deprived of adequate data on poverty. This is a huge problem because the poor, who often lack political representation and agency, will remain invisible unless objective and properly sampled surveys reveal where they are, and how they're faring. The lack of data on human and social development should be seen as a form of deprivation, and along with poverty, data deprivation should be eradicated. Aleem Walji notes that recent poverty estimates are available for only half of the 155 countries [where] the World Bank monitors poverty. United Nations IEAG Report "A World That Counts" argues that a lack of data can lead to a "denial of basic rights." [And] 77 out of 155 countries measured do not have adequate poverty data. In summary, about half of the countries surveyed—77 of 155—are deprived of adequate data, 57 of them quite acutely. The goal of ending extreme poverty by 2030 must be accompanied by the end of data deprivation. These targets are ambitious but possible by exploiting advances in knowledge and technology, utilizing resources for capacity development, and improving coordination of efforts among key actors to mobilize sustainable development.[20]

Any prospect of doing more to achieve a better balance between homogenous and qualitative poverty approaches would have had to take into account the fact that the World Bank had not invested in the creation of a comprehensive worldwide database for qualitative data comparable to the database that facilitated the institution's economic work. Nor have the World Bank assumptions about $1.90 a day been regularly backed up by international purchasing power studies showing what could be bought for $1.90 a day.[21] There are, of course, very few people who regularly receive only $1 or $2 a day in poor countries. Receipts, particularly from seasonal activities like agriculture, will be lumpy. What really needs to be understood is the way money is used by the poorest. In countries where government is not close to the people few poor people will want to tell government census or household enumerators what they receive. Expenditure data is much more useful than income data but is harder to collect.

At the national level, aid agencies do need to know if the quantitative and qualitative assessments of poverty were mutually consistent or divergent.[22] In order to verify World Bank assumptions and claims it would have been necessary to collect not only objective measurement of poverty factors such as incomes, health, and education status, or basic needs access, as is now the case, but also the subjective perceptions that poor people have of their own circumstances. Obviously, there could be differences between town and country,[23] between social classes, between ethnic groups, and between landless peasants and landowners.[24]

Banking for Money-Moving

Cheap money, at least cheaper than any regular bank could offer, has always been the key factor providing the World Bank with a unique competitive advantage. In addition, fifty years ago it was the attractiveness of the technical analysis that was persuasive. This was succeeded by an emphasis on the quality of the economic analysis and the policy dialogue between the World Bank and client countries. Merchandizing poverty has become more and more important. Merchandizing is the process of showing the variety of intellectual and lending products available for sale and the display of those products in such a way that it stimulates interest and entices client countries to make a purchase by accepting loans.

Borrowing has been accelerated by financial innovations designed to increase the attractiveness of borrowing. Funds that have been collected for the replenishment of the International Development Association (IDA) and lent at a quarter of a percent can be mixed with funds that the World Bank has had to borrow at a higher rate of interest. This blended finance is attractive because it is still cheaper than the funds that may be available from commercial banks. As more and more money has been collected the World Bank has managed to package it into larger and larger loans and investment vehicles.

The World Bank continued throughout the 1970s and into the 1980s to emphasize the volume of activity focused on the elimination of absolute poverty and the encouragement of equitable economic development. Under McNamara, the World Bank grew into a very large institution occupying an ever-increasing portion of prime real estate in downtown Washington, DC. In the early years of the World Bank the majority of loans were for infrastructural development, for hydroelectric works, for roads, bridges, railways, and ports development. Within the past decade the World Bank has turned away from loans and lending in order to rebrand the institution as a "knowledge organization."[25] This emphasizes that the World Bank can provide unparalleled technical skills and knowledge. McNamara looked around the world for innovators who could accelerate economic growth in the sectors of the economy where he wanted the World Bank to invest heavily. He started the training and visit system for agricultural extension, both of which were developed by David Benor.[26] He engaged the Australian economist Sir John Crawford to see what regional planning could do to accelerate agricultural production.

While the World Bank was doubling, tripling, and quadrupling in size as a result of its global poverty mission, member countries were constantly reminded about the need for competition, small lean public institutions, accountability and transparency, shrinkage of state functions, private sector development, level playing fields, market-based this or that. World Bank expansion was promoted by officials who wanted to deal with big bold ideas, global commitments, planetary considerations.

The World Bank financed more education projects than Educational, Scientific and Cultural Organization (UNESCO), more agriculture projects than the UN Food and Agriculture Organization, more environmental projects than the UN Environment Programme (UNEP), and made the UNDP appear to be a very junior partner. Given its public visibility, the World Bank managed to get more and more of the aid money of bilateral aid agencies of countries such as Britain and the Scandinavians who, although they have convinced their citizens that it is their moral duty to give lots of money for poverty alleviation, do not seem to be able to spend all that money on useful investments.

Soon after war was declared on global poverty the walls of Bank offices were covered with pictures of poor people. Now that the World Bank is vastly larger, the offices are not covered with pictures of suffering. There are, instead, postcards of nice places staff have visited, primitive art, photographs of roads, dams, bridges, and flat fields bursting with an improved variety of this or that. In the middle of the day, as with other banks, there are lectures by famous economists and music concerts.

Poverty alleviation, especially poverty alleviation that was presented as a solvable problem as long as very large sums were spent on infrastructural projects, provided a major boost to the raising and spending of very large sums of money. The World Bank expects to spend $59 billion in 2018; in 1968 it raised and lent about $1 billion to client countries. The World

Bank has now lent around $400 billion and the only chance of getting the money back seems to be to lend more. It has been able to raise and spend because the institution has advantages that ordinary banks and development agencies don't have: it raises money on the world's bond markets backed by the full faith and credit of the rich countries. Economic growth generated by the World Bank's economic investments in the developing countries is intended to help the poorest people in the world to achieve higher incomes. The money to fund these investments has been collected from the rich countries to give to the poor in recognition of a moral commitment to help the very poorest.[27]

Manufacturers and suppliers in the industrialized countries were accustomed to getting 80 or 90 cents from every dollar that went into the World Bank's infrastructural development projects. When Robert McNamara wanted to have lots of loans for social development he found that this was not popular among the manufacturing and key private sector supporters in the industrialized countries. Low-spending social development attracted no such enthusiasm in the industrialized countries because condoms, mosquito nets, and primary school teachers did not cost a great deal whereas infrastructural development created jobs at home in the commodity supply chain, in the provision of training, and for consulting companies. Poverty alleviation involving large-scale infrastructural development, which had a less obvious link with effective alleviation, was popular with the rich and powerful at home. Abroad, developing countries also wanted large wads of cash to provide visible signs of progress for the voters that strengthened the power and the positions of the politicians who had negotiated the loans.

Why, citizens in the developed countries might wonder, are there so many expatriates and foreigners involved in development assistance? Are poor country nationals not in a better position to handle their own poverty? One reason is that the World Bank stipulates that consulting firms that are full of foreign nationals and frequently very expensive, be used to supervise and sometimes prepare projects. Another reason is that many of the key personnel in the government have trained and spent much of their careers overseas and may well know little about how poor people in their own country live. Poor countries may themselves employ large numbers of expatriates in key ministries. One secretary for finance in Papua New Guinea said that he had sent so many expatriates from his department to Washington that he ought to charge the World Bank a training fee.

The World Bank has garnered support in the industrialized countries by promising to eliminate poverty and support in the developing countries by providing cheap billions for economic development. Governments did not disagree with the World Bank's promises to end poverty even though they knew that elimination would not happen. After all, poor countries can save the money they themselves would have used on poverty alleviation and can then spend those funds on items with a higher priority for the government such as military hardware. And surely it is the case that World Bank poverty alleviation may well be encouraging a number of developing country governments to think that their citizens' severe poverty is somebody else's problem.

To attract larger and larger sums of money from the industrialized countries the World Bank has to present global poverty as a problem that could, at a cost, be fixed because the causes and cures are known. At the same time, the World Bank has to exert sufficient influence and control over poor country governments to ensure that they pursue economic growth—which they often want to do if the process is not too painful—accompanied by the right measures. These initiatives inevitably involve a reordering of political and social priorities and a willingness to listen and act on World Bank advice to a point that some might think impinges on a country's sovereignty.

The idea that more money can do the job has been questioned by former World Bank economists such as Bill Easterly in his book *The White Man's Burden.*[28] Obviously, as far as poverty alleviation is concerned, economic development by itself could not be expected to be sufficient because its benefits might not reach the poor. Implementation needs a high degree of government commitment and few countries have the technical capacity or the political will to do what is required for a comprehensive program of poverty alleviation.

A strong policy dialogue with developing countries in which the World Bank's economic views usually prevailed was thought to be in the public interest. The substance for these conversations came from the World Bank's country economist who monitored national income, the exchange rate, consumption, savings, investment, profits, imports, exports, and rates of population growth. Special attention was paid to debt management and the proportion of the national budget that was required to service loan obligations. Every few years the country economist was responsible for an economic memorandum dealing not only with creditworthiness, but also with what the World Bank's leading strategy should be for the next few years. At the sectoral level other economists looked at strategies for the sector by examining costs, utilities, prices, and quantities in order to identify interventions and investment opportunities.

In common with other big corporations the World Bank is now beginning to rely on risk analysis. Risk analysis aggregates and relies on the views and opinions of a few at headquarters; it survives and grows because of the suggestiveness of the language, the impression that there is a method driving all the uninformed opinions, and because it can be forgotten about as soon as the charts have been circulated to those who matter. Risk analysis is usually conducted too early or too late or with too little frequency and too little imagination.[29]

The World Bank in Washington became a counting house as more and more money was collected. The World Bank said that without its development skills and its comprehensive development framework, and more money, the systemic problems that cause poverty could not be addressed.[30] Bilateral development assistance agencies followed the World Bank's example by making the ending of poverty a mission priority. For example, in 1997, a few years after McNamara's Nairobi speech, Clare Short, Britain's then secretary of state for overseas development, produced a White Paper showing how the UK could help to eliminate global poverty.[31]

The World Bank example was followed by other UN agencies as they became aware of how addressing poverty could expand their budgets. UNEP, UNDP, UNICEF, and UNESCO all regularly make bids to help. The Office of the UN High Commissioner for Human Rights (OHCHR) says that poverty is an infringement of Human Rights.[32] The quest for funds is not confined to public sector sources: UN agencies have begun to approach the public for funds. On overseas commercial flights passengers are asked for money to help UNICEF though they are not told that it can cost that agency close to $500,000 a year to keep a staff member overseas.

Capital Transfers

The Bretton Woods architects supposed that the World Bank would provide a bridge over which capital could safely flow from the developed to the developing countries, but for much of the 1980s more money was coming back to Washington for repayment of old loans than was going out in new loans. Private sector investment then entered and this was thought to restore the balance in favor of developing countries since foreign direct investment did not have to be repaid like a World Bank loan.

The private sector has now become the largest supplier of finance in the developing countries. Good companies have learned to avoid creating dependency and that they need a dedicated workforce of community practitioners who have hands-on skills and who have been schooled to listen to and learn from poor people before engaging with them. Emphasis is placed on relationships and reciprocity with both company and locals gaining something of value because experience has shown that community goodwill cannot be bought. Companies need to behave in a consistent manner, a need supported by written commitments. In and of itself the fact that there is two-way communication with poor people represents a considerable advance over the management-by-seclusion practices of the big donors.[33]

In 2000 UN Secretary General Kofi Annan launched a massive private sector initiative when he invited the CEOs of the world's largest corporations to join a global compact whose main object was to prevent corruption, avoid human rights abuses, and protect the environment while implementing the Millennium Development Goals (MDGs).[34] The World Bank was slow to appreciate the need to enter into partnership with the private sector. Despite talking about the importance of working with the private sector the World Bank organized meetings of the Paris Club in Paris—between the World Bank and borrowing countries—without inviting the private sector to attend. Although thirty years ago the flow of funds from the rich to the poor countries was largely dependent on official aid flows, that is no longer the case. Private sector funds are now more significant than official flows.

The private sector, in addition to its wealth creation capacity, had several distinct advantages over institutions such as the World Bank. First, many private sector firms are in for the long haul and are not, like UN agencies, looking for change within the short life of a project. Second, the private sector is looking for employees and opportunities to make a difference and is therefore more likely to look for the positive dimensions of local poverty—the assets rather than the negatives. Third, the private sector will say what it can't do as well as what it can do and this sort of assessment is long overdue in poverty alleviation. Companies with a good record for social performance also have a role to play; they already have much more focus on communities than official development assistance.[35] As shown by Hickel,

> The flow of money from rich countries to poor countries pales in comparison to the flow that runs in the other direction. In 2012, the last year of recorded data, developing countries received a total of $1.3 trillion, including all aid, investment, and income from abroad. But that same year some $3.3 trillion flowed out of them. In other words, developing countries sent $2 trillion more to the rest of the world than they received. If we look at all years since 1980, these net outflows add up to a massive total of $16.3 trillion—that's how much money has been drained out of the global south over the past few decades. To get a sense for the scale of this, $16.3 trillion is roughly the GDP of the United States. What this suggests is that the usual development narrative, which highlights money going from the rich to the poor countries, has it backward.[36]

Projects

By the early 1980s, and due to an energetic sales effort, the World Bank was turning out around 300 projects a year. The average size of these projects was around $80 million although some were more than $100 million and others were less than $5 million. Over the course of the past thirty years the trend has been toward larger and larger loans. Projects and programs could not get the money out quickly enough to meet the expansion targets for lending and the World Bank began what was called policy-based lending. Policy-based lending, which might involve up to $1 billion, involved situations where a government agreed to change its policies or to draft new policies to benefit the poorest, in return for which the World Bank provided finance. Typically, financing covered a three-year program. Policy-based lending, which was sometimes called Structural Adjustment Lending (SAL), became the new popular vehicle for poverty funds. SALs were made to member countries in return for promises to reform economic management. Reforms covered the budget, state enterprises, subsidies and the civil service.[37] In return for the funds, governments were supposed to use the money for the good of the poor. Anecdotal accounts of the time suggested that less than 50 percent of the list of conditions attached to SALs (referred to as conditionalities) were met.

Where fifty years ago USAID recognized the need to alter project procedures to accommodate the special needs of the very poorest, the World Bank did not. What was needed, and what the World Bank has never developed, was a project delivery system capable of the mass delivery of benefits directly to the very poorest using average or below-average resources. World Bank projects used above-average financial and human resources; they took center stage; they required a great deal of the time of a country's most able civil servants. And, in addition to the time of senior civil servants, the World Bank was usually also able to ensure the participation of the best consultants. Few governments can afford to spend that amount of time on all the projects that would be needed to produce benefits for the well-off, let alone the poorest.

Traditionally, project design looked at the needs of potential participants in an investment in order to assess what level of income or health and education would constitute an improvement as well as a contribution to local, regional, or national goals. It was usually assumed that if opportunities were offered they would be taken up. What was missing in this way of looking at projects, and what anthropology was often able to supply, was an idea of what participants had to learn to do in order for a project to be a success. Did they have to learn new methods of animal husbandry or new personal hygiene practices? When looked at in this way it was clear that each development project was—yes—about cultural change but it was also about securing some changed behavior on the part of project participants that would remain in place after the project was finished. A project was not only an experiment in social change, but also had to be a learning experience that aimed to institutionalize new ways of behaving in order to secure income, health, and education improvements.[38] Consequently, projects could be looked at in terms of constraints: Were there beliefs, values, and attitudes that would make the behavior changes that were needed difficult to achieve? On the other hand, were there factors that could be used to increase the chances that the new methods, techniques, and forms of behavior would take root?

What project designers needed to do was to recognize—and this was particularly true for poverty alleviation—that each and every project needed to change behavior; the challenge for analysis was to identify who had to change and how that change could best be introduced and secured. In this process, relationships that facilitated the creation of rapport and the hands-on skills and knowledge of aid agency personnel had vital roles to play. First, and as a result of experience with relationships among the target population, personnel needed to help with project design. Second, personnel needed to facilitate the learning and change process as implementation proceeded. In this way it could be seen that staff with local knowledge and skills had a vital role to play—one that provided substantive content for project relationships. When this behavioral factor was recognized it could, of course, be used to speed up, slow down, or adjust the project implementation process.

Public Administration and Local Government

Local government is the government that is closest to poor people.[39] From Bretton Woods onward, the World Bank pretty much neglected local government, in particular rural local government. IBRD's Articles of Agreement preclude lending to local government and the World Bank concentrated its lending at national level. Central government usually takes to itself all the most easily collected sources of revenue, leaving local governments in a very difficult situation indeed. If and when World Bank money was borrowed by a national government and then passed on local government usually faced having to pay a hefty on-lending charge. Of course, when metropolitan areas wanted transport or educational institutions or social housing or new sewerage arrangements costing hundreds of millions of dollars, then the World Bank was interested in lending.

From a public administration perspective there was little point in persuading client countries to adopt the "right" policies if they did not at the same time acquire the capacity to change those policies as circumstances changed. What aid officials often did not seem to appreciate was the importance of not looking only at the policies, but also at the administrative machinery that was available to translate those policies into action. Instead, in the years since the World Bank's 1983 *World Development Report* (WDR) on public sector management, interest in administration was largely confined to the extent to which the public service could advance the economic and financial objectives set by the World Bank. Reducing the size and cost of government became important, as did the creation of special efforts to generate revenue while local government was, as already mentioned, shamefully neglected. The World Bank supported privatizing, downsizing, rightsizing, and getting the policies right but frequently the emphasis on accountability and managerialism also served to promote skills and ways of behaving that took the public service farther and farther away from the notion of service to the public.[40]

Visiting World Bank staff needed to understand how government was supposed to work and how it actually did work, but few had the overseas experience that this understanding required. Administrative capacity and the administrative requirements for poverty relief ought to have been a starting point for strengthening the World Bank's appreciation of what was needed for poverty relief. In 1983, and even earlier, internal recommendations were made in the World Bank for the creation of administrative overview papers that would have begun to provide the first building blocks for such a database. These would, in effect, have been administrative ethnographies, accounts of how the public service works, how it is supposed to work, and the values, beliefs, and attitudes of officials.

When I was chief technical adviser for civil service reform in Tanzania I discovered that World Bank and UNDP staff knew so little about the workings of a civil service that they designed the wrong management arrangements for the project. They had created and filled a post that they called Executive Chairman for the Civil Service Reform Project (CSRP) because they wanted their appointee to look as if he had all the authority that reform might need. To attract the right candidate, they offered a high salary. Neither the World Bank nor UNDP (nor the UK Department for International Development, DfID) realized that in any former British colony the executive authority that wanted the Executive Chairman to have was by law invested in the permanent secretary of the civil service department. When I pointed this out to the permanent secretary of the civil service department he really did not want to upset the donors. The World Bank was happy to soldier on with the defective arrangement and so were the Danish and Swedish donors. A later evaluation of CSRP glossed over the mistake the World Bank and UNDP had made. Their review said,

> Initially, the independent secretariat arrangement of the CSRP provided a "quick start" for the programme, as it bypassed normal Civil Service proce-

dures. However, it soon ran into difficulties implementing new policies as it lacked credibility within Government. In effect it was duplicating the role of the Civil Service Department [CSD] (which has the statutory management responsibility for the Civil Service) without CSD's authority. Although CSRP was located within CSD, the institutional linkages with it were weak, and little was done to develop the capacity of departmental staff within CSD who had line responsibility for core CSRP activities such as pay reform and restructuring. A key factor in this poor relationship was the perceived unfairness of the pay arrangements, such that CSRP staff (including recently retired Civil Servants) were enjoying pay levels which were a multiple of 10 or 20 of that of regular civil servants in CSD."[41]

World Bank economists did not have a good understanding of how the Tanzanian bureaucracy worked and how it might be improved.[42] Although the project was supposed to be about civil service reform I had the greatest difficulty persuading the donors, and the Tanzanian government, that local government should be included in the package. When working on the 1983 WDR whose theme was public sector management, I had to press for the inclusion of some mention of local government. The inclusion was agreed but without much enthusiasm. World Bank economists wanted the Tanzanians to dismiss 50,000 civil servants; the country knew that if the money was to keep coming they had little choice other than to obey. Nobody really knew how many civil servants there were because there were so many "ghosts."[43] What was known was that the amount of money the World Bank wanted to be saved could have easily come from retrenching a small number of those who were highly paid at the top of the service. In the end, it was the little people at the bottom of the service, those who had few skills and few job prospects, who were fired.[44] One difficulty was that much of the salaries contained numerous allowances, and these did not count towards pension entitlements.

NGOs

National disasters such as that in Haiti, and good causes such as clean water or better protection against deadly diseases, have seen NGOs working closely with UN agencies and the World Bank. As Swithern's Humanitarian Report notes, "International humanitarian assistance rose for a second year running to a record $24.5 billion in 2014. All of 2013's largest donors gave more in 2014, and many gave their largest amounts."[45] NGOs must continually face the challenge of raising money, but in meeting this challenge they have to try to ensure that they do not do better with the building of skills to raise funds than in maintaining the capacity to spend those funds to good advantage.

Social development has been most strongly associated with the smaller NGOs, particularly the national ones, which have tended to be taken for granted by the big international players. However, it is the big international payers, the Oxfams and the CAREs (Cooperative for Assistance and Relief Everywhere), that have campaigned on behalf of the issues for which the World Bank has now developed responses. They have been extremely effective with emergencies, with drawing attention to unnoticed environmental problems that, if left unchecked, will pose a global threat, and with educating and informing the public about what support is needed.[46]

The World Bank's virtual monopoly on the aid money of industrialized countries has resulted in crowding out NGOs who do work well with the poor. The World Bank sucks up most of the available aid money so that NGOs have to beg for money on evening TV. These organizations have the capacity to work much more closely with poor people than the World Bank and are often prepared to do small projects with poor people, something that it is very difficult for the big agencies to contemplate.

Growing Challenges

After the turn of this century the World Bank faced a number of new competitors. These included China, the EU, and the Republic of Korea (South Korea; hereafter Korea); these countries have become big sources of financial assistance to poorer countries, private consulting firms, private investment banks, and private foundations, including the Bill & Melinda Gates Foundation. The new development banks were offering quicker and cheaper financing and as a result were getting more and more new business. However, the World Bank retains a slight competitive advantage because of its financing arrangements, which are backed by the governmental guarantees of the industrialized countries, enabling the flow of funds to increase each year. The US and other industrialized countries would like the World Bank to stop lending and providing concessional finance and assistance to the BRIC countries (Brazil, Russia, India and China).

Lending to countries that are capable of looking after their own poor should be phased out. The BRIC countries have the technical capacity and financial muscle to address their own extreme poverty without external assistance. China, for example, has established the Asian Infrastructure Development Bank, so continued World Bank lending to that country makes little sense. Indeed, quite why the BRIC have continued their World Bank association is hard to fathom since all BRIC countries could, like Korea, probably well afford to set up their own development banks. The BRICs in general, and Chinese-funded development assistance in particular, may not have the same concern for safeguards work. European and US firms have discovered that, when it comes to African or Asian developing countries, new lenders such as China do not play by their rules; they do not seem to worry much about worker safety nor do they want to do exhaustive and expensive environmental and social analysis. India has world-class computing skills and China may shortly overtake the US in terms of economic importance. Where the BRICs can be expected to focus much of their effort will be on the twin tasks of developing and sustaining policy leverage and a market for their goods and services. This will bring out and make more obvious the political nature of the development process as well as the domestic commercial advantages that large infrastructural projects provide and that have so far been seen to go to the US and Europe.[47]

Grants or Loans

In development assistance circles there was a growing debate over whether the World Bank should provide grants or loans to the world's poorest countries.[48] While discussing the possibilities the World Bank has stuck with lending. The World Bank has two lending rates: the higher rate, which is for middle-income countries, and the IDA rate, which is loaned at a very low interest rate to the poorest countries. As Radelet has commented, "Countries are classified for IBRD or IDA funding based on two criteria: (i) income levels, with the IDA cut-off at approximately $900 annual income (with a few exceptions), and (ii) creditworthiness, based on Bank staff judgments about a country's ability to borrow on private capital markets."[49] Providing grants rather than loans to the very poorest countries would reduce debt and encourage those countries to become more self-reliant.

World Bank reliance on IDA funds, recently replenished to the tune of $54 billion, have given the institution a considerable competitive advantage. At a quarter of a percent over 40 years the IDA money is virtually grant money. It has not been difficult for the World Bank to collect IDA money from industrialized country governments; many don't know how to spend the money they set aside for aid. Giving those funds to the World Bank suggests value for money, but it is shortsighted. It would make more sense for these agencies to learn how to do their jobs properly or to stop the silly and wasteful practice of giving a fixed proportion of national income for development assistance.

In 2000 the US Congress appointed a task force to examine international financial institutions, including the World Bank. The commission, chaired by Allan Meltzer, recommended reforms, since it found that aid was mainly going to the rich and the better off in poor countries and that increases in the amount of money would probably make the situation worse.[50]

Micro-Finance

Could the World Bank mobilize micro-credit for poverty alleviation? Only to a limited extent, it seemed. Supporters of micro-finance initiatives want to try to ensure that "poor and socially marginalized people and households have access to a wide range of affordable, high-quality financial products and services, including not just credit but also savings, insurance, payment services, and fund transfers."[51] The microfinance industry is estimated at $60 billion–$100 billion, with 200 million clients, but the results, even including well-known examples such as Grameen Bank, have been mixed. Critics cite modest benefits associated with microcredit, overindebtedness, and a trend toward commercialization that is less focused on serving the poor. Obviously one of the major constraints on using finance to alleviate poverty is the fact that poor people have to pay very high interest—usually thought to be in the nature of 30–70 percent—to get access to money, and even large institutions like the World Bank cannot hope to overcome the problem with subsidies.

At the beginning of my overseas career, cooperatives were popular; they worked well when I was in the Solomon Islands, particularly when the members, who never understood the concept of a share, had someone who could keep the books.[52] When governments began to try to help small businesses by making small loans they had a growing mountain of bad debts until they learned to find out what local moneylenders were charging. When they adjusted their rates to what the moneylenders were charging the default rates declined dramatically. Savings associations and self-help organizations have worked here and there but without any model or approach becoming dominant. Experience suggested that lending to both individuals as well as groups was successful and that women were good at saving.

When working in Sri Lanka USAID procedures made it possible for me as chief-of-party to give very small grants. In Sri Lanka I was able to give a $200 grant to men and women who recycled aluminum cans collected from Colombo rubbish dumps. Those loans were followed by a small grant of a few hundred dollars to the Maharagama three-wheelers association who wanted to lobby the Colombo authorities for permission to park their vehicles in a spot that would help their business. Big aid agencies find it very hard to have hands-on contact with small clients or to give out small amounts of money, even though small amounts are often exactly what is needed.[53]

The Recurrent Cost Problem

Many of the grants and loans made by the World Bank had a satisfactory anticipated rate of return, but too few produced the steady stream of revenue that enables a government to pay for the costs of maintaining these new investments. Further borrowing, regardless of whether it is a loan or a grant, usually does nothing to improve the health of the recurrent budget. On the contrary, increased further borrowing will further weaken the recurrent budget, because the borrowing will generate additional loan repayment burdens. The major reason why recurrent budgets are weak is because of too much unproductive borrowing. Even in the case of highly concessional lending, donor activities frequently cause more problems than they solve. But World Bank staff push their projects regardless of the fact that even "free" money further weakens the public finances of the recipient country.[54] Beginning in 1996 the World Bank, in part as a response to the growing recurrent cost problem, began to cancel the loans of some of the most highly indebted countries; this trend is likely to increase. However, in some instances the countries whose debts have been forgiven begin to borrow unwisely again.

Roads and schools must be maintained. Depending on the climate and use factors the annual cost of maintaining a building might be equal to 10 percent of the construction cost, and the amount that would be needed to maintain a road might be 5 percent of the capital cost. The link between the capital budget (money spent on construction and what economists think of as deferred consumption) and the recurrent budget (money for the annual running costs for the civil service) was not adequately included in the financial analysis in projects work. Many developing countries did not budget for the recurrent costs of capital development in their recurrent budgets. Each time a capital project was approved and undertaken, a contribution for recurrent costs needed to be added to the recurrent budget. In many instances the new investments remained on the capital budget because the borrower did not have sufficient revenue to support maintenance costs from the recurrent budget.

Consultants

Projects work was increasingly outsourced to consulting firms as lending expanded. The consulting services provided by the big accounting firms have grown rapidly in order to meet the increasing tide of World Bank-financed business. Some 25–30 percent of World Bank personnel are temporary employees, either individuals or from firms, and the cost of their services has now reached between $15 billion and $20 billion a year. These costs are usually added to the cost of the loan; unsurprisingly, the World Bank's habit of recommending expensive European and US consultants to do required work has not always been popular with borrowers. For the World Bank the big accounting firms are highly convenient; they can if necessary be badged as local firms or international firms and so it is easier to use them in countries where contracting is difficult unless it flows through a locally owned or controlled company. The big accounting firms—Deloitte & Touche, PricewaterhouseCoopers, KPMG, and Ernst & Young—tackled anything the World Bank wanted: health, museums, the administration of justice, tax, trade, growing flowers, floating shares, sinking funds, or anything where large sums of money are involved. Probably what the big accounting firms liked best was privatization. In many countries they earned millions by supplying advice on how to downsize the state. If and when that failed they advised on upsizing. They had tremendous comparative experience. Solutions, which were usually based on best practice from all over the world, were tightly written, studded with pithy PowerPoint capsules, and delivered on time.

A big consulting company can provide one-stop services: it can handle macro-level economic issues as well as social safeguard issues at the community level. Of course, the danger is that since World Bank guidelines and policies are fairly general, scope is provided for the consulting companies and the consultants to put their own ideas and interpretations into practice. When it comes to social development the World Bank has limited in-house community-level capacity; anthropologists and sociologists, 90 or 100 in number, may personally know a particular area in depth but the number of project demands for local information far exceeds their knowledge base. In fact, as the World Bank has grown, more and more anthropologists and sociologists with a fondness for a particular area have preferred to work with consulting companies since they believe that this employment makes better use of their fieldwork skills. Private sector businesses working in remote areas have found that the World Bank often relies on exactly the same consultants that they are using.

The time is fast approaching for the World Bank and other development assistance agencies to develop a strategy for managing the intellectual consequences of outsourcing. More and more pieces of work that ought to be handled by Bank staff are being assigned to consulting firms and individual consultants who are mostly based in the rich countries. It is these firms and individuals that are gaining a competitive commercial and intellectual advantage rather than the World Bank staff who manage and backstop the work or the developing countries where much of the work is carried out. The consulting companies are becoming price-givers rather than price-takers; in many areas of social development the preponderance of knowledge and experience resides outside the World Bank with companies and individuals who have more up-to-date and comprehensive, as well as specialized, knowledge than exists within the World Bank itself. This makes the development of new policies and procedures based on World Bank experience much more difficult than was the case thirty years ago.

Donor Management

Tanzania, which has gained a great deal of revenue from aid, and intends to continue to do well, seems to sense, and quite rightly, that important World Bank visitors do not like to see their favorite ideas fail, and so they continue to offer support even when things go wrong. Of course, all the while the international agencies take over more and more of the running and ruining of the country while wringing their hands and protesting that they want to reduce dependency, that they only intend to facilitate, and so on. And even when things go very wrong, Tanzanians are good sports. They will murmur *pole sana* (very sorry), a nice elegant ki-Swahili expression of regret. They can sense that when donors get angry with them they still care; there is thus still more money to be had.

When Tanzanians are lambasted at international meetings for poor revenue collection or corruption they quietly accept the blame. They would never suggest that, after thirty years of aid, perhaps the donors should share some of the blame. Unique skills have been developed by Tanzanians in the handling of relationships with donors that usually result in a maximization of concessional aid inflow and a minimization of change to areas where local opinion is quite happy with things as they are.

Tanzanians manage donors very effectively; they study them, and consequently seem to be able to get the donors to initiate something that the donors really want to do. They know what donor personnel need to show their home ministries in order to advance their careers. They manage to ensure that all the plans, the ideas, the detail, and the funding come from the donors, so that the donors develop a suitable sense of responsibility for the outcome. There is reluctance on the part of donors to admit that they don't know the answers, to go back to the drawing board. Nobody, neither the aid agencies nor the Tanzanians who keep agreeing with them and then doing nothing, is prepared to dispel the illusion. And illusion has been part and parcel of the World Bank approach, as well as the Tanzanian approach, to development. The best strategy would be to stop the aid and let Tanzanians begin to sort themselves out. But Tanzanians have never had to come to terms with sorting out their own affairs because the World

Bank and the other international agencies and the Scandinavians have never had to come to terms with their own failed innovations.

As a country that has become more dependent on aid than most, Tanzania has been exposed to a bewilderingly broad array of innovations from aid agencies and their staff: Swedes from that country's *folk* (people's) colleges; Soviet advisers who offer planning help; New Zealanders anxious to shrink public sector functions; Australian stockmen who are highly concerned that locals be taught how to put up a stout fence; Canadians fascinated by agricultural engineering; South African surveyors, proud of their ability to "close" at 1:250,000, who are hard on their crews and reluctant to believe that any local surveyor could meet their professional standards; Polish advisers from the United Nations Industrial Development Organization, determined to demonstrate their understanding of computer technology; Indian economists, determined to show what their discipline can do; Sri Lankan accountants who are sticklers for procedures; Americans who want to harness satellite technology; Pakistanis who believe that a good civil service staff college could solve many problems; Chinese engineers who try to construct Olympic facilities, or some other symbol of everlasting friendship, quickly and very cheaply; Germans who try to reproduce the dual training partnership they have known between industry and chambers of commerce; Irish advisers who want to show what their Industrial Development Authority thinking can do; Finns who build, equip, staff, and train entire hospitals; and Japanese agriculturalists anxious to grow rice or produce a master plan of something important for the future where their private sector construction or engineering industry can play a prominent role.

Accountability

The World Bank marks its own homework, and there are no institutionalized arrangements for genuinely independent evaluation. Externally, objective analysis is supposed to be provided by the highly visible, and aggressively promoted, Independent Evaluation Group, but it is operated by World Bank staff members. Internally, complaints about projects are handled by a three-person inspection panel, an arrangement that was started after the Indian dam controversy in the 1980s. The panel is usually drawn from former World Bank staff or those who have worked at other UN agencies. These two evaluation mechanisms do not have the right appearance. The increasingly urgent need is for comprehensive and authoritative evaluation mechanisms whose membership, procedure, work schedule, and reporting are beyond any suspicion of being influenced by the World Bank and its major shareholders.

Corporations have gradually learned that society expects more than financial probity and a good balance sheet. The private sector has faced fierce criticism, which so far the World Bank has escaped, because business executives have not managed to persuade NGOs that they will not put profits before principle. Why should an organization tackling poverty be any different?[55] The World Bank's accountability is not to voters but, like any other corporation, to the institution's shareholders, who are national governments. If you supposed that an organization whose raison d'être is to work to eliminate poverty would be in some way answerable to poor people, you would be wrong. The Board of Governors of the World Bank comprises directors who vote their country's wishes in the case of the big shareholders while other directors convey the interests and instructions of groups of small countries who have been elected to represent a group of minority shareholder countries.[56] The directors perform as delegates who pass on their views of their home country. Ministries of finance seem to be representatives passing on what they have been told to say and vote for and against rather than behaving as representatives who can be expected to use their own judgment and experience even when their views may not be precisely those of their masters. Maynard Keynes is reputed to have said that the World Bank needed to avoid behaving like a bank if it wanted to gain recognition as a development institution but, on the other hand, it was not clear how the institution would be able to succeed if it gave all its money away.

The internationalist character of the World Bank and its backing by the full faith and credit of the richest industrialized nations made the institution look as if it was an accountable public entity. However, the ministry of finance officials from member countries who serve as governors of the World Bank are not persons who are always very knowledgeable about what should be happening on the ground nor are they inclined to be terribly tough on the World Bank since it raises its own money, albeit with the guarantee of member countries. This makes it unnecessary for the member country finance officials who like to be visionary, without raising taxes or having to spend their own money, to agree to most of what is recommended by the President of the World Bank. US congressional committees do weigh in from time to time but their views do not necessarily carry weight these days with the BRIC countries who want World Bank voting rights to more accurately reflect their economic status.[57]

Obviously it would help if aid agencies in general, and the World Bank in particular, were discouraged from promoting their approaches, products, and wares in the media because such activities seldom present a balanced view. Much of what is released by aid agencies is, not surprisingly, self-serving. Surely the public interest would be best served by high-profile third-party opinion? Despite the fact that development assistance involves a great deal of public money and tough choices, it is largely a matter of, as with the World Bank, one set of bureaucrats answering to another set of bureaucrats. Development assistance could certainly do with a transparency initiative like that adopted by extractive industry.[58] After all, it is easy enough to access all the positive things that are said by the World Bank, Oxfam, and other aid agencies and NGOs about their own performance but where does the citizen go to find the not-so-positive news and how is a sensible balance between the good and the bad to be achieved? Should we believe that the World Bank has been able to spend several hundreds of billions of dollars without there once having been any questionable conduct on the part of a staff member? Despite intense concern in the industrialized countries in the performance of police, doctors, and nurses, there is no such concern about the way World Bank staff carry out their duties overseas.

Emphasis on reputation management and advertising have contributed to a failure to inform the public about what can and cannot be done. Where can the citizen easily find how much of the aid money is spent at home? How much of the aid budget goes toward promoting trade? How much for foreign policy objectives? There is a general failure on the part of governments and aid agencies to supply the public with the information needed to understand the objects and reasons behind the national objectives and purposes of development assistance. Why should the test for the relevance of a development assistance agency be any different from the test applied when one media company wishes to acquire another? Will the public receive a balanced and objective view or will there be an unhealthy concentration of power and influence if the views of one actor become dominant? Despite numerous think-tanks and other organizations having been established to further the public interest in gaining a better understanding of what aid agencies do, their delivery is too infrequent and too selective and too general to provide an adequate accounting the public can rely on.

In rich countries the public is subjected to an ever-increasing barrage of demands for financial assistance, support, and understanding from organizations claiming to be or about to be eliminating serious world problems— hunger, disease, access to clean water, gender equality, education, poverty, environmental protection, and plain suffering—if only they can get a little regular money from viewers or readers. Unfortunately, there is no international or national assistance-rating agency where we can look up the organization that wants money to see its track record, whether or not good use is made of the money, how much is spent on administration and management, and why, if it is such a worthy cause, the agency does not get some of the official aid budget. The average citizen has little or no opportunity to assess the reasonableness of the avalanche of requests because usually the public knows only when an organization has failed to deliver, and if and when some regulator or whistle blower says so. Aid is such a given, and the lack of information so generally accepted, that political parties do not even debate the issue other than to question How much? instead of What for? It is this unimaginative accountability regime that has produced the present quite ridiculous situation where industrialized countries measure their commitment, their decency, and their humanity in terms of the proportion of their national income that is spent on foreign aid.

Notes

1. The war on poverty is discussed in Weisbrod, *The Economics of Poverty*.

2. Halberstam, *The Best and the Brightest*. Tendler, *Inside Foreign Aid*, described money-making behavior at USAID.

3. Shaw, *Back to Methuselah*, Part 1, Act 1.

4. See Spicer, *Human Problems in Technological Change*.

5. Brown, *The Social Impact of the Green Revolution*.

6. Sharma, *Robert McNamara's Other War*, 54–58.

7. World Bank [1971], press release, September 27. Alan Berg, the World Bank's first nutrition adviser, had little impact and little institutional visibility. See Berg, *Nutritional Factor*, portions with Robert J. Muscat.

8. Streeten et al., *First Things First*.

9. World Bank President Kim, who was president of Dartmouth College before going to the World Bank had, in addition to medical qualifications, an anthropology PhD from Harvard. He has followed the McNamara expansion tradition and has shown less interest in social and cultural factors than Jim Wolfensohn, who was an investment banker in Australia with experience of conditions in the outback before arriving in Washington. World Bank [2015], "World Bank Forecasts Global Poverty to Fall Below 10% for First Time," press release, 4 October.

10. On efficiency and effectiveness, see Waldo, "Development in the West."

11. Warren Baum, interview by John Lewis, Richard Webb, and Devesh Kapur, World Bank History Project, 13 November 1990.

12. Wade, "Western States in Global Organizations."

13. Cochrane and Noronha, "Recommendations on the Use of Anthropology"; Cochrane, "What Can Anthropology Do for Development."

14. On 25 July 1986, Richard W. Van Wagenen was interviewed on behalf of the World Bank Archives Oral History Program by Robert W. Oliver.

15. Between 1968 and 1973 the professional staff increased from 767 to 1,654. By 1981 the figure was 2,552. World Bank, *Annual Report 1981*.

16. My late friend Stan Batey used to say that bright visitors from the headquarters of aid agencies and corporations with limited overseas experience of living in a poor country could, all too easily, get their ambitions mixed up with their capabilities.

17. Visvanathan Rajagopalan, interview by William Becker and David Milobsky, World Bank Archives Oral History Program, 1 January 1993.

18. When I worked on the 1983 WDR I think I was the only person who had been a regular civil servant. One had been a planner in a developing country.

19. Within the past ten years, books on the World Bank and UN agencies have included Hancock, *The Lords of Poverty*; Rich, *Mortgaging the Earth*; and Meren, *The Road to Hell*.

20. Yoshida, Uematsu, and Sobrado, "Is Extreme Poverty Going to End?"

21. For an indication of the work that should have regularly been updated if this incomes approach was to work, see Kravis, Heston, and Summers, *International Comparison of Real Product and Purchasing Power.*

22. A number of old and more recent articles deal with measurement but not with the assets and relationships of the poor. See Baster, *Measuring Development*; Chambers, *Rural Poverty Unperceived*; Drewnowski, "Poverty"; Glewwe and van der Gagg, "Confronting Poverty in Developing Countries"; Galbraith, *The Nature of Mass Poverty*; Mencher, "The Problem of Measuring Poverty."

23. Lipton, *Why Poor People Stay Poor*; Balogh, "Failures in the Strategy against Poverty"; Mangin, *Peasants in Cities.*

24. Kay, "Achievements and Contradictions of the Peruvian Agrarian Reform." Peruvian land reform took land from the rich and gave it to the landless, but the landless, even those who had been day laborers, were also poor in terms of their agricultural skills, so production fell and small farmers failed.

25. See, e.g., Mehta, "The World Bank and Its Emerging Knowledge Empire."

26. See Benor and Harrison, *Agricultural Extension.*

27. Global poverty was expected to have fallen from 902 million people or 12.8 percent of the global population in 2012, to 702 million people or 9.6 percent of the global population in 2017. World Bank Independent Evaluation Group, *Growth for the Bottom 40 Percent*; World Bank [2015], "World Bank Forecasts Global Poverty to Fall Below 10% for First Time," press release, 4 October.

28. Easterly, *The White Man's Burden.*

29. Kloman, *A Brief History of Risk Management.*

30. Wolfensohn, "A Proposal for a Comprehensive Development Framework."

31. See "Eliminating World Poverty." This policy paper followed more or less the same line that had been set by the US Congress with its New Directions in Foreign Aid legislation in 1973.

32. OHCHR and the World Bank both set out their stalls at a poverty conference organized by the Council of Europe in Strasbourg some years ago. See *Poverty: A Violation of Human Rights.*

33. Cochrane, *Anthropology in the Mining Industry.*

34. Williams, "The UN Global Compact"; Black and White, *Targeting Development.*

35. Cochrane, *Anthropology in the Mining Industry.*

36. Hickel, "Aid in Reverse."

37. See Ascher and Mason, *The World Bank Since Bretton Woods*; Baum and Tolbert, *Investing in Development.*

38. This approach to projects is discussed in Cochrane, *The Cultural Appraisal of Development Projects.*

39. Cochrane, "Policies for Strengthening Third World Local Government."

40. Malinowski was right to point out that one should "never forget the living, palpitating human being that remains somewhere at the heart of every institution;" Malinowski, *Introduction to Ian Hogbin*, 5.

41. Teskey and Hooper, "Tanzania Civil Service Reform Programme Case Study," 8.

42. Unlike Therkildsen, *Watering White Elephants?*

43. Ghosts were names on the payroll for people who did not exist but whose salary ended up with a real civil servant.

44. There was irony in an organization that said it was devoted to poverty elimination undertaking a CSRP that ended up creating rather than reducing the number of jobless poor people.

45. Swithern, *Global Humanitarian Assistance Report.*

46. Smillie, *The Alms Bazaar.*

47. Izquierdo, "BRICS Nations to Form Bank"; Bolton, "BRICS Development Bank."

48. "In 2004 the World Bank committed about $20 billion in new funding, of which $11 billion (55 percent) were IBRD loans and $9 billion (45 percent) were from IDA. Traditionally, IDA provided its financing almost exclusively as highly subsidized loans, but it began to expand its use of grants in 2003, and in 2004 it committed grants worth $1.7 billion (19 percent of IDA's total commitments)." Radelet, *Grants for the World's Poorest*, 1.

49. Ibid. IDA funds are concessional and have been lent at around a quarter of a percent for 40 years, which has made them little more than grant funds. Although they are supposed to go the poorest countries, they have also been used in rich countries in order to sweeten a loan deal. The World Bank discovered that it could compete very effectively with commercial banks by using a blend of soft IDA money and hard loan money. Recent reports in the press suggest that IDA funds have been replenished to the tune of $54 billion.

50. Radelet, "Grants for the World's Poorest," 1:

> Treasury Secretary Lawrence Summers under President Clinton made the first official US proposal on grants at the annual meeting of the IMF and World Bank in Prague in September 2000, calling for "the creation of a 100 percent concessional window for the provision of pure grant finance within IDA"—that is, for a subset of IDA funds (that he did not explicitly define) to be provided as grants. Ten months later the new Bush administration adopted a modified version of this proposal as its own. President George W. Bush, in a speech at World Bank headquarters in July 2001, called for 50 percent of IDA funds to be provided as grants for education, health, nutrition, water, and sanitation. Loans are based on the idea that the funds invested will generate enough resources through economic growth to repay the loans. But the very poorest countries, by definition, have not been successful in generating sustained growth, despite improved policies. Even when funds are invested wisely the country may not always be able to repay loans, since the poorest countries tend to be the most vulnerable to (and less able to cushion against) climactic and commodity price shocks. Progress in one area may be more than offset by unexpected setbacks elsewhere. Until countries have a proven record of sustained growth, grants may be more prudent than loans. (Ibid.)

51. Christen, Peck, Rosenberg, and Jayadeva, "Financial Institutions," 2–4.

52. See Worsley, *Two Blades of Grass*.

53. Bateman, *Why Doesn't Microfinance Work?*; Dowla and Barua, *The Poor Always Pay Back*; Maimbo and Ratha, *Remittances Development Impact*; Wright, *Microfinance Systems*.

54. Cochrane, *Issues in Budgeting*.

55. Schumpeter, "Principle before Profit."

56. Wade, "Western States in Global Organizations."

57. Meltzer, *Report of the International Financial Institution Advisory Commission*.

58. The Extractive Industries Transparency Initiative (EITI) was established to monitor and make public the financial flows from mineral, oil, and gas operations. It shows or is supposed to show where the money goes and who owns what. Eiti, "Upholding the Standard Internationally."

Chapter 2

REPUTATION MANAGEMENT

If senior management in Chase Bank announced that the organization was going to dedicate itself to poverty alleviation in Mississippi while securing a decent return on their invested funds and maintaining a Moody's AAA credit rating, most sensible people would assume that this was a publicity stunt. But by some sort of media-inspired trompe l'oeil the World Bank is able to earn billions in interest on past loans to some of the poorest countries in the world while claiming that its poverty paradigm can work.

The reputation management skills used by corporations are now used by the World Bank to simplify, aggregate, and communicate to citizens of developed countries the problems poor people face in different ways and in different societies and cultures without necessarily separating the things that could reasonably be expected to be achieved by economic development from the things that 10,000 or 20,000 aid agencies should not be expected to solve. Old problems had to be presented in new policy papers. Inevitably, the urge to communicate with the widest possible public to perfect the methodology of comparison, to quantify, to be significant, resulted in the end-product not being usable in anything other than a glib manner. Time was spent perfecting the technical neatness of proposals, the clarity of language, the compelling instructions, the solid supporting data, and so on. What was usually neglected was the necessity of engagement with the poor that could improve the chances for successful implementation. Wide-ranging proposals made by a few clever people seldom result in results on the ground. Insufficient time was spent developing a sense of ownership among those who would have the burden of implementation because improvement needed to have social roots.[1]

In March 1973 William Clark was appointed director of external relations at the World Bank and then quickly became a vice president and the primary spokesperson for McNamara and the World Bank. He laid the foundation for the World Bank's very significant and not yet fully appreciated reputation for management expertise.[2] Reputation management skills have become more and more important in elevating and maintaining the World Bank's public profile; this is essential for the institution's money-raising. Clark came from the Overseas Development Institute in London where he had been critical of the World Bank. McNamara had, as US Secretary of Defense, painful first-hand experience of what a hostile press could do. Under Clark the World Bank's publication business boomed.[3] He brought in professionals like Jim Feather who had been a director at the Oxford publisher, Blackwell.

Conventional wisdom in the private sector in general, and in oil and gas companies in particular, has been that it does not pay to sing your own praises; third-party advocacy is thought to be essential. Although bilateral aid agencies such as USAID or DfID are not permitted to advertise, the World Bank's extensive media coverage of its own activities suggests that, when done on a massive scale, self-advertising can drown out opposition and keep the institution's name in the public eye. With the arrival of Clark, World Bank messages were increasingly well placed in the world's press. A global posture was projected with, for example, the World Bank, together with the Group of Eight industrialized countries, mulling over the fate of Eastern Europe, or saying what relief could be offered for a country ravaged by war or a disease like Ebola. These carefully choreographed events have helped the World Bank become a charmed institution and have frequently played a much more important role than its actual performance on the ground. Imagery has become more and more important.

The international standing and visibility of the World Bank was helped by the fact that by the 1990s the President of the World Bank was, de facto, seen as the equal of an important head of state in a big country and a Bank vice president was seen to be equal to a head of state in a small country. Nothing was ever placed on paper that makes this clear—it can only be inferred from looking at what actually happens. The World Bank would usually make sure that the civil servant in charge of finance in a member country was made aware that his status was less than that of a Bank division chief; a Bank department director was on a slightly higher level than a minister for finance. This could be seen not only when World Bank staff visited the country but also at the annual meetings of the governors and at the Paris Club meetings of aid donors that looked for pledges of new aid for a borrower.[4] World Bank senior people have moved into vice presidential jobs or better in Indonesia, Nigeria, Panama, Pakistan, and Turkey in recent years.[5]

Statistical evangelism also helped, and, for example, provided data on the number of children in the world who failed to develop because they didn't get the proper nutrition before the age of five. Then there was usually a straightforward and obvious solution requiring World Bank leadership and more money. At first advertising was used to mobilize public opinion for aid, since development assistance is something that has simply never been popular. Then old development problems had to be presented in new ways to jaundiced and cynical legislatures in order to win new money for lending. War was redeclared on poverty, illiteracy, disease, hunger, gender inequity, and so on. The language of mountaineering was popular with crests, peaks, valleys, and the abyss; seismological metaphors were generated by the 1973 oil crisis with shocks, swings, and aftermaths; marine language was a perennial favorite with waves and troughs. In an effort to catch up, UNDP began to produce the *Human Development Report*, a document that tried to go one better than the World Bank by putting everything in the world into a graph or table.[6] But poor countries do not advance by means of significant coffee-table reading, nor in fact does our understanding of those countries' problems.

Evangelism could be seen on two fronts: one was in the developing countries where the aim was to increase economic growth, the second was at home in the US and Europe where the aim was to secure favorable public opinion in order to raise more and more money. Telling the story and putting the World Bank at the heart of that story has played a critical role in the promotion of the World Bank, enabling that institution to begin to shape the intellectual debate over aid. The World Bank's big-name economists began, and have maintained, a strong relationship with departments of economics at many of the world's great universities, thereby contributing to a situation where there has been very little criticism of the institution from academic economists. Staff from these institutions get research contracts and Bank staff spend sabbaticals at these institutions. Prize students are hired by the World Bank. The World Bank became a major publishing house providing an image of the institution at the cutting edge of thinking and practice related to poverty; books, articles, and press releases publicized the things that the World Bank wanted publicized, making it possible for them to raise and spend more and more money.

Positive Spin

Disciplinary and technical expertise has increasingly been organized as a publishable research activity that can be expected to have greater impact on the institution's external reputation than on ongoing operations. This research can be used to protect and extend the World Bank's position as the premier repository of poverty and development assistance know-how. Anthropology, for example, helped the World Bank to put a human face on poverty alleviation.[7] Well-promoted Bank publications with titles such as *Putting People First* and *Listen to the People* were intended to look like examples of normal practice though that was not universally the case.[8] As anyone who has worked in the World Bank well knows, its own self-interest, rather than people, are put first. The publications of Bank anthropologists have been deployed to good effect because they have conveniently conveyed the image of a World Bank that takes culture seriously, though not too seriously. Cultural difference, and explanations of cultural difference, if undertaken in one or two small instances, were indeed useful in a public relations sense. However, a systematic cultural analysis of differences in client countries around the world would have complicated and delayed lending while putting at risk the credibility of the statistical evangelism.

President of the World Bank, James D. Wolfensohn, provided an example of how reputation management could be used to make World Bank social performance appear to be better than it actually was. In 1999 he said, in an address to the governors, "My colleagues and I decided that, in order to map our own course for the future, we needed to know more about our own clients as individuals. We therefore launched a study entitled 'Voices of the Poor' and spoke to poor people about their hopes, their aspirations, their realities. Teams from the Bank and from nongovernmental organizations have gathered the voices of 60,000 men and women in 60 countries."[9] The World Bank found that

> the poor are the true poverty experts. . . . People explained wellbeing and illbeing in terms of five related dimensions: material wellbeing, physical wellbeing, security, freedom of choice and action, and good social relations. . . . Not surprisingly, lack of food, shelter, clothing, poor housing and uncertain livelihood sources were critical and mentioned everywhere. . . . Physical health, strength and appearance are of great importance to the poor. . . . A startling finding of the consultations was the extent to which poor people experience the police not as a source of help and security, but rather of harm, risk and impoverishment. . . . Households across the world are stressed. . . . The poor typically have few assets to make a living. . . . It is exceptionally difficult for the poor to be upwardly mobile.[10]

If the World Bank had been listening to the poor, then this publication would not have been necessary. Wolfensohn's statement was an extraordinarily candid admission that the World Bank and its anthropologists were out of touch with the poor and that the social and cultural substance in its regular data collection, country reporting, and loan procedures were not sufficiently well-aligned with the World Bank's primary mission of poverty alleviation.

For those who contribute to the reputation of the World Bank by turning out publications, the organization provides advantages that most universities would find hard to match. They have unrivalled access to data. They can employ expert consultants and use their work in publications—without, it was widely said, worrying too much about giving the consultants credit for their work. A World Bank author could spend five to ten years writing a major book, unlike a junior academic who must worry about a looming tenure decision. What academic would not like having no students to teach, regular pay increases, and travel without having to write a grant application? And have you noticed that, unlike the case with a conventional civil service, World Bank publications are no longer anonymous? Authorship is good for career advancement in the World Bank.

As World Bank development assistance has begun to use the same skills as commercial corporations, more and more staff have come from these corporations; they want to use their experience at the World Bank to return to the life of a business executive but at a higher level. Social scientists and professionals in the health, education, transportation, or logistics fields were encouraged to maintain and burnish their professional and disciplinary credentials since they contributed to their portability and their ability to transfer to another organization. Consequently, individuals have concentrated on maintaining and upgrading their portability rather than spending time and effort on the development of the special skills and capacities that might only be of value to the World Bank; those gained from living and working in remote areas or learning unusual languages had a low priority. Global poverty alleviation experience did not feature at the top of many head-hunter lists.

Demonstrating passion, public purpose, and commitment to poverty alleviation does little to advance disciplinary reputations. Tolstoy put it well in *Anna Karenina*:

> Levin regarded his brother as a man of vast intellect and culture, as generous in the highest sense of the word and endowed with a special faculty for working for the public good. But in the depths of his heart, the older he grew, the more intimately he knew his brother, the oftener the thought struck him that this faculty for working for the public good, of which he felt himself completely devoid, was perhaps not so much a quality as a lack of something—not a lack of kindly honesty and noble desires and tastes but a lack of vital force, of what is called heart, of the impulse which drives a man to choose one out of all the innumerable paths of life and to care for that one only. The better he knew his brother, the more he noticed that Koznyshev, and many of the people who worked for the welfare of the public, were not led by an impulse of the heart to fare for the public good but had reasoned out in their minds that it was the right thing to do to take an interest in public affairs, and consequently took interest in them. Levin was confirmed in this supposition by observing that his

brother did not take questions affecting the public welfare, or the question of immortality of the soul, a bit more to heart than he did chess problems or the ingenious design of a new machine.[11]

Meanwhile, the poor countries were bombarded with projects and rich countries with more and more statistics showing how the war on poverty was proceeding. George Santayana can convey the flavor. He recalls having been stopped one day at the beginning of term by the president of Harvard College who asked him how things were going. Santayana prattled on about the sort of student who was doing well, how nice they were and so on. A look of irritation came over the president's face as he said, "I meant how many do you have in your class?"[12]

Each year the organization's flagship publication, the WDR, is carefully framed to catch the attention of the public. So seriously was this task taken that for many years an editor from *The Economist* came to Washington to help to put the final report in order. Thirty years of WDRs on poverty have not turned up conclusive evidence of the relationship between economic growth and redistribution or of ways in which equity can be ensured. Rather than pointing to a solution that could be made to work, the evidence seems to suggest that economic growth increases inequality. Michael Walton, World Bank director for Poverty Reduction, said a few years ago, "We do not have any direct estimate of how many poor have been lifted out of poverty as a result of World Bank loans." The number of absolute poor in India had increased by 40 million in ten years. Walton went on to say that in Latin America less than 3 percent of the region's wealth went to the poorest 20 percent of the population.[13] The first WDR reviewing developments from 1970 till 1980 said, "Nothing can make absolute poverty melt away overnight. Any human development at best can do only part of the job."[14] The second poverty-focused WDR written in 1990 said, "This report suggests that many of the world's poor . . . will continue to experience severe deprivation."[15] The World Bank's WDR for 2000 showed that little or no progress had been made with global poverty. Lifting the poor out of poverty is not the whole story since there is growing evidence that the billions spent on global poverty alleviation are creating new poverty. Despite the fact that more and more money has been collected, the number of people living in absolute poverty has been increasing rather than decreasing.[16]

Poverty in the US Undermined Bank Claims

Can poverty in poor countries be ended when there are still growing numbers of poor people in the US? The fact that studies by the Brookings Institution have shown that there are large numbers of people in the United States living on less than $2 a day suggests that the World Bank promises to end poverty need rethinking.[17] Of course, economic growth has lifted some poor people out of poverty, but are they the absolute poor? What may well have happened is that a number of poor people have graduated to incomes above the $1.90 or whatever figure is being used to define poverty and so they are no longer counted in surveys. But the absolute poor may well remain and may well have increased in number. Instead of calculating the number and the income of this group and comparing it to the $1.90, the World Bank surveys find fewer people on incomes of $1.90 because some are now earning more and others continue to be missed by the enumerators, while the homeless and those living in institutional care are not usually counted at all.

Brookings Institution researchers took issue with the World Bank's estimates, which show that, between 1981 and 2008, the population groups of sub-Saharan Africa, India, and China have consistently accounted for three-quarters of the world's poor. They said,

> Poverty estimates for each of the three suffer from glaring problems: insufficient survey data, flawed surveys, and faulty [purchasing power parity] conversions. . . . If we cannot believe the poverty estimates for Sub-Saharan Africa, India and China, then we cannot believe the World Bank's global estimates, and we must admit that our knowledge of the state of global poverty is glaringly limited. . . . Bank's numbers for country and global poverty have important consequences because they can affect the allocation of aid dollars. . . . They define areas of focus. . . . And they are used to justify funding expansions of the concessional windows of the multilateral banks and capital increases for these aid agencies.[18]

Safeguards

In the 1980s the World Bank's reputation was threatened by organizations such as the Sierra Club and the Environmental Defense Fund, which objected vociferously to a number of Bank projects. In 1992 World Bank board of executive directors met to discuss the Sardar Sarovar projects on India's Narmada River. The board reviewed the recommendations presented by the independent review panel headed by Bradford Morse, and the World Bank management's proposals for the next steps to be taken. The Morse Commission was appointed in June 1991 at the recommendation of World Bank President Barber Conable; that commission conducted the first independent review of a World Bank project. The independent review concluded, inter alia, that a new World Bank approach to resettlement was needed, stating, "Performance under these projects has fallen short of what is called for under Bank policies and guidelines and the policies of the Government of India." [19]

The initial World Bank response by President Lewis Preston was that continued support of the project was warranted, although with a vigorous response and remedial actions to solve the shortcomings of the projects. Management response concentrated on improvements in policies, organization and management, and implementation of resettlement and rehabilitation; tighter linkage between resettlement and rehabilitation and the progress on the construction of the dam; and strengthened environmental planning. (Bank participation in the projects was cancelled in 1995.) [20] Later, after more NGO pressure, the World Bank introduced safeguard policies for Indigenous peoples and cultural heritage protection.

NGO campaigns provided private sector companies with a vivid example of what could happen if they got on the wrong side of NGOs. In 1995 the Brent Spar incident in the North Sea provided Shell Oil Company with a lesson on public perception that company executives are unlikely to forget. Shell wanted to decommission an obsolete oil platform and had done rigorous feasibility studies, all of which indicated that disposal at sea was the safest option. The onshore disposal that Greenpeace, who did no studies, eventually obliged Shell to accept, found no significant platform hazards such as large amounts of oil though it did create risks for worker safety and the environment that sea disposal might have avoided. Greenpeace got the science wrong but won over public opinion on evening TV by inviting viewers to imagine what would happen to a pristine marine environment if a massive oil-spewing platform sank beneath the clear blue sea. [21]

Promises, Promises

The 2017 WDR was interesting because it pointed to how complex policy-making was without in any way acknowledging the contrast with the idea that poverty was simply all about $1.90 a day. The WDR made a case for better government action and a greater sense of responsibility for economic growth and poverty alleviation.

The 2017 WDR asked,

> Why are carefully designed, sensible policies too often not adopted or implemented? When they are, why do they often fail to generate development outcomes such as security, growth, and equity? And why do some bad policies endure? This *World Development Report 2017: Governance and the Law* addresses these fundamental questions, which are at the heart of development. Policy making and policy implementation do not occur in a vacuum. Rather, they take place in complex political and social settings, in which individuals

and groups with unequal power interact within changing rules as they pursue conflicting interests. The process of these interactions is what this Report calls governance, and the space in which these interactions take place, the policy arena. The capacity of actors to commit and their willingness to cooperate and coordinate to achieve . . . socially desirable goals are what matter for effectiveness. However, who bargains, who is excluded, and what barriers block entry to the policy arena determine the selection and implementation of policies and, consequently, their impact on development outcomes. Exclusion, capture, and clientelism are manifestations of power asymmetries that lead to failures to achieve security, growth, and equity. The distribution of power in society is partly determined by history. Yet, there is room for positive change. This Report reveals that governance can mitigate, even overcome, power asymmetries to bring about more effective policy interventions that achieve sustainable improvements in security, growth, and equity. This happens by shifting the incentives of those with power, reshaping their preferences in favor of good outcomes, and taking into account the interests of previously excluded participants. These changes can come about through bargains among elites and greater citizen engagement, as well as by international actors supporting rules that strengthen coalitions for reform.[22]

Notes

1. Lewis and Madon, "Information Systems."

2. William Clark was press secretary to Anthony Eden during the Suez crisis and the first director of the Overseas Development Institute in London (1960–68). He is the author of a novel, *Number 10*.

3. I had a number of meetings with William Clark as he relaxed in his trademark lavender shirt and red socks. He used to say, in response to any question about what McNamara might do, "Bob is as American as apple pie."

4. Despite frequent references to the need to attract and help direct private sector capital, the Paris Club was a World Bank and donor affair and concentrated on public sector finance.

5. Anthropologists have been advisers to the presidents of large countries. In Indonesia, Jim Fox of the Australian National University was close to President Gus Dur; and Scott Guggenheim, formerly of the World Bank, became an adviser to (former) World Bank economist Ashraf Ghani, president of Afghanistan.

6. See World Bank 1999. Each year the WDR has a different theme. See also World Bank 1993, 1994, 1995.

7. Jim Wolfensohn had been an investment banker in Australia before becoming World Bank President. In Australia he became familiar with mining; when he was World Bank President he made the point that the miners were the first people to take services to, and stay for years in, very isolated and remote communities and as a result they deserved support.

8. Cernea, *Putting People First*; Salmen, *Listen to the People*.

9. Wolfensohn, in 28 September 1999 address to the Board of Governors at the annual meetings of the World Bank and the International Monetary Fund, *Voices for the World's Poor*, 156–157.

10. World Bank, *Poverty Trends and Voices of the Poor*, 1–54.

11. Tolstoy, *Anna Karenina*, 234.

12. Santayana, *Santayana on America*, 173.

13. Walton, "Do the World Bank, IMF and WTO Help the Poor?," 1.

14. World Bank, *World Development Report 1980*, 12.

15. World Bank, *World Development Report 1990*, 3.

16. World Bank, *World Development Report 2000/2001*.

17. Chandy and Smith, *How Poor Are America's Poorest?* Redistribution, like sustainability, can be useful; if that is to happen, though, the term has to be seen as more than a slogan. Most economists would probably agree that they have not worked out how to tackle redistribution. You can take money and things from the rich and give them to the poor, but you cannot take skills from the rich and give them to the poor.

18. Chandy and Kharas, "The Contradictions in Global Poverty Numbers."

19. Morse and Berger, *Sardar Sarovar - Report of the Independent Review*, 350.

20. World Bank Group Archivists' Chronology, 1944–2013. http://pubdocs.worldbank.org/en/186241442500110286/PDF-World-Bank-Group-Archivists-Chronology-1944-2013.pdf.

21. Lofstedt and Renn, "The Brent Spar Controversy."

22. World Bank, *World Development Report 2017*, 19.

Chapter 3

DISCIPLINES

Technical expertise and social science, including economics, were pushed to one side as money-moving and reputation management skills were used to justify World Bank expansion. The decline in the influence of economics in project lending was underlined by the fact that cost-benefit analysis and tight requirements for economic analysis had, by 2010, fallen into desuetude. The use of cost-benefit analysis in World Bank projects had declined by 75 percent. Interviews with Bank staff revealed that cost-benefit analysis was usually prepared after major decisions had been made and thus had little influence on those decisions. Cost-benefit analysis was often delegated to consultants: senior staff showed little interest in cost-benefit results and a great deal of interest in areas where reputation management was important such as safeguards, procurement, and financial management.[1] Anthropologists were seen as a constraint on accelerated spending and, as a result, the discipline has been more useful to the organization as a component of reputation management, and a shield against possible NGO attack, rather than as a mainstay of the global mission to alleviate poverty.

Economics

Technical specialization, country knowledge, hands-on skills, and the values, beliefs, and attitudes one associates with a public service institution were in place until the 1980s when economists took over. The period during which economists were preeminent was shorter and less influential than is commonly assumed—ten to fifteen years at most—because, due to a rapid expansion of lending, new skills were needed to move the mountains of money the World Bank was raising and obligating in loans.

For much of the 1970s, development economics had a questionable reputation similar to that of applied anthropology; there was continuing disagreement over what was the best way to promote economic development.[2] In 1974 the World Bank published *Redistribution with Growth*, an antipoverty strategy paper discussing income distribution and economic growth. Hollis B. Chenery, vice president for Development Policy, was the primary author, and described the book: "The main thrust of the book is the need for fundamental reorientation of development strategies so that the benefits of economic growth can reach a wider range of the population of developing countries. The book is intended as a progress report on our work towards formulating viable strategies for redistribution and growth. We hope that it will make some contribution to the growing debate on these vital questions by sharpening the issues and providing the framework for further analysis." Acknowledging that the increase in income per capita had increased but that this had meant little to a third of the population of developing countries, Chenery proposed a new analytical framework for the study of income distribution and growth, income inequality, and the relationship to poverty. The book concluded with policy recommendations and analysis of several countries that had implemented income redistribution policies.[3]

The Chenery book was suggesting something politicians in the rich countries had never succeeded in finding—a recipe for economic growth without increasing social inequality. What was noticeable—and nobody disagreed with the idea that growth with redistribution was an excellent thing—was that somehow the redistribution part of the analysis never seemed to get beyond model building. It remains the case that the World Bank knows a good deal about how to promote economic growth, but that how the benefits of that growth can be delivered to those at the bottom of society remains unclear. Half a century on, the World Bank's economists are still working on the problem; in the absence of good theory supported by on-the-ground practice they seem to want to survey every household in the world. World Bank staff were sure that Chenery would get a Nobel Prize for economics, but he did not, and the link between economic development and poverty alleviation is still neither clear nor convincing. In 1983 Chenery was replaced by Anne Krueger, an economist's economist, and, as the emphasis on quantitative poverty deepened, the World Bank was no closer to a solution on redistribution.[4]

A number of chief economists—and there have been a large number of well-known economists who have spent short periods in the post—have had a greater impact on the intellectual visibility of the World Bank than on the way it engages with the poor. The same observation can be made about the use of anthropology. As lending expanded, the World Bank's economists had to spend more and more time in their Washington offices; very few had the time or the opportunity to develop deep country knowledge and relaltionships with poor people. In 2007 the brief prepared for incoming World Bank President Robert Zoellick alerted him to the fact that in order to move money more quickly and meet what the competition was doing, managers wanted to spend less time on cumbersome safeguards procedures.[5] Project lending had become highly regulated by the World Bank and involved thirty internal processes, approvals, and documentation requirements. These safeguards had to be applied irrespective of the level of risk, borrower capacity, or the country track record. The average project preparation time was 16.7 months, and an average preparation cost on the World Bank's side of $391,000.[6]

Social change and situations where land, labor, and capital were not transacted by market forces were not necessarily well understood by many development economists. Post–World War II thinking in the up-and-coming development economics discipline supposed that the introduction of taxation would create a workforce whose exposure to making and using money would result in workers' desire to keep on earning. In what was then the New Hebrides (now Vanuatu) in the South Pacific, those who needed to earn money went to work on coconut plantations whose output, copra, fetched a good price on the world market. However, contrary to the assumptions that produced the rationale for taxation, the demand for money turned out to be inelastic. Men worked until they had enough money to pay their taxes, buy a bicycle or shells for their shotgun or perhaps a radio, and then they stopped working. There were limits to what the authorities could do to stimulate a desire for store-bought goods.[7]

Anthropology

Homogenized poverty encouraged the idea that poverty elimination on a global scale was possible without the qualities, attitudes, and efforts previously thought necessary—in other words, that economic development was possible without cultural change.[8] To play a key role in the World Bank anthropology would have had to play a key role in the continuous expansion in money-moving. Could the community competence of the discipline be upscaled to do this? Unsurprisingly, as we shall see, given the influence of the poverty paradigm, "no" was the answer; this fact has continued to constrain World Bank use of the discipline. Homogenous poverty was a watershed moment for anthropology in the World Bank.[9] It represented a departure from the more balanced traditional view held by Bank staff who had substantial developing country experience in the early years of the institution; they recognized the importance of cultural diversity and personal choice in assessments of well-being.[10]

Even the influence of economists has been reduced as more reliance has been placed on the skills needed to raise and spend more and more money. In fact, today, good writing can do as much for career advancement in the World Bank as technical or social science expertise. Doing small things well, using strong relationships with local people, which used to be at the heart of development assistance, no longer seems to be important in the World Bank's style of management by seclusion.

Acephalous Anthropology

The scattering of the anthropologists, sociologists, and others around the World Bank, and the lack of a senior intellectual leader or anyone able to provide a strong visible presence for the discipline throughout the World Bank was a constraint. Although anthropologists became well-known for their work with individual activities such as resettlement, population studies, Indigenous peoples, or land tenure, the discipline lacked an institutionally acknowledged czar.

Anthropology, pretty much left to its own devices at the World Bank, has lacked strong leadership, imagination, and an emphasis on using the discipline's unique skills in poverty alleviation. There was no anthropologist with overall responsibility for the discipline and none managed to assume such a role or to leave a strong mark on the way the institution does business. Successive World Bank chief economists who were, in effect, the institution's chief social scientists, did little to expand disciplinary boundaries, while the non-economists did little to change the way the World Bank worked. Anthropologists earned a reputation for always wanting more studies; even after all that work had been completed, they seemed to be reluctant to make a firm prediction.

It has been hard for outsiders to track what has been happening to anthropology because few of the early professionals have left much of a public record beyond occasional articles. Not surprisingly there was little institutional imperative to make use of anthropology since the poverty paradigm suggested that the institution needed to get more and more money out to client countries who were expected to implement World Bank–inspired economic development.[11] Anthropology was counted on to alert the driver to problems on the track that required slowing down or rerouting slightly, but anything more fundamental than that was, unfortunately, hard to see. When NGOs stopped active campaigning, World Bank anthropology began to fossilize.[12]

Popularity and demand for a discipline in an institution that wanted to move money and maintain a high public profile depended on cutting corners, relying on hunches, taking small chances. Worse still, for managers in a hurry, they knew that if you put five anthropologists in a row you might well get five different opinions. Economists took to the World Bank bureaucracy like ducks to water, but anthropologists did not. Each anthropologist wanted to do things his or her own way. If, for example, a common procedure or policy should be followed—on Indigenous people for example—they would try to put something distinctive of themselves into the way the work was written-up or presented. This individualism did not help the discipline to project a common approach that could take advantage of the weight of the number of anthropologists working at the World Bank. The university training of most anthropologists did not prepare them for teamwork. They had been taught to work as individuals, a style that was not always helpful in a large complex bureaucratic organization whose output—loans—required combined pooled effort. In an organization such as the World Bank, anthropologists find that many of their thoughts and experiences that in an academic setting might have resulted in a paper or a publication become a part of the output of a team. Although teamwork at the World Bank has limitations, it is essential. Teamwork affords its members the opportunity to challenge each other's ideas and suggestions in order to come up with a common solution that contributes to a successful conclusion of a mission. Working cooperatively provides team members an opportunity to acquire new skills and knowledge. This working together reduces individual workloads. When members pool their ideas and proposals this can build mutual understanding and respect as well as team cohesion.

The skill sets required for money-moving were popular with managers and resulted in anthropology not being seen as a core discipline in the World Bank. Senior World Bank economists did not see sociologists and anthropologists as the go-to people in the institution when new ideas were needed.[13] Anthropology did not manage to reach the top echelons of the World Bank where, in addition to the heavy hitters from economics, Robert McNamara favored environmental, medical, and agricultural scientists whose innovations could, he believed, help millions of people. What the history of World Bank anthropology illustrates is that the use and well-being of the discipline has been a reflection—not of what Bank managers, economists, environmentalists, or even anthropologists themselves have wanted and argued for—but of NGO pressure and the World Bank's desire to produce publicity that shows a concern for the softer side of development.

Social Development

It was no surprise that social development has not managed to achieve authoritative voice or a persuasive identity within the World Bank. The social development soubriquet had little practical significance and became a title for all those who were not economists.[14] The UN use of the term "social" has been problematic; in the past fifty years it has been a residual category, a dumping ground for things that do not lend themselves to global solutions or quantification, such as cultural heritage. Social has followed UN fashion by being other than economic, and social performance, like financial performance, has been defined by lending targets and the project pipeline.[15] However, the difficulty for a highly centralized organization is not just recognizing the social importance of lending for health and education in client countries but also in saying what kind of education or health, in what quantity, where, and for whom. (See appendix C, "World Bank Social Development Group.") This is hard to achieve without strong local dialogue and contribution.

World Bank office organization and the personnel system reflected the old-fashioned idea of economic *and* social development. Thus, economists dealing with economic development lived in the center of town while anthropologists lived in what was very much seen as the suburbs. Internal reviews of the social network conducted between 1995 and 2005 showed a social development function with practitioners who appeared unclear about their work and how it should fit into Bank operations.[16] Discussion kept going back to first principles over and over again, defining, for example, what was meant by "social." Could one imagine economists asking for a definition of "economics"? The reputation and institutional use of the discipline depended on its practitioners being able to contribute to project investments. However, the members of the network appear to have conveyed an impression that they would delay and complicate projects work since they were unable to agree on a simple easy-to-understand form of project analysis other than to talk very generally about "sociological variables," without saying exactly what these were, how they would be selected and used, and what value they would add. Confusion was inevitable with the proliferation of terms, few of which had an agreed meaning: "social assessment," "social analysis," "social capital," and "social risks," that were applied at project, national, and global levels; as well as a profusion of possible perspectives and starting points: individual, family, tribe, community, ethnic, nation, and gender. Social relationships did not seem to have any particular pride of place in network discussions. As far as relationships were concerned, those that were most frequently mentioned were with the government of the borrowers, consultants, university-based academics, and NGOs.[17]

Making engagement with the poor a key component in poverty alleviation and in general lending operations could have helped to address the deskbound state of World Bank development assistance. The World Bank might have added to what it could offer clients if attention and focus had been placed on social engagement rather than on social development. "Social development" was not a term or approach that was operationally helpful to the World Bank. Inevitably, in an institution dominated by economists the term has ended up as little more than a subset of growth and economic development concerns, something that is done *to* populations, rather than something done *with* them. The vision and the objectives have been pretty much limited to improvement to health and education in the hope that this will result in increased productivity in the workplace. Moreover, because the World Bank's version of social development has been the result of internal debate and discussion, the term has lost generative potential. Genuine social development is not internally determined; it can and should emerge from the process of engaging with all levels of society in order to address the social expectations of employees, communities, and society. An assumption that the World Bank can improve society is often implicit in what the World Bank does, though such an objective does not usually represent any activity where development assistance has any obvious mandate or comparative advantage.

Introducing Anthropology

In the 1970s I assumed, along with others, that as a result of a shift in development assistance policy there was a major opportunity for anthropologists with good interdisciplinary skills to convince policymakers in aid agencies such as the World Bank that anthropology could help to illuminate, understand, and come up with innovative ways to help poor people. The expansion in international development assistance during the 1970s suggested that aid agencies with a global remit who had to handle more and more population, nutrition, and rural development projects would be unable to continue to rely on solitary academic anthropologists who were often available only during the long summer vacation. This was not a viable long-term option for aid agencies during a period when they were doubling their staff numbers and their expenditures every few years. Although some of these individual anthropologists managed to persuade global organizations of their personal utility, and thus the need for their own further engagement in particular locations or particular types of project, this did

not result in the greatly increased use of anthropology or increased awareness of anthropology's broader applicability and potential among senior
staff in the large organizations.

I wrote to the World Bank in 1971 explaining what I wanted to do and
received a polite, if not terribly enthusiastic, reply from John King, who
worked in the Central Projects Division. Although a lawyer by training,
King had written a book about World Bank projects and was very much
an institutional loyalist.[18] His diffidence was understandable because anthropologists were assumed by Bank staff to be rather impractical folk who
were interested in the lurid, sexual deviance, bizarre rituals, and equally
strange practices. World Bank staff kept sending me cuttings from news-
papers describing, for instance, a situation where an African chief was said
to be engaging in strange rituals or providing headlines about exotic poly-
andry. I suspect there was also some thought given to the financial motives
of the authors since Bank staff saw their institution as a pile of money and
assumed that any visitor wanted some.

In 1972 and 1973 I spent fifteen months in the World Bank before
writing a report, with recommendations, on the use of anthropology in
project operations.[19] My assumption had been that the successful institutionalization of anthropology at the World Bank or USAID required three
sequenced steps. Step one involved taking the existing work of the organization in areas where staff admitted they were facing challenges and showing them how anthropology could add value. Step two was to draft and
have inserted as a mandated part of project procedures the innovation that
called for an anthropological input. Step three was to design and deliver
fit-for-purpose training to ensure that staff could make confident and good
use of the new social procedures. USAID achieved all three of these steps,
but I do not think the World Bank got beyond step one.[20]

I entered the World Bank together with Raymond Noronha, a graduate
student of mine who had just finished his PhD with a dissertation on the
legal aspects of land tenure in Fiji. I assured John King that Raymond and
I were prepared to bear our own expenses.[21] I decided to fly from Syracuse,
where I taught, to Washington each week during term time for a few days
and to spend vacations at the World Bank. This was the pattern I followed
for almost two years. Before taking to anthropology, Raymond had been a
frugal Indian lawyer who, during his time at Syracuse, bought a bag of rice
at the beginning of each fall semester and made it last till spring. He did
the same in Washington.

We had very good access to the top people in the World Bank; as they
began to understand what we were trying to do, they helped us to meet
their colleagues who they believed could also be helpful. With the help
of Bernard Chadenet, who was the head of what was then known as the

World Bank's projects division, I managed to talk to large groups of staff who dealt with agricultural lending, transportation, power, and communications. Commenting on the 1972 study Raymond Noronha and I had done, Gloria Davis, the first anthropologist to be employed by the World Bank in 1987, and who became the director of the Social Development Department, said in 2004:[22]

> This [report], written by Glynn Cochrane and Raymond Noronha, was based on an examination of the World Bank's problem projects and the World Bank's quarterly review of projects from 1968–72. Based on this survey, the team concluded that there was a need to add an anthropological or social dimension to project operations, and that there was fairly widespread recognition of such a need in the World Bank—but staff did not know how to do so. The paper was among the first in the World Bank to describe the influence of culture on human behavior and to point out the social impacts of land acquisition and resettlement, which were major causes of project delay. The paper also made a number of practical observations and recommendations including increasing staff sensitivity to social issues, preparing a library of resources, constructing a roster of available consultants, hiring anthropologists as Bank staff, and including them in the young professionals' program. Whether as a result of this paper or the broader issues that precipitated it, over the next five years the first generation of social scientists was hired by the World Bank.[23]

By the 1990s there were about 100 social specialists throughout the institution, or less than 1 percent of the total staff number. About a quarter of these worked in the Environmentally Sustainable Development Vice Presidency, while another 15 percent worked in the Asia Technical Department; thus, just two divisions accounted for about 40 percent of the World Bank's social specialists. Moreover, half of the World Bank's social specialists were long-term consultants, and 70 percent had been in the World Bank for less than three years.

Since homogenous poverty had suggested no obvious role for anthropology, practitioners were forced to become service providers to projects and area departments for safeguards work, surveys, gender issues, governance, and special projects. The use of the discipline depended very much on what potential users believed was the quality of the anthropologist. This pattern of use resulted in fragmented performance with little institutional learning. Bank colleagues said that working in the institution was like working in a series of villages: sometimes you did business with the people in the next village and sometimes you did not. What was important was whether the size of your village was growing. Was its work being mentioned in speeches, quoted in publications, receiving interest from donors with money to spend? In a bazaar there could be many people selling the same box of matches, but in this bazaar each seller is trying to be noticed.

Anthropologists who had done fieldwork, who had an earned doctorate, and who saw themselves as specialists expected to be treated like specialists but then found that they were not highly regarded at all. In the eyes of seasoned Bank staff an anthropological specialist was a luminary like a Raymond Firth on economic anthropology, a Harold Conklin on agriculture, or a Thayer Scudder on dams. A generalist who wanted more stature and status had to gain it by earning what the Australians very aptly call personally earned authority. That meant being a good team player, doing your share on mission, and collecting data that might help others.

Interdisciplinary Shortfall

My emphasis in development anthropology was on the importance of interdisciplinary skills because my experience suggested that this was what the World Bank and other development assistance agencies would need to succeed. However, since many of the World Bank's anthropologists had not had training that emphasized interdisciplinary skills, the results have been disappointing both in terms of the contribution of the discipline to Bank operations and in terms of the impact that these graduates might have had on improving university training. There were notable exceptions. Monica das Gupta, an anthropologist/demographer who worked at the World Bank from 1988 to 2012, provided an all-too-rare example of what an anthropologist with an interdisciplinary focus could achieve. She was a member of the World Bank research group and contributed to a number of key publications in the health field.[24] Monica did her doctorate at Sussex with Scarlett Epstein, who was working on a large World Bank population research project.[25] Next to her I would probably put Raymond Noronha, who combined the skills of a lawyer and an anthropologist. Raymond spent his career at the World Bank where he had some interesting assignments. Sir John Crawford, who Robert McNamara asked to help the World Bank with regional development, took him to Iran for six months to work on an agricultural development plan.[26] Then, since the World Bank was lending for tourism, he was asked to spend some months on Bali trying to work out what was needed to sustain public Balinese rituals as a tourist attraction.[27]

One might have expected a good number of significant contributions to economic anthropology from professionals working in the World Bank but that has not been the case. Raymond Firth made a useful contribution to the debate over the involvement of anthropologists in development assistance when he said,

Another attitude, sharing the same general definition of development aims and methods, is more sceptical of the performance and claims of anthropologists to contribute to the process. On the whole the argument is for greater involve-ment—that the "academic" anthropologist who straddles the gulf between his permanent career and his occasional immersion in the field cannot be effective as an adviser, and even his analysis of, say, economic problems is liable to be distorted by his unfamiliarity with any level except the merely local scene of his fieldwork. . . . Theoretically, then, an anthropological approach should re-define its area of interest to embrace national and not simply local community structures and relations. Pragmatically, the role of the anthropologist is to ex-pose the true conditions of this pseudo- development-possibly also to indicate and support radical measures to help in rectification.[28]

Scarlett Epstein suggested that the ideal marriage would see the econo-mist look at the big picture and the anthropologist look at the community level.[29] Richard Salisbury, reflecting on his James Bay, Canada, mining in-dustry experience, saw a role for the anthropologist as societal ombuds-man.[30] James Ferguson doubted that involvement made any sense at all.[31] Constructive exchanges between those who liked to work at the local level and those who believed in global perspectives was unlikely because those interested in the worm's-eye view wanted to burrow more deeply into the social soil while those who believed in the bird's-eye view wanted to rise higher to get a better view and to be better seen.

According to Antje Vetterlein of the Copenhagen Business School, who has analyzed the World Bank's position on poverty over the past forty years by contrasting its discourse and policies with operational and organiza-tional data,

The World Bank continuously falls into discredit when it comes to the quali-tative meaning of the "social" . . . for its continuing econocentric culture . . . [and] for only dealing with issues that can be quantified, often offering stan-dardized policy solutions based on technocratic economic modelling. . . . In the World Bank "economic knowledge" . . . wins over social and more complex knowledge about poverty. . . . It is more manageable for the World Bank to measure poverty in terms of income, life expectancy, school enrolment and so on than employ social knowledge. . . . Distingushing between the norma-tive and organizational dimension of the problem and acknowledging that economic growth and poverty reduction are not causally linked might help to improve the World Bank's dealing with poverty and social issues.[32]

For a while when Robert Zoellick was president there was talk of the World Bank becoming a knowledge organization, but that idea did not last long; money-moving did more for the World Bank's public visibility and market share of development assistance. Top management at the World Bank failed to bang heads together in order to come up with genuine in-terdisciplinary approaches to poverty. World Bank economists have shown little enthusiasm or aptitude for interdisciplinary work; leaving poverty thinking and the evolution of the strategy and tactics to them has resulted in too little thinking outside the disciplinary box. The World Bank hired too many anthropologists who were not really familiar or comfortable with economic concepts, and too many economists who were unwilling or unable to think outside their disciplinary box. This contributed to the general failure of senior managers, economists, and anthropologists to recognize the importance of putting in place a working relationship between anthropology and economics—something beyond the occasional publication—on poverty-related issues.

Paul Streeten, a prominent contributor to World Bank's thinking on poverty thinking, and strategy, said:[33]

> I suspect that some economic method could illuminate anthropological work and probably the other way too. . . . It is quite clear, for example, that an agricultural production function in many underdeveloped countries should count among its inputs, not only land, labour, fertilizers, water and power, but also levels of education of farmers, nutritional standards, distance from town, health systems of land tenure and family kinship. All these variables are likely, in some societies to be systematically related to agricultural production.
>
> But it may turn out that the whole notion of a production function is wrong or misleading. . . . It may be that output depends on variables that have been constructed or analysed by anthropologists: the relationships between majority and minority groups; religious beliefs (The Protestant ethic), or kinship systems. . . . The society may have opted for an alternative style of development, in which the ever-growing production of material goods is rejected. It prefers containment of wants and aspirations to growing production to satisfy ever-growing wants and infinite aspirations. Or, through a shift in valuations, unemployment may be converted into leisure. If this is the case the crucial questions will have to be asked by the anthropologist or sociologist. He has to construct the concepts and it may be that it is then the economist's turn to fill in the boxes constructed by the anthropologists.[34]

Scarlett Epstein,[35] trained in economics by the economist Arthur Lewis, said,

> Many development economists based their analyses and plans on the economic man model found appropriate to industrialised societies and they barged in where angels feared to tread. . . . Deductive reasoning based on the economic man model cannot provide the right formula for ensuring a more equal distribution of income either between different parts of the world or within any one country. . . . McNamara in an address to the Governors of the World Bank said that increases in the national income—as essential as they are—will not benefit the poor unless they reach the poor. . . . There is a growing realization among many leading development economists of their discipline's inadequacies. Why is it that the Third World has defeated so many development economists while advanced societies still lend themselves fairly readily to economic analysis? . . .

In contrast to industrialized societies in lesser developed societies the majority of people still live in highly localised communities. Within these small-scale societies inter-personal relations tend to be multiplex to a far greater degree than they do in developed countries. The small range of social links is reflected in a greater density of relations between a limited number of rural dwellers: economic relations linking the same individuals as master and servant as well as creditor and debtor are frequently parallel and reinforced, for instance, by kinship ties, political patronage, and ritual relations. It is this multidimensional linkage between different economic, political and general social variables within the large number of rural microcosms in the Third World, which constitutes the major stumbling block to the economist and his retention of the "economic man" model macro-approach.[36]

Any assumption that economic growth, combined with the provision of access to better health and education, or even the installation of better governance and the securing of less corruption would automatically result in a more equitable distribution of the benefits of growth depended on serious collaboration between economists and anthropologists that unfortunately was not encouraged. The beliefs, values, and attitudes and the relationships that act as a constraint on the upward mobility of the poor all needed to be better understood.

Anthropologists were no strangers to statistics and were in a position to be able to provide advice on the construction of questionnaire surveys, questions that could not be asked, response rates, and administration of survey instruments. The real strength of the discipline was in the collection of high-quality data related to the meanings that poor people attached to their deprivation. There was no good substitute for working out the meaning of poverty in the old-fashioned way by anthropologists doing the hard yards on the ground, talking and listening and being alert to exactly what is being said. There do not seem to be any shortcuts that can be relied on to do better with the very poorest than would be the case if participant observation methods were used in conjunction with the information that can be gleaned from completed fieldwork.[37]

Environmentalists Were in the Top Bunk

World Bank managers who had looked at how the social and environmental functions should be organized, assumed that they ought to be working closely together because both functions deal with issues and matters that were often the subject of worrying NGO activist campaigns. In 1972 I was told that decisions about anthropology had to await the arrival of the first environmental adviser. Although World Bank environmentalists shared with the anthropologists a concern for avoiding harm, the environmentalists were usually more concerned with exogenous factors such as setting and following national and international regulations, whereas anthropologists were concerned with local environmental perceptions. To the environmentalist these local perceptions—and this was particularly true when they departed from science—were thought to lack rational justification. Local people have their own knowledge of the environment and it has often served them well.[38] Stuart Kirsch, one of the few visible anthropologists working in the environmental area, has supported the importance of local environmental knowledge.[39] Hopefully, more environmental professionals will pay attention to what might be called local environmental science. While it is essential that social and environmental issues are coordinated, it is also essential that both remain intellectually independent.

The environmentalists had the upper hand in their relationships with anthropologists—not just because Robert McNamara favored them rather than anthropologists, but because the environmentalists had hard numbers. They also had standards for social development function; this indicated a degree of precision and measurement that was somewhat in advance of the facts. The environmentalists could, to be sure, develop standards for pure air and clean, potable water; they could measure toxicity and pollution, but they could not measure relationships or social institutions such as marriage.[40] The standards promoted by the World Bank in relation to social development echoed the problem of the drunk who has lost his keys and then looks for them near the illumination provided by a street lamp because that is where it is easiest to search. The World Bank social standards provided for universality but it was a universality that, like homogenous poverty, was unable to accommodate cultural diversity.

Dr. Jim Lee, who was the first environmental adviser, had virtually no impact inside the World Bank and had been unable to correct adverse consequences of dam construction and resettlement.[41] Lee, who arrived at the World Bank in 1972, was expected to look at health hazards associated with Bank projects, but not at issues related to the natural environment. Lee later described his relationship with project managers as adversarial, and acknowledged that McNamara's Bank was not effectively handling environmental concerns. McNamara had an overly optimistic view of Lee's role. Effective programs regarding the environment did not enter into Bank projects until well after the creation of the Environment Department in 1987. Although Lee and his colleagues were ambitious and committed to environmental protection, their role in the World Bank's activities appears to have remained marginal. Their enthusiasm for environmental issues never permeated the World Bank's institutional culture.

Throughout the 1970s and 1980s and into the early 1990s the World Bank's Office of Environmental and Scientific Affairs, established as a result of McNamara's conversations with Barbara Ward and Rene Dubos, had attempted to play an active role in reviewing Bank projects. Lee, the office's director, was eager to prove that his office was more than window dressing. All Bank projects were subject to that office's review, and in early 1974 the office published an exhaustive catalogue, "Environmental, Health, and Human Ecologic Considerations in Economic Development Projects." The "green book"—as it was called—was required reading for all Bank staff members. Every country division director had to show that his or her projects conformed to its guidelines. It is true that environmental provisions were included in all loan agreements after 1970, but they were largely formalities. Implementation of these provisions was far from consistent and follow-up evaluations were hurried and incomplete. There is no evidence that the World Bank rewarded those staff members with the most environmentally friendly projects. While Lee tried to overcome these problems, his operations evaluation capabilities were limited.[42]

In addition, Lee emerged as a leading advocate for the financing of purely environmental projects. In 1971 the board of directors approved the first of these ventures, which was a loan to Brazil for water pollution control. In his address to the 1972 United Nations Conference on the Human Environment (also known as the Stockholm Conference), McNamara expressed the basic conviction that would continue to guide policy at the World Bank through the 1970s. McNamara believed that his institution had already satisfactorily responded to the challenge of the growing environmental movement. He ended his speech with a strong declaration of the World Bank's commitment to finding an optimal balance between economic growth and environmental health. The environmentalists had to deal with matters involving entomology, soil science, hydrology, zoology, botany, invertebrates and vertebrates, air, sea, and water.[43]

Social Impact Assessment

Anthropological fieldwork was an early casualty of the liaison with environmentalism. The need to get loans processed quickly and to hold down costs persuaded World Bank managers that traditional anthropological fieldwork was impractical because of time and cost factors and because it was difficult to scale up results.[44] The alternative to fieldwork called Rapid Rural Appraisal did on occasion have advantages but it often produced information of low quality and doubtful validity even on those rare occasions when it was done by an anthropologist.[45] The problem was that the decision to do or not to do fieldwork was not always in the hands of anthropologists but instead in the hands of staff members who often knew little about the community involved or the discipline.

Of course, the reasons for not doing lengthy and expensive fieldwork were often valid. Instead of leading to a weeding out of what was not essential, though, the unintended consequence of the virtually blanket introduction of this approach was that qualitative data collection, which had depended on collecting a sufficiently broad number of facts that might suggest theory or explanation, was replaced by data collection that had at its heart an already established economic need or purpose.

Emphasis was placed on the identification of project risks and these were supposed to be analyzed as a result of Social Impact Analysis (SIA). A single consultant, often an environmentalist, was frequently given responsibility for both the social and environmental assessments that World Bank projects work required. The idea that all fieldwork has to take years was a straw-man argument and usually an exaggeration, particularly when anthropologists with local experience were available.

The Nixon administration's 1972 Environmental Protection Act introduced the idea of SIA.[46] Impact analysis became commonplace in the work of anthropologists in the field, despite the fact that it is a crude and blunt tool for looking at social change. In communities where modern employment and its rituals may not be at the center of local lives, social change may be slow and almost imperceptible, taking place over several generations, as is sometimes the case with marriage customs and practice, or with land tenure.

SIA can all too easily be used in ways suggesting that it is possible to predict and produce social change without the necessity of really understanding local communities.[47] SIA suggests a desired outcome rather than providing an objective way to assess costs and benefits. The language is that of a crash—mitigation, compensation, and so on. But projects also have benefits and this form of analysis does not usually do justice to positive features of a project. SIA was born in 1970 when President Nixon signed the National Environmental Policy Act into law. Section 102 of the Act required federal agencies to make "integrated use of the natural and social sciences in decision-making which may have an impact on man's environment." Just how this integration was to be achieved remained uncertain. Reporting on an acquisition of 130 acres, the US Army Corps of Engineers said the proposed use "will affect the human population that resides there and also some mouse, rat and domestic habitat that is normally associated with intense human use areas."[48]

It is important to note that the impacts that were of interest all, or mostly, had to do with the consequences of physical construction. "Have you thought of everything?" seemed to be the point of view rather than,

"What are you trying to get away with?" Development activities were viewed very positively in the US and there was an idea that they could be managed in such a way as to have the benefits outweigh the risks. SIA was obviously useful for large construction projects where new transport, housing, or public utility supply issues needed widespread discussion. Relocation due to dam and highway construction featured in the early years, as did the mining industry. In 1985 a $4 billion transfer of coal leases in the Powder River Basin of Wyoming and Montana was set aside by a federal judge on the ground that the social, cultural, and economic impact on the Northern Cheyenne Tribe had been ignored.

Broadly speaking, the question SIA was supposed to answer was, "Is the new development going to be good or bad for the community?" In fact, this is a question that hardly justified the "social" label. It is, in any effect, usually a community issue rather than a social issue. Moreover, few of those who worked in this area had the skills to be able to balance what might be good for a nation with what might be undesirable for a community. Anthropologists have no calculus that enables them to answer this question with any degree of authority. In fact, what was and is needed is the widest possible public discussion and elimination of any suspicion that those with the most education should have the greatest say.[49]

In the US the function to be performed by SIA was answered by broad-ranging inquiry and guesswork by committee, which was then tested in public meetings. Social scientists in the US were well aware that the prediction and production of social change was quite beyond the capability of their science. In the poor countries, although there was less work of a broad-ranging nature, fewer public consultation pronouncements were made by individuals whose social science background was often questionable.[50]

In poor countries the private sector frequently faced a substantial trust deficit because industry critics started from the position that companies would try to cut corners. Whereas in the rich countries the questions and the answers were supposed to emerge from the objective assessments of the observers, in poor countries the investigative agenda was often heavily influenced by critics. In the poor countries the SIA burden is for the developer to discharge. The public consultation process is of less prominence than in the rich countries because the authorities, rather than the public, have the final say and it is they who impose various conditions. A further distinction is the fact that, unlike the rich countries, civil society organizations can be expected to play a prominent role. In fact, in many cases those organizations took it upon themselves to argue that they were the representatives of local people without ever taking the time and effort to clear this with those in whose name they purported to act.

SIA was overwhelmingly structured in terms of an assumption of harm. Those using the concept talk about harm even though they may have little understanding of how harm features in local ethnography and they certainly do not have the time to remedy this deficiency when carrying out an impact analysis over the course of a few weeks. SIA was supposed to measure or assess harm, and since impact assessment came from the environmentalists it was associated with metrics and standards. While it was and is possible to set a standard for pure water or clean air, treating relationships as if they could be reduced to a number was a very different matter.[51] In addition, and despite attempts to say that impact analysis was also capable of examining opportunities and positive developments, the universal use of the mitigation and compensation language in SIA analysis continues to confirm the negativity of this environmentally influenced approach.[52]

Papua New Guinea can provide an example of why this approach was not necessarily suitable in situations where social change process was bubbling away. When cocoa producers on the Gazelle Peninsula in Papua New Guinea stopped selling their beans to a new and expensively built fermentery the reason turned out to be that the patrilineal inheritance system was changing slowly in favor of matriliny.[53] As a result of this slow change, farmers had begun to want the sale proceeds to go to their sons whom they had begun to see as their heirs rather than to their nephews who might be the heirs under a matrilineal system. Sales would be registered by the fermentery, and the information made public, which would make it impossible for a farmer to give the money to his son.[54]

How would a two- or four-week SIA undertaken by an environmentalist using Rapid Rural Appraisal methods discover how a community makes decisions when local customs are far removed from democratic decision making and focus-group thinking? How would they estimate the likely consequences of land registration that aims to transfer land traditionally held under collective tenure by a lineage or other corporate kin group into individual titled tenure? Whereas the thinking dominant in industrialized countries suggests that an individual can sell or dispose of his or her interest in land, in traditional societies the individual—who is like a shareholder—has no identifiable estate to sell or lease. When trying to look at traditional tenure through our eyes, the most obvious fact is how limited and circumscribed the rights of individuals are with respect to what they can do with land. The attitudes and beliefs just mentioned obviously make it difficult to turn land into a commercial commodity, especially where traditional beliefs are still strong. The response from economists in aid agencies has been to ignore traditional rights and to convert land held under traditional tenure into ground held under our principle of primogeniture, thereby ensuring that the ground can be bought and sold and used as collateral for loans.

The result of going along with environmental thinking and practice such as SIA was that World Bank anthropology has begun to give the appearance of having become in tune with, or intellectually subordinated to the environmental sciences. Of course, paying attention to avoiding harm is important but not at the cost of failing to also devote time and effort to showing what could be done to promote beneficial social change. As a result of spending too much time on avoiding harm and too little time on social change, it was the case that apart from safeguards procedures there were few anthropologically inspired alterations and innovations to the traditional project cycle. The occasional mention of sociological variables by Bank anthropologists was seldom a key determinant of how SIA was conducted. The role of the anthropologist began to look like that of the loss adjustor in the insurance business.

Safeguards

Safeguards showed that NGOs had a more decisive influence on the use of anthropology at the World Bank than the institution's own professionals and senior management. Although Bank anthropologists tended to suggest that they themselves had come up with the safeguard social and environmental policies and procedures that were used, the reality was that the policies and safeguards were forced on the World Bank by civil society campaigns.[55] After the safeguards policies were put in place the job of the anthropologist in the World Bank became one of identifying, selecting, briefing, and debriefing the consultants working in the field on safeguard issues. Poverty assessments were carried out by consultant anthropologists for some sixty-two countries and were said to cover 80 to 90 percent of the developing world's poor people.[56] While these assessments had shown that, in addition to material impoverishment, poverty involved feelings of isolation, personal insecurity, and vulnerability to violence, they did not result in any fundamental adjustment of the homogenous paradigm.[57] For the anthropologists, not only was there a loss of hands-on contact, which resulted in the fossilization of community competence, but also when they were overseas the anthropologists had most of their contact with the officials of central government, rather than with poor people.[58]

As a consequence of the NGO campaigns, the World Bank developed eleven key operational policies and associated bank procedures that are critical to ensuring that potentially adverse environmental and social consequences are identified, minimized, and mitigated during the World Bank's project preparation and approval process. The World Bank now says that safeguards provide the cornerstone of work on investment projects and are helping to ensure strong protections for people and the environment. The new policies were supposed to identify, avoid, and minimize harm to people and the environment. Examples of these policy requirements include conducting environmental and social impact assessments, consulting with affected communities about potential project impacts, and restoring the livelihoods of displaced people. As stated in an April 2017 Press Release, "World Bank safeguards are widely regarded as an effective way to ensure that environmental and social concerns and community voices are represented in the design and implementation of our projects."[59]

Resettlement

In response to NGO pressures the World Bank developed safeguards for resettlement. The sociologist Michael Cernea played an important role in this development; he became well-known to applied anthropologists, as did his anthropologist associate Scott Guggenheim.[60] The use of the guidance was ensured when a group of banks declared that they would not provide finance for private- or public-sector resettlement that did not follow these guidelines (called the Equator Principles). The guidance was all about the individuals to be resettled and a listing of their material requirements. As time went by, both the World Bank and the International Finance Corporation (IFC) arm of the World Bank Group each developed its own guidance because client countries found it easier to obtain finance if and when they followed the international guidelines. In no time resettlement became a nice little earner for the Asian, African, and Inter-American Development Banks.

Strangely, there did not seem to be much anthropology in the way the World Bank handled resettlement. Neither the World Bank nor the IFC approaches to resettlement said much about relationships, morale, and motivation, or the importance of thinking about the need to move social organization as well as settlers. The impression was gained that World Bank resettlement was about moving a number of individuals who had entitlements rather than moving a community with its social organization intact. These relationships are critical to success in resettlement—relationships between settlers, relationships with helpers, and relationships with the authorities.[61] The World Bank and IFC envisaged all conversation and contact taking place between the government, which was referred to as the proponent, and the World Bank. The settlers, who were not seen to be important in this dialogue, were kept well in the background. My experience suggested that it would be very difficult to recompose community life on the basis of this guidance.[62] Like homogenized poverty, the World

Bank's approach to resettlement did not do justice to the importance of social factors. A problem with the resettlement guidance was that it did nothing to recognize the importance of relationships between those helping the settlers to adjust to their new environment. Nor did the approach, and its listing of the entitlements of those moved, mention the case for making sure that those who were moved to allow economic development to proceed in their old home area should receive a share of the wealth generated. For example, shouldn't those moved to make way for a dam surely have been entitled to receive free, or subsidized, electricity?[63]

While safeguards were important, that only seemed to be the case as long as they promoted, rather than hindered, lending. Certainly, although the social consequences of large-scale resettlement merited serious longitudinal analysis and international debate, the World Bank's assessment of its own resettlement efforts remained loan-focused, short term, and in line with the project cycle. Few big strategic or long-term questions were asked about Indonesian transmigration and its effect on Papua, for example—and that was surprising in view of the World Bank's resettlement and Indigenous safeguards policies. One possible explanation for the World Bank's positive and high-profile assessments of its own resettlement performance was the large amount of past and possible future Bank lending for dams in resettlements in BRIC countries that the work of the World Commission on Dams, which met between 1997 and 2001, might question.

After independence in 1949, the Indonesian transmigration program under President Soekarno aimed to resettle subsistence farming families from densely populated islands such as Java to areas with low population.[64] Transmigration resulted in Papuans being outnumbered by Muslim settlers, who were mostly from Java, in their own homeland in less than fifty years. This migration was stopped by President Widodo in 2015, causing open conflict between migrants, the state, and indigenous groups due to differences in culture, diet, and religion. Among other differences, the Papuans are pork eaters and fond of beer, and the Muslim settlers are neither.

Long-term social analysis also appeared to be absent in large-scale World Bank–funded Chinese resettlement. This resettlement was seen as a relatively easy option in the short term. It involved the construction of urban dwellings, planned for the convenience and cost-effectiveness of service delivery with access to potable water, electricity, and paved roads rather than to express traditional settlement patterns. Because of an assumed increase in settler incomes, the World Bank believed Chinese resettlement performance had improved and could serve as a model elsewhere. However, quite apart from a serious examination of matters of taste and preference, we do not know the consequences of relocating millions of diverse cultural groups and forcing them to adapt to new environments. For example, the assimilation of village farmers, and especially farmers with different cultures and spoken languages, into urban citizens who can work in new industries with a different value system and lifestyle, is a generational, rather than a short-term project challenge. Promising urban employment for the displaced from the Three Gorges Dam in Yima City failed to deliver, resulting in urban poverty; half of the displaced people had to return to farming.[65]

Indigenous Peoples

The 1972 study that Raymond Noronha and I had performed had contributed to World Bank awareness of the need to develop a response to the indigenous challenge.[66] Shelton Davis, who trained with David Maybury-Lewis and was familiar with the concept of cultural survival, assumed the intellectual responsibility for the development of the World Bank's safeguards response to the indigenous challenge.[67] The United Nations Declaration on the Rights of Indigenous People (UNDRIP) put Indigenous peoples in the driving seat when it came to making decisions about their future. The declaration passed by the UN General Assembly in 2007 was the culmination of many years of work by the Indigenous people themselves at the UN in Geneva.[68] As was the case with resettlement, change came from outside the World Bank: it was the Indigenous peoples and their campaigns that forced the World Bank to accept that transparent regulatory procedures and safeguards had to be put in place when dealing with them and their cultural heritage.[69] I believed then, and still do, that UNDRIP provided the gold standard for the way extractive industry, or aid agencies, or NGOs, had to engage with Indigenous peoples. Rather than being seen as a unique set of arrangements for unique peoples, the UNDRIP needed to be seen as establishing how relationships with all poor peoples should be conducted.[70] Why should engagement with poor people be conducted with less foresight and care than engagement with Indigenous peoples?

UNDRIP is ambitious, and it is as yet unclear whether resources will be available to Indigenous peoples for implementation. Australia, New Zealand, the US, and later Canada (Canada ratified UNDRIP in 2010) voted against adoption of UNDRIP, as did African countries that did not believe in the whole ideology of indigeneity. UNDRIP is not a legally binding document. States will, however, be expected to pass supporting national legislation, as was the case with the 1948 Declaration on Human Rights.

The US Supreme Court has ruled that certain Indian groups already have the legal status of sovereign nations. New Zealand has the Treaty of Waitangi, and Australian and Canadian courts have recognized indigenous land rights. Yet in a number of South American countries, Argentina and Panama for example, the constitutional safeguards for Indigenous peoples have performed poorly.

Prior to UNDRIP, indigenous communities were seen as being unable to handle their own affairs. Article 22 of the Covenant of the League of Nations said that "safeguards" were needed for "Native Peoples who were unable to stand on their own under the strenuous conditions of the modern world," and the term "safeguards" was then adopted by the World Bank.[71] As was the case with involuntary resettlement, World Bank involvement was expected to minimize and mitigate any harm. Indigenous peoples now got what might be called the World Bank's Indigenous Project, a consultant-intensive experience that provided good material for World Bank publications but, like resettlement, did not obligate large amounts of money. The World Bank had to update and upgrade its resettlement and cultural resources management advice after UNDRIP; it was obvious, even to the World Bank's own management, that in relation to cultural heritage matters the institution had no comparative advantage at all.

Indigenous peoples were not inclined to accept the idea that others knew what was best for them or that others needed to do the heavy mental lifting. The World Bank was a spectator not a major player; it was the First Nations people themselves in Canada who started the healing lodges to combat alcoholism, and it was the Indians who have led the pushback against dependency and the deterioration in their way of life caused by alcoholism funded by regular royalty payments from oil and gas companies. Indigenous people who are small in population and vulnerable to outside influences speak a quarter of the 6,000 languages in the world. Many of these languages are used by fewer than a 1,000 people each, and are expected to disappear at the rate of one a month over the course of the next century.

Indigenous peoples were a genuine global issue involving rich and poor countries. I have heard that in Western Australia, prison planners reckon that Aboriginal people, who make up less than 2 percent of the population, will take up half the places in tomorrow's jails. It is also said that the average lifespan of Aboriginal people is twenty years shorter than that of European Australians. Some Indigenous peoples preserve their local cultural heritage while acquiring the knowledge and skills required to journey to the outside world to earn a living for short or long periods. North American Indian groups have been doing this with some success for many years.

The Mohawk, who retain a fierce pride in their cultural heritage, have developed a talent for working on the construction of steel girders at great heights in big cities. Social change that is the result of some indigenous people wanting isolation while others want to participate to a limited degree in mainstream society cannot be stopped by leaving Indigenous peoples alone or trying to keep out the outside world with a cordon sanitaire, or a reservation. Indigenous people rather than well-meaning outsiders will make their own choices.

The situation of Indigenous peoples made it hard to see how they would be able to maintain their unique cultural identities. Experience suggested that Indigenous peoples have searched for an accommodation with the outside world to provide them with insulation against the effects of social change. Examples of this approach would include nativistic movements such as the Ghost Dance of the Sioux. But this, although peaceful, caused panic among surrounding settlers and led to the slaughter of Indigenous people without much cause.

The United Nations used the definition of Indigenous people applied by José Martínez-Cobo, the special rapporteur to the Sub-Commission on Prevention of Discrimination Against Indigenous Populations. Cobo states, "Indigenous communities, peoples and nations are those which having a historical continuity with pre-invasion and pre-colonial societies that developed on their territories, consider themselves distinct from other sectors of societies now prevailing in those territories, or parts of them. They form at present non-dominant sectors of society and are determined to preserve, develop and transmit to future generations their ancestral territories, and their ethnic identity, as the basis for their continued existence as peoples, in accordance with their own cultural patterns, social institutions, and legal systems."[72] In practice, self-definition was usually taken to be the most important element in deciding whether a people is or is not entitled to be called indigenous. No single definition exists that is capable of capturing all indigenous peoples.

Impact on the Project Cycle

World Bank anthropologists never managed to make their concerns a mandated part of project procedures as happened at USAID. Of course it was not unusual for the qualitative dimension of poverty to receive limited attention when project lending was for bridges, railways, and dams.[73] World Bank infrastructural investment projects could be engineered with relative certainty and their successful construction did not depend to any great degree on the behavior of local people.[74] With infrastructural development it was usually the case that needs were so great that project identification was like shooting fish in a barrel. With social projects there was a need to identify forms of behavior that exist throughout the country and agreed to constitute a constraint on development.

It was hard for World Bank anthropologists to supply the missing social meanings for the global poverty statistics because the project cycle did not call for such data and these sorts of views were usually the result of special studies designed to avoid harm or damage to project participants. The loss of intimate contact with a known community and its inhabitants made it hard to either explain or do anthropology. Without inclusion in the mandatory analysis required for big projects the use of anthropology could not be increased by simply issuing well-meaning guidance and lists of things that deserved to be looked at in projects work.[75] The increased use of anthropology depended not only on mandated procedures in projects work that, apart from safeguards, were minimal, but also on institutional change that was driven at the presidential level, and that never happened. At the same time, training did not familiarize economists and others with social issues. The anthropologists had no external champion or intellectual heavyweight with a substantial reputation outside the institution, unlike the case with the economists, who had Nobel Laureate Joe Stiglitz.

Social Movements

Early in the World Bank's history, projects, particularly those in agriculture or transport, that focused on the elimination of bottlenecks were exactly what was needed: a precise technological innovation that focused resources and attention on a high priority area.[76] But national or global development is not easily accomplished by means of a patchwork quilt of projects; and projects, while successful, too often have had little impact on other areas of the economy. Good standards of management in a project have not always improved regional or national standards of management.

For fifty years the development project has been the main method of delivering economic development and poverty alleviation. World Bank project documents usually describe the need for change as the result of weak staffing, a lack of motivation, poor organization, inadequate knowledge and skills, unsatisfactory space and facilities, outmoded or poorly maintained equipment, and, of course, a lack of finance. It takes about two years to get the materials, equipment, and staff in place. Then a new set of visitors with a new set of career needs appears and new documents, which describe the old problems in new ways with new approaches, can be processed.

As an alternative to conventional projects, the World Bank and other aid agencies might have considered making more use of their own experience with social movements, and to also make greater use of the work of anthropologists and other social scientists who have studied these movements. As David Korten said,

> We might reflect on what might have been accomplished over the past three decades if there had been more development movements and fewer development projects. . . . The qualities of a movement gradually gave way to the qualities of a publicly funded and centrally administered program with centrally sponsored projects. It would be interesting to know more of the dynamics of this process. True movements draw their energy and resources from the people and have little definable organizational structure.[77]

The Korean war of the 1950s helped to produce a revival of the traditional Saeumaul Undong movement in rural areas of the country. Though in the 1970s it was an obvious success, the movement declined in the 1980s after President Park Chung-hee died.[78] Since then the movement has played an important role in the increasingly ambitious development assistance offered by Korea.

J. C. "Jimmy" Yen, a Yale graduate, succeeded in mobilizing the poor people of Tsing-Hsien province in China in 1934 in order to promote economic development. His rural reconstruction movement created jobs and raised incomes, and improved literacy and public health. An essential part of the program was the development of political institutions that could promote democratic development. Participation was voluntary. Yen built a volunteer organization staffed by academics and Chinese elders long before Mao came to power. He persuaded academics from the cities to come and join his movement. Yen's experience demonstrated that the best and the brightest in a country had to be involved in the task of rural reconstruction. In China he had no time for those who wanted to be paid, and he had no time for those who wanted to make helping the rural poor just another job.[79] Yen was a charismatic man and the sort of movement he founded required charismatic leadership.

In the 1930s, while working in China, Yen believed that improvement was not simply a grim matter of edging forward, a matter of all work and no play. Yen believed that people had to be brought to realize the commonalities that existed among themselves. He used drama, putting on plays to bring humor to the work and to remind people of their cultural heritage; he used the radio as a means of reaching out.[80] Sent to France during World War I to help organize more than a quarter of a million Chinese laborers, Yen decided that if their lot was to improve, they must learn to read. Even though the idea of teaching coolies to read was then unthinkable, he succeeded in reducing the Chinese alphabet to around 1,000 functional characters. Yen then used these characters to teach the laborers so that they could write home. The laborers were highly impressed that a scholar like Yen would help them. The program was outstandingly successful. Jimmy Yen's use of the role of scholar in his literacy campaign was a brilliant stroke because scholars were venerated by the public in China. He did not have to explain who he was or what he was doing to those he was trying to assist. Inspired by this progress, Yen returned to China where he helped to improve the standard of living in rural areas. His work attracted powerful support from backers in the United States, and as a consequence the movement that he founded later became known as the International Mass Education Movement.[81] After China had been taken over by the Communists, Yen moved to the Philippines, where he and his thinking were put to work to combat the Huk Communist insurgency. Early in the 1960s Yen founded the International Institute for Rural Reconstruction (IIRR) which has its world headquarters in Silang, Cavite Province, just outside Manila.

The Yen movement drifted away from its unique movement approach and its global aspirations and became bogged down in the Philippines doing more or less what all the other NGOs and donors were trying to do. Although, like many other NGOs it was possessed of a strong sense of independence, when Yen's movement lost vitality and became bureaucratized the movement's survival was linked to doing what the donors wanted. Yen's movement reached its apogee during the years when it was involved in China. It never achieved the same resonance in the Philippines. Since the early 1960s its claim to global prominence became weaker and weaker as the organization has fallen behind the CAREs, the Oxfams, and so on. The twin strands of US anti-Communist interest and fascination with China handicapped further growth.

Recently, using money from the World Bank, the IIRR has been experimenting with a novel population-control project in an area of Ethiopia where many women have an average of seven children. Rather than using traditional family planning approaches and techniques that involve facilitators trying to persuade individual women to adopt contraception, IIRR has attempted to try to influence community understanding and behavior so that outcomes become the result of community discussion and consensus. This initiative is interesting because rather than, as is so often the case, project ideas and the way of securing change come from outside, the community is seen as the originator and implementer of change. Obviously, the idea that a community can learn our way out (LOWO) could have implications for the way a number of aid agencies deliver assistance.[82]

Social Movements in the Health Sector

When working on a World Bank research project into the organization and management of tropical diseases I discovered that the energy and enthusiasm that was evident in NGO campaigns has also been used in public health campaigns such as the one that eliminated smallpox.[83] Campaign organizations harness substantial social forces using what Ronald Knox called "enthusiasm," an energetic vision created by society that is more important than self.[84] Campaigns evoke widespread enthusiasm and support, particularly from the poorer elements of society; they have shown that enthusiasm and widespread social mobilization and participation can be maintained over a period of years. This in itself is no mean feat, since in many poor countries there is suspicion about the motives of government agents at the local level. These public health campaigns demonstrated the importance of administrative performance as a result of years spent building a fit-for-purpose organization and a dedicated staff from the grassroots upward, beginning with those who were expected to form relationships with the at-risk public.

World Bank support for public health campaigns may be capable of broader application. Public health campaigning has involved a number of interesting social dynamics that show how development assistance can work more effectively with poor people. In Brazil in 1987, 88 million people were protected from tropical diseases; this protection was the result of 55 million house-visits and 30 million kilometers of travel on foot, bicycle, horseback, motorbike, small truck, canoe, and small riverboat. Operations covered 7,700 municipalities. The Brazilians had at one time or another produced maps of every dwelling in the country.[85]

A public health campaign is not just a delivery device, a way of giving people what they want. The results that are achieved represent a product that is the joint outcome of collaboration between the community and health workers. Covering a community house by house offers a useful way of dealing with communities. The use of the house as a workplace by residents, program personnel, and auxiliary assistants permits concentration on a narrow range of household behaviors, beliefs, and attitudes. Household contact helps residents forge personal relationships with health workers. Disease control shows that top-down silver bullet technological solutions can produce impressive results when medical personnel have established social relationships with those at risk that are characterized by mutual trust, understanding, and respect. Nor is this emphasis on relationships confined to public health: corporations are becoming more aware of their own social performance responsibilities.

The poor become part of the solution. They are made part of the health organization. They are not the passive recipients of assistance—they are participants. Public health organizations in Brazil target the household. Social solidarity is promoted when health workers visit the family regularly in their home, when the health workers know each member of the family, and when all family members work together on disease eradication. The health workers try to change behavior; there is always something that they want participants to do differently.

The partnership between public health personnel and the household residents is reinforced with intensive supervision. Where health education is important, house visits provide the messages in a relevant and understandable manner. Personnel invest their personal reputation and are aware that all their work will be checked. The work is nonintrusive in a cultural sense—it does not affect existing relationships or power or status, nor does it run counter to important religious or ideological beliefs or values. Personnel are not in a position of authority over residents, but instead must work with the residents and be judged not only by their supervisors, but also by the residents.

Public health officials focus on individual poor people. They study them, listen to them, continually make judgments about what they will and will not do, and constantly try to ensure that what they do has roots in ordinary life. They know how to work with a wide variety of people, how to explain, and how to generate support and understanding. They work with and for people. Administrators must have personal skills not only in the conduct of social relations. They must also have leadership capacity. They must demonstrate personal beliefs, strong feelings, and a commitment to an important national purpose. They succeed because the achievement of a social purpose that all agree to be important is their highest priority. The role of expertise is simply to help achieve this objective.

Success in disease control requires concentration on predictability and reliability, making sure that small though important tasks can be satisfactorily performed. It cannot be assumed that these small tasks are unimportant, that they are boring, that they have no complexity, that they are simply mechanical and routine. In institutions that have been designed to accommodate policy skills, employees who spend time on small things run the danger of their superiors believing that these small tasks are the sort of responsibility and level of complexity best suited to their capabilities. Officials who see themselves as important need to gain a competitive edge, and so they do not want to be bothered with visiting unimportant people living in hard-to-get-at locations.

Public health organizations cannot afford to have a high degree of tolerance for errors. Accuracy and reliability in program execution and in record keeping are absolutely essential. There is little hope of achieving a reduction of transmission unless a large proportion of an infection can be treated in a short time. Spreading treatments haphazardly over time, within the framework of a therapeutic service responding to perceived symptoms, would have no significant effect on transmission. In Brazil employee responsibilities were clearly laid down and clearly understood. There were no shortcuts taken or allowed. Employees were expected to do their jobs in the way they were trained. If they did not perform, or if they broke the rules, then they were dismissed.

The key to campaign success was the production of a system that encouraged individuals to discipline themselves. Throughout the beginning of their professional careers, staff were exposed to good work; they discussed good work and bad work so that they could see what was expected. The sense of professionalism that was engendered in employees made them want to do well, which in turn lowered the propensity to do bad work.

Poor people were co-opted as volunteers in Brazil and provided more than half the treatments. Each campaign recruited and managed its own community volunteers. Brazilian salaries were low compared to the private sector, and they were low compared to the rest of the health sector. Two factors accounted for personnel effectiveness and helped counterbalance remuneration difficulties. First, the prestige and image enjoyed by the organization in the eyes of the public as a consequence of more than fifty years of effective field service. It was an organization that people were proud to work for; the work was worthwhile. Those contemplating leaving invariably anticipated and spoke about the sense of loss they expected to feel. There was an immense reservoir of good will. The second factor was the commitment to public service expressed by employees. Employees believed deeply in the importance of their public service. They believed the work was important and they wanted to keep doing it.

Notes

1. World Bank Independent Evaluation Group, *Cost Benefit Analysis*.
2. Woo, "The Art of Economic Development."
3. Chenery, quoted in World Bank [1974], "Press Release, September 30"; Chenery et al., *Redistribution with Growth*. Andrew M. Kamarck worked for twenty-six years at the World Bank and was director of the Economic Development Institute. "Kamarck contended that most economists today strive for a mathematical precision in their work that neither stems from nor leads to an accurate view of economic reality. . . . Subtle realities of the individual, social, and political worlds render largely ineffective both large-scale macroeconomic and microeconomic models of the consumer and the firm. Fashionable cost-benefit analysis must be recognized as inherently imprecise. Capital and investment in developing countries tend to be measured in easy but irrelevant ways. Kamarck concluded with a call for economists

to involve themselves in data collection, to insist on more-accurate and more-reliable data sources, to do analysis within the context of experience, and to take a realistic, incremental approach to policy-making." Kamarck, *Economics and the Real World*.

4. Would it not have been equally possible to invent a global smiling concept based on an assumption that all jokes have a relatively homogenous quality and that one could, country by country, work out how much laughter was needed for individual well-being?

5. Personal communication from an economist staff member.

6. The anthropologists might continue to hope that their concerns would achieve priority, but the realpolitik suggested that money-moving and speed of execution would continue to run the institution no matter what public statements were made. As Attorney General John Mitchell said at the time of Watergate, "Watch what we do, not what we say." For the more hopeful anthropological view see Davis, "Bringing Culture ."

7. Cochrane, review of Wilson, "An Economic Survey of the New Hebrides," 217–18.

8. Bauer and Ward, *Two Views of Aid*, 49.

9. Stern, "Beyond the Transition." UNDP gives a similar view in *Poverty Alleviation in Asia and the Pacific*.

10. Chambers and Conway, "Sustainable Rural Livelihoods," 296.

11. See, for example Mosse, *Knowledge as Relational*, which mirrors my own impression that World Bank anthropology, deprived of fresh contact with communities, has become weaker and weaker over time.

12. See the concluding remarks to Cochrane, *Anthropology in the Mining Industry*.

13. Rosalind Eyben, who was chief social adviser in British Overseas Aid, met economists who were skeptical about the value of anthropology because they didn't believe anthropologists had been trained to ask the right questions. Eyben, *A Guide to Social Analysis*.

14. Some context is provided by Mosse, "Localized Cosmopolitans."

15. The NGOs' view of social development responsibilities has focused on compliance with safeguards policies, international norms, and conventions, as well as on the avoidance of harm. In the mining industry, discussion has been about social performance rather than social development with performance being defined as a "company's interactions, activities, and outcomes with respect to local communities. Performance is supported by systems, data, and capability that align with international standards and locally negotiated commitments, with the objective of avoiding harm to people and ensuring a stable operating environment in which communities and companies can prosper." Kemp and Owen, "Social Performance Gaps," ii.

16. Burki et al., "Social Development and Results on the Ground"; Davis et al., "Social Development Update"; Davis, "A History of the Social Development Network."

17. On relationships, see Strathern, *The Relation*.

18. King, *Economic Development Projects*.

19. Cochrane and Noronha, *The Use of Anthropology*. See also Goodland, "Social & Environmental Assessment." Later work with the World Bank and USAID in Washington and overseas is covered in appendix A.

20. USAID had a long history of using anthropologists and of realizing the value that they added. What was missing was a way of making this use systematic. The 1973 New Directions in Foreign Aid legislation required the development of a new project manual, and to this manual was added a training component.

21. In comments presented together with my paper "Policy Studies and Anthropology," Louise Morauta referred to my "international paymasters" since she assumed that I had been paid to do the study by the World Bank.

22. Michael Cernea began his account of anthropology at the World Bank, *Sociology, Anthropology, and Development*, in 1975 and ignored the study that Raymond Noronha and I had done in our 1972–74 work.

23. Davis, "A History of the Social Development Network," 2.

24. das Gupta, "Gender, Poverty, and Demography"; das Gupta, "How Well Does India's Federal Government Perform?"; das Gupta, *Health, Poverty and Development in India.*

25. I became familiar with this project when Scarlett asked me to be a discussant on the project's results at Sussex.

26. Sir John, who was from the Australian National University, pulled me aside when we first met in Canberra with a comment about how Raymond got on with his other Iran study team members. I explained how I thought an anthropologist would probably work best in the Iran assignment. He was an inspirational figure and I still remember a paper he had written comparing economic development in the Nile Valley with western Australia; his paper included the interesting observation that both areas had camels.

27. Noronha, *A Review of the Literature*; Noronha, *Social and Cultural Dimensions of Tourism.*

28. Firth, "Methodological Issues," 473.

29. Epstein, "The Ideal Marriage."

30. Salisbury, "The Anthropologist as Societal Ombudsman."

31. Ferguson, "Anthropology and its Evil Twin."

32. Vetterlein, "Seeing Like the World Bank," 54. See also Mosse, "Social Analysis as Corporate Product."

33. Streeten, *First Things First.*

34. Streeten, "Why Interdisciplinary Studies," 8–9.

35. Epstein, "Economic Development and Social Change."

36. Epstein, "The Ideal Marriage," 15–16.

37. Gupta has a similar view about the importance of collecting this information on the ground, Akhil Gupta, "The Construction of the Global Poor."

38. Cochrane, "Review of Brokensha, Warren, and Werner."

39. Kirsch, "Lost Worlds"; see also Brosius, "Analysis and Interventions."

40. See Goodland, "Social & Environmental Assessment."

41. Lee had been appointed by McNamara personally and was much better placed to act than the first sociologists and anthropologists who joined the World Bank without having been selected by the president.

42. Dr. James Lee and Olive Nash, interview by Boegomir Chokel, World Bank Archives Oral History Program, 4 April 1985.

43. I found Jim Lee to be very open-minded and receptive to having a close working relationship with anthropology. That was not the case with a later director of the environmental function, Ken Piddington, who became a victim of the Indian dams controversy. Ken was the son of well-known New Zealand anthropologist Ralph Piddington.

44. "For example, poverty within a region can vary across districts. This makes small-area estimates of poverty very appealing. However, often we are unable directly to compute poverty estimates for small areas like districts. Instead, we usually have poverty estimates for regions or entire countries only. The main reason that poverty measures are computed for large areas and not usually available for small areas is data availability." World Bank Institute, "Analysis of Poverty," 79.

45. Chambers makes a case for this alternative in "Rapid Rural Appraisal." See also, on long-term fieldwork, Shokeid, "From the Tikopia to Polymorphous Engagements."

46. Alm, "NEPA"; Caldwell, *The National Environmental Policy Act*; Glasson, "Environmental Impact Assessment."

47. World Bank environmentalists obviously believed in the "Think Globally, Act Locally" slogan, which assumed that global strategy could form the basis for local action. This suggests that global goals could and should be aligned with local preferences, something that few anthropologists were likely to agree with. The phrase has been attributed to town planners and environmentalists associated with Friends of the Earth. However, *The Daily Telegraph* suggested it was coined by David Brower. *Daily Telegraph*, "Obituary for David Brower."

48. Freudenburg, "Social Impact Assessment," 454.

49. Franks et al., *Leading Practice Strategies*; Burdge and Robertson, "Social Impact Assessment."

50. Luther, "The National Environmental Policy Act."

51. Influenced by the ability of the environmentalists to measure, the anthropologists began to talk about standards and, after all, was poverty not all about standards of income for the individual? The idea has unfortunately been taken up in the private sector despite the obvious fact that relationships do not lend themselves to this kind of analysis. Standards for relationships? Marriage?

52. Franks et al., *Leading Practice Strategies*.

53. Epstein, *Capitalism, Primitive and Modern*.

54. See Epstein, *Matupit*.

55. A number of observers have not appreciated the fundamental force and significance of NGO campaigns. See Edwards, *NGO Rights and Responsibilities*; Lewis, "Political Ideologies"; Smillie, *The Alms Bazaar*. An important fact that does not always emerge is the nature of the relationship between the big international NGOs and their local affiliates, a relationship that is often contentious since local organizations often feel that they are treated as the junior partner.

56. Aronson, *Participation in Country Economic and Sector Work*.

57. "A country poverty profile sets out the major facts on poverty (and typically, inequality), and then examines the pattern of poverty, to see how it varies by geography (by region, urban or rural, mountain or plain, and so on), by community characteristics (for example, in communities with and without a school), and by household characteristics (for example, by education of household head, or by household size). Hence, a poverty profile is a comprehensive poverty comparison, showing how poverty varies across subgroups of society [such as region of residence or sector of employment]. A well-presented poverty profile can be immensely informative and extremely useful in assessing how the sectoral or regional pattern of economic change is likely to affect aggregate poverty, although it typically uses basic techniques such as tables or graphs." World Bank Institute, "Analysis of Poverty," 66.

58. Of course a few anthropologists managed to get themselves posted to interesting places and managed to do interesting work. But these were somewhat rare exceptions to the deskbound pattern.

59. World Bank [2017], "Press Release, April 5."

60. See Guggenheim, "Resettlement in Colombia."

61. Cochrane, "Administration of Wagina."

62. See Cochrane, "Resettlement."

63. China has put legislation in place to ensure free power for resettled people.

64. Gloria Davis worked on Indonesian transmigration. See Davis and Garrison, *Indonesia*.

65. Merkle, "Ningxia's Third Road"; Wilmsen, "Development for Whom?"; Zhang and Zhang, "The Practice of Accepting Rural Resettlers."

66. Thanks to early work, the World Bank was well-prepared to respond to the indigenous challenge. See Goodland et al., *Economic Development*.

67. Davis, "The World Bank and Indigenous Peoples."

68. Each summer for five years, from 2002 to 2007, I joined the annual meetings of Indigenous peoples in Geneva that were working on finalization of the draft UNDRIP. I do not remember ever seeing a significant representation or a significant contribution from the World Bank. Details of this annual event are found in Burger, "Standard-Setting: Lessons Learned for the Future."

69. A pre-UNDRIP view is given by Davis, "The World Bank and Indigenous Peoples."

70. Purcell, "Indigenous Knowledge."

71. Callahan, *Mandates and Empire*, 213.

72. Cobo, *Study of the Problem of Discrimination*, 3.

73. USAID did pay attention to qualitative issues. Hageboeck et al., *The Manager's Guide to Data Collection.*

74. The cost-benefit calculations involved in UN projects work were a business school tool, not much different from those made when a sales rep sells a car on credit. Cost-benefit analysis involved identifying and quantifying a stream of costs and a stream of benefits in order to ensure that the return on the investment represented the best use of the funds. The project cycle, based on engineering and refined by the international agencies, went through a number of well-defined stages. Projects were identified by the country as a result of technical assistance, but increasingly as a result of staff suggestions while in the field. It was the responsibility of the country that wanted to borrow to prepare the project so that it could be reviewed by an aid agency. The project was then appraised; if the appraisal was satisfactory, then the project proceeded to the negotiation stage. Negotiation involved the aid agency and the borrower sitting down and hammering out all the fine details. The loan then went for final approval. The international agencies mounted supervision missions throughout the life of the loan to ensure that the funds were applied in a manner that fulfilled the loan agreement.

75. Cernea, "Operational Manual Statement"; Jacobs et al., *Methods and Tools*; Davis et al., *Social Assessment.*

76. King, *Economic Development Projects.*

77. Korten, quoted in Mayfield, *Go to the People*, 11.

78. Boyer and Byong, *Rural Development in South Korea.*

79. Hershey, "Jimmy Yen."

80. Yen, *The Ting Hsien Experiment*, 23–30.

81. Yen's career is summarized in Buck, *Tell the People.*

82. The LOWO concept was developed by Jane Boorstein, a board member of IIRR. The LOWO project received a grant from the Bill & Melinda Gates Foundation to help with a population project in Ethiopia. I have been working with IIRR to see what follow-up arrangements should be made.

83. Liese, Sachdeva, and Cochrane, *Organizing and Managing.*

84. Knox, *Enthusiasm*, discussion, 400–409.

85. Liese, Sachdeva, and Cochrane, *Organizing and Managing.*

Chapter 4

PUBLIC SERVICE

W orld Bank staff are skilled bureaucrats with all the foibles of bureaucrats. They know how to survive and thrive in their bureaucracy. In
no time after McNamara's money-moving was introduced, a whole class of
courtiers had emerged vying with each other and vying for attention. Since
McNamara's time at the World Bank, the quick fix has been in a well-
written idea, a catchy policy idea, abject loyalty—these are the things that
are rewarded. Being a favorite was soon seen as a way to get rapid promotion. The resulting self-interest prompts competition with coworkers,
encourages staff to blow their own trumpet, and to make sure that as many
people as possible know of their virtue, their capacity, and their accom-
plishments. Officials spend their time looking for gaps in the defenses of
coworkers, estimating where rewarding attacks may be made. Where colleagues are involved, cooperation is viewed with caution in order to ensure
that an actual or potential competitor does not gain an advantage.

Can the World Bank be considered a UN International Civil Service?[1]
I don't think so, because a civil servant needs a society to serve and World
Bank staff are expected to represent and serve more than 180 societies.
Erving Goffman made it clear that for a civil servant to represent his own
country is difficult enough. He said that the official is normally representative of public ideals, qualities, and attributes associated in the public mind
with society. "Thus, when an individual presents himself before others his
performance will tend to incorporate and exemplify the officially accred-
ited values."[2] How can a UN civil servant do this for a hundred or more
societies? The unique cultural constitution of the World Bank provides an
equally unique constraint on public service.[3] As the World Bank has grown
larger and larger, it has become more and more difficult to make operational
use of the cultural heritage of the World Bank's individual staff members or
their client countries. The World Bank's global bureaucracy must try to get

a recognizably common performance from Americans, Australians, Zambians, Argentineans, Englishmen, Dutchmen, Indians, Pakistanis, and even Irishmen from both sides of their border. In fact, as we shall see, the World Bank is best understood as a large corporation animated by the desire to have a healthy bottom line and supported by staff who follow a commercial, rather than a public-service-oriented, code of conduct. World Bank retirement notices often state, without apparently appreciating the irony, that so and so has "retired from the service of the World Bank."

The continuous expansion in lending has had a considerable impact on the World Bank as part of the UN International Civil Service.[4] My sense is that World Bank has, over the past forty to fifty years, changed its essential institutional characteristics from those of a public institution with notional public accountability to the commercial attitudes, values, and beliefs of a global corporation.[5] As time passed, the burgeoning World Bank bureaucracy in Washington has become more concerned with its own internal issues such as expansion and market share than with the provision of public service in client countries. Like any other corporation, the World Bank can be seen to provide value for the institution's national shareholders. Inter alia, this raises questions for research related to the cultural constitution of the World Bank and its capacity for public service.

Beginning professionals in the World Bank want to start at the top or as near to the top as they can as assistants, advisers, or bag carriers for the top people. They want to start by working on policy and other big issues. Many appear to be like young politicians. After all, above all other walks of life, the career of politician is the one that offers the quickest rewards and visibility to those with the smallest amount of real-life experience and accomplishment. Staff members believe that if they are to advance in the organization, then they need to be noticed. Self-interested staff members keep the reins of their careers and their welfare in their own hands, making rapid connections between results obtained in their work and their own personal advancement. These staff tend to view colleagues, superiors, and even the public as opportunities to be exploited or obstacles to be overcome.

It is unrealistic to expect an international organization like the World Bank, particularly one without a strong cultural identity, to provide the sort of service to the public that Nyerere suggested was wanted in the new nation of Tanzania:

> If there is a common attitude of service, helpfulness, and sympathy with the basic objectives of the Nation, then politicians and Civil Servants together make a team which can lead the people triumphantly into the building of a new society . . . but the way instructions are carried out can make all the difference in the world to the man whom they intimately affect. When a Civil Servant is

dealing with the public directly—either in person or by correspondence—his courtesy makes essential difference both to his own position, and to the understanding with which his words are received, even a firm "No" said kindly, and if possible with an explanation, can make a citizen feel that his own importance has been recognized by those in authority. In dealing with files too, the attitude of the civil servant can contribute to or sabotage, the general work of the Government. Promptness and a willingness to make constructive suggestions of how a policy could be made to work in the most expeditious manner, can save the ordinary citizen unnecessary frustration and contribute to the overall development of Tanganyika.[6]

Former UK prime minister Jim Callaghan suggested that a civil service that did not have common values, beliefs, and attitudes would not be effective. In evidence to a House of Commons Committee on the state of the British Civil Service, he warned that new values such as cost-efficiency might be seen as replacements for traditional values of impartiality, integrity, and incorruptibility resulting in a much less responsive civil service than in the past. The atmosphere would be less conducive to the transmission of shared values.[7]

Although USAID has economists every bit as hard-nosed as those in the World Bank, the agency is staffed by Americans with more or less the same values, beliefs, and attitudes. I believe this has helped to produce a poverty performance that is often more in touch with social circumstances than that of the World Bank. My sense has been that USAID personnel instinctively seek to get close to those they want to help. They want to feel their way to solutions that seem to fit in with what they have seen on the ground. Even though the agency has had global programs in areas such as health or agriculture, the opinion of the director of the local USAID mission has usually been influential. A further cultural advantage comes from the fact that the consultants that are used are US-based and there is heavy reliance on US universities. USAID personnel do have a strong sense of public service despite the fact that their strange position in the US Foreign Service in the past often made them appear to be second-class citizens.

The culture-free environment has contributed to the institutionalization of management-by-seclusion behavior that is inimical to public service at the World Bank. Over the past twenty or thirty years, as presentation skills have increasingly replaced hands-on work with poor people as the experience to look for in new recruits, personal qualities such as consideration and helpfulness have become less evident. Staff want to be seen to excel in intellectual activities, publications, organizing conferences, and managing large research projects because these activities help with lending and promotion. The result of recruiting young staff members who have learned how to look after themselves is that it is hard for them to put the interests of the public first, nor can they award high priority to the interest of their colleagues because they are competitors.[8] After this training, it becomes natural to realize that if careers are to prosper, staff have to make sure that their work is noticed by their main superior. That means that they have to have assignments that provide good publishing opportunities or opportunities to shine. The training and experience do little to enforce the idea that teamwork is fundamental.

Worse still, bilateral aid agencies are now full of the same people in the same bureaucratic mold. They are equally at home in the public or private sector. They have highly portable qualifications. It is less and less the case that the industrialized countries select and train young men and women for a life in development assistance nor do they offer a career with advancement commensurate with ability and experience. Increasingly, new entrants have backgrounds and experience suited to corporate life or the World Bank.

Aid agency and NGO personnel who have never lived and worked in a developing country are at a disadvantage when it comes to working out how locals may react to a new initiative or knowing why an ongoing initiative is not doing well. World Bank staff who visit for only a few weeks may be fascinated by the new experiences. If the visitor is a very important person, he or she will be shown the show places, will be pampered and petted, and may believe the hosts when they speak about progress and the hard work to be done. They stay in hotels and associate with nationals and officials who speak their language and are polite and respectful to foreigners. What their stay is unlikely to provide is an insight into the quality, attitudes, and practices of those much lower down in the government—those whose efforts may be essential to the success of a new project. It is essential to be able to know when hosts are being polite and saying what they believe foreign donors want to hear, and when they are being straightforward.

An overseas apprenticeship is an essential rite of passage.[9] What is learned by those aid agency personnel who have spent some years living and working in poor countries is professionally invaluable, though often frustrating at the time. New arrivals must make their way from ministry to ministry, office to office, dealing with frequently indifferent, and sometimes hostile or suspicious, civil servants. The newcomers have to acquire lots of permits to live and to drive in the country. They need to secure a lease for an apartment or house for which the landlord may wish a year's rent in advance. Large wads of hard currency will be spent on personal vehicles. Proof of marriage may be required even for those who have been wed for many years. Starting an account with a bank manager who recognizes that even the best of employers do not pay salary and allowances on time is a must. Electricity and water supply must be secured and hard bargaining may be necessary to be able to make overseas telephone calls. Friends may provide the names of reliable tradesmen, servants, or house staff who can actually do what is wanted. Initially there is bound to be mail trouble as letters and parcels go astray for weeks of forever. School may present curriculums and other challenges for children in local schools. Language lessons become increasingly urgent and increasingly hard to fit into busy schedules. House trouble grows because of breakdowns and landlords don't want any responsibility for fixing or even maintenance. Vehicles develop major faults that were not pointed out at time of sale and warranty does not apply. Familiar comfort foods are not available. Those who were thought to be friends and colleagues seem largely indifferent to all these troubles. There are more revelations to be had as one learns just how many holidays, religious and otherwise, staff and colleagues believe they must follow when all hands are needed on deck. A surprising number of staff at home, and at work, want short-term financing for family troubles. Meanwhile, at home the tea and sugar and petrol never seem to last.

These essential experiences provide a good idea of what works and what does not work well in a country. They provide a good idea of how foreigners are regarded, how the government is regarded by ordinary people, and, in particular, how the government is regarded by those at the bottom of the social pile. What is invaluable about settling in, and staying for a few years, is that personal experience with the amount of time taken to get things done, which may be months, with the boredom and indifference of the officials, with the absence of paper, paperclips, and copying facilities in offices, all help to illustrate what the average citizen has to endure.

Efficiency and Effectiveness

Instead of having societal expectations and traditions of public service providing guidance and a standard to aspire to, World Bank staff have tried to ensure that their decision making reflects universal efficiency and effectiveness thinking, rather than the values and beliefs that civil servants usually get from their societal affiliation. A difficulty emerges when an attempt is made to define what "efficiency" or "effectiveness" actually mean, because whether defined in terms of getting results such as the relationship between inputs and outputs or in terms of the relationship between what is or what might be, it soon becomes clear that these supposedly rational terms are hopelessly mixed up with values, and values are not the object of a precise science.[10] And "rationality means or implies the elimination of the traditional, the mystical, the magical, the sacral, the development of causal-scientific ways of thought, the adoption of modes and patterns of action which relate means to ends with minimum waste and maximum efficiency."[11]

The reality is that performance in a civil service will rise or sink in order to meet popular standards and expectations. It is quite impossible to have a highly efficient civil service in a society whose other social institutions place little value on minimizing costs or maximizing output. The World Bank has encouraged the civil service in developing countries elsewhere to give priority to the new imperative of economic growth and material development; this econocentric imperative can ultimately exercise a considerable influence on the way the public is served and the way the poor are regarded.[12] In these circumstances the civil servant becomes a technician more concerned with the principles of budgeting and accounting, planning, reporting, and evaluating than of listening to and learning from the public.

Had they been asked, senior World Bank staff would probably have agreed with Margaret Thatcher when she said there was no such thing as society, since for many of them society does not seem to really exist. Society's opinions, values, beliefs, or hopes are thought to be constraining or irrelevant. Public opinion is seen to be primitive, uninformed, contradictory, and lacking in intellectual and analytical authority. The public is something to be convinced, improved, educated, fed better, given a higher income. The financial needs of developing countries are considered to be so great that the supply and delivery of finance is seen to be the most important responsibility of client countries. Under these circumstances, cultural considerations and social arrangements are irrelevant. When people are starving, the supply of food is what is important. The same thinking has been extended far beyond poverty. The assumption, usually unspoken, is that any society that cannot look after its citizens really has no business having cultural considerations or spendthrift political ideas.

Colonialism, despite fashionable continued criticism and rejection, made a local contribution; socialism built health and educational provision with habits of service that survived for a time after capitalism triumphed. What is disappointing about the impact of the World Bank in developing countries is that there is little evidence that it strengthens a sense of public service. Indeed, the effect is often quite the opposite because Bank officials want to pay the highest salaries and allowances to those who handle money in government—in other words, to people like themselves. Instead of believing in a sense of service, Bank staff have made no secret of the fact that they think that a country gets what it pays for in terms of public service. This is simply not an affordable proposition for many poor countries.[13]

In the upper echelons of the World Bank there are officials who believe that there are governments in developing countries that need to be viewed as failed states. They will continue to fail to deliver basic services to their citizens. It is therefore incumbent on the great and the good in the World

Bank to try to make up for the governance deficit. Exchange rate decisions and many other political issues cannot be decided simply on the basis of technical criteria. Political factors also affect the whole implementation process, particularly where different parties have strong geographical or sectoral affiliations. Inevitably, the decision making over large grants and loans involves judgments about the political stability of a government, and about the political risks involved in the imposition of terms and conditions.

Politicians Seen as Competitors

Civil servants work for politicians, but do the World Bank's staff think that politicians are their masters? World Bank economists do not see politicians in a kindly light; they are, after all, competitors for power who should be pressured to accept that their highest duty is to follow the revenue and expenditure advice of Bank country economists. It is possible that the apparent lack of enthusiasm for democracy stems from the fact that policy analysts and most economists see political processes as an inefficient way to manage resources. This interpretation is also suggested by the fact that the countries that the officials like, because they do what is needed to promote the World Bank's favorite prescriptions, have tended to be authoritarian regimes such as Korea, Singapore, or Uganda.

> Politicians intervene excessively in the operations of the public and private sectors to the point where they often end up acting against their own political interests. This is because politicians act following a partial or short-term perspective. . . . Another way of making the same point is that there might be more effective ways to meet the (public and private) goals of politicians at lower cost to society and with higher benefits to the politicians themselves.
> Equally important, the political establishment has to understand that to saddle agencies, central institutions or public enterprises, with an excessive number of often contradictory economic, political and social objectives often makes their effective management impossible. . . . To have a sporting chance of being successful, political agendas have to be modest and objectives pursued preferably one by one. . . .
> What could be done to improve the quality of politics? . . . Strengthening the technocracy (inside and outside the government), particularly with regard to policy analysis, design and implementation, could provide not only information necessary to improve the quality of political decision making, but also act as a de facto countervailing power, as it happens in many developed countries.[14]

Senior Bank staff are not used to working for politicians. They do not try very hard to find out what the minister's ideas are and how they could help with their implementation. Ministers sometimes become frustrated by the lack of cooperation. Strong ministers try to run their ministries without external advice. Some invent their own programs as an alternative to those of the external advisers. The result of indifference to the political process has been to undermine and trivialize the normal working relationship that ought to exist between civil servants and their ministers.

Part of the instinctive dislike that both politicians and World Bank economists have for each other, and that both are good at disguising, has to do with the fact that both depend for their future well-being on their success as great persuaders. Politicians wrap themselves in culture; they embrace the core values, trumpet the beliefs, and try to be seen to live lives that demonstrate the expression of core values and beliefs. Culture is a musical instrument for politicians, a mighty mobilizer, a medium usually denied to local civil servants, always denied to Bank officials. People in very poor countries need ideals to believe in and leaders to represent those ideals. The poor countries need inspiring political leadership.[15]

Politicians are those who by word and gesture can depress large groups of people; they can also make them angry or dependent, hopeful or hateful. Like the World Bank economists, the politician also seeks to persuade that he is the right person to do this or that. The tools of the politician are not written, though they involve memory, imagination, an ability to judge people, a sense of timing, and oratory. It is a sobering thing to take on a politician on his own ground. The battle will be fought on his terms. It will benefit a protagonist little to mention logic or contrary facts, because the politician can invoke much stronger cultural and social feelings. The politician will seek to put the entire weight of the country, its culture, its experience, its humiliations, and its triumphs on his side.

The difference between Bank officials and the politician lies in the fact that the former succeeds by conveying an aura of impartial objectivity without even a hint that the outcome has anything other than the remotest professional curiosity, while the latter succeeds by conveying believable partiality, that he is a friend, that he will protect, advance, or do whatever else is necessary. The politician succeeds by pretending to be everyone's friend, the World Bank economist succeeds by having no friends or even the appearance of friends. The politician succeeds by embodying culture, the policy analyst succeeds by denying culture.

Of course, it is the case that World Bank staff often wield more power than politicians; unlike politicians, though, their decisions seldom go in front of the electorate. For many small poor countries, the sort of school their children will have, the sort of health care that will be made available, the sort of public transport that serves the public are just a few areas where decisions have been influenced by World Bank staff. What the World Bank official is unlikely to mention is the importance of leadership, political leadership. Instead the impression is gained that economic development is the result of sound economic advice. In reality projects are not scientific documents—they are documents of advocacy designed in ways that ensure their approval. There can be no doubt that investment projects, particularly in terms of the generation of jobs and economic opportunities, have consequences that are extremely important for politicians, and World Bank staff.

Self-Interest

For World Bank officials, the process of advancing in their bureaucracy has become a technology with charm, consideration, hospitality, and so on being strategically supplied when something is needed. These emotions and exhibitions vanish without a trace as suddenly as they appear when the staff member decides that career prospects may not be helped by the relationship. Officials become wimps as they search for the solution that will please their masters. The organization does not create certainty; instead it usually contrives to expose the UN official to the maximum feasible uncertainty. One day a career is sure and job performance fine. The next day a career may appear to be in ruins or going nowhere. The way to survive and to get ahead is by working closely with a powerful person, by providing personal service. In an uncertain world, staff members try to have a protector, someone far up the organization for whom they can act as a pilot fish and who, in return, can help their careers. Reciprocity is the fossil fuel of the bureaucracy. Patrons often steer clients toward issues that are about to be popular and help them avoid danger areas. Clients alert patrons to opportunities that can be seen at their level.

It is in the medium-size countries where the World Bank's strange form of public service has the greatest consequences and where there is most scope for staff members to further the World Bank's and their own self-interest. But even in the medium-size countries the scope for imposition of views may be limited if the country simply thinks that the technical package that the World Bank is presenting is weak, or if they think the World Bank's money is too expensive compared to other commercial lenders. There is a conspicuous absence of policy advice and nostrums for the big borrowers. World Bank staff could lose in competition on policy issues with the big countries, so they don't really try very often. The World Bank does not have very much policy leverage with Brazil, China, or India. They have economists and bureaucrats who have little to learn from the World Bank and they don't welcome any attempt to impose controls. Countries that are very poor, like Bangladesh, are those the World Bank pushes around.

Reports and Missions

It is important for the World Bank to turn out significant numbers of high-quality reports telling client governments what they should do. Poor countries receive more and more World Bank missions because staff need to be seen to have led important missions whose conclusions have been accepted by member governments. Instead of visiting the poor, listening to them and learning from them the priority when visiting poor countries is to get on with economic development and to produce documents that show this intention. World Bank staff do not listen to poor people or learn from them not because they do not want to but because there are other stronger pressures that they must contend with. The view is global and so World Bank staff must listen and learn from their own thinkers. These thinkers have to catch the eye of the public, have to show that the World Bank is on top of things.

Missions to gather data for the advice serve both institutional and personal self-interest. Mission documents determine the success of the institution and the success of its individual staff members; the documents provide the basis for public reputation of the agencies as well as the possibility of their receiving enhanced resources. The World Bank's reports on the economy, bits of the economy, or projects are documents of advocacy, written to be approved. Several hundred of these documents must be produced each year. Reports represent a major investment of time and effort. As much as a hundred person-years may go into a major economic report on a country such as China.

World Bank missions would assume that they should have center stage, that they should have the time of top officials, and that their report should be regarded as the last or the latest word on the subject. Since team members have often not worked together before, the safest form of conduct is to exemplify the professional standards of the economist. Contact with local civil servants is minimized in favor of more contact with mission members, since these contacts are likely to result in more-positive career benefits. Where there is overlap between tasks, staff members do not help each other—quite the contrary. Staff members might withhold information that would help fellow mission members. Mission members concentrate on data collection because they know that any loose thinking unsupported by data will be criticized. The standard to be aimed at both in the thinking and in the presentation tends to be the same no matter where in the world the mission is taking place. Novelty is not encouraged; the aim is not to set new standards, which might be seen as an implied criticism of an established economic superior back at headquarters. Instead, the aim is to meet standards already established.

A time will come when Bank officials will be able to use satellite communications to interview their clients in poor countries. They will be able to look closely for signs that political commitment to some project or other is wavering, that information is being withheld. The presence or absence of key officials in the room will telegraph whether a new global initiative is well on the way or whether another bright idea must be rolled down the slipway. Unlike medical facilities in the US, the World Bank has not yet managed to avoid house calls on grounds that diagnostic equipment needed is at the office. So younger officials must travel regularly.

Bank officials arrive at one of the main hotels in a poor country looking important. They frequently have an air of slight impatience. They send and receive faxes. They usually seem to be taut, like the strings of a violin. They are in constant staccato motion rushing through the hotel with files and folders, backward and forward, with many tightly coordinated instructions about how to get together as if they were on maneuvers in a vast unknown country. They have a constant need for meetings with each other. When they have a meeting, they sit as if they were tournament chess players: underneath the table, their limbs are writhing and wrapping around table legs; above the table bodies have been schooled not to betray the slightest twitch. They write important things on yellow legal pads. Each seems to take care not to talk too much, not to laugh too much. They demonstrate task orientation. They are polite to hotel staff, but not friendly. Each morning and each evening they eat together and exchange whatever information they have agreed to share. It is essential for the mission leader's reputation that the product be finished on time, within budget, and to a standard accepted by peers. Missions provide tangible evidence that staff can take inputs—raw data from poor countries—and turn it into output, a professional product whose quality is generally acknowledged within the aid community. World Bank reports drip with data, tables, and boxes. Few are examined closely.

When World Bank staff and the consulting firms they engaged began pouring into former socialist countries such as Sri Lanka and Tanzania, the new visitors did not have to understand the country in any great detail: they only had to keep stressing the importance of stabilizing the currency, privatizing, reducing the functions of the state, establishing sustainable development, safeguarding the environment, mainstreaming women, and so on. Instead of trying to find out about Sri Lanka's rich history, for example, the visitors are more likely to spend their spare time pondering questions such as why it was that Ceylon (Sri Lanka's previous name), which was economically more advanced than Singapore in the 1960s, should have fallen behind in terms of its economic development. Meanwhile, for those involved in the new countries, there were new foods, new airports, new hotels, new presents for those at home, and new daily allowances to establish.

As the reality of life in the poor countries recedes, the volume of statistical data seems to increase as if in some way it could create meaning where none was intended. The tone is always measured, the judgments reasoned, the conclusions orthodox. There is no question of including emotional statements or indeed any opinion that is not backed by data. The mission member knows that she or he is simply a means to an end. The distillations in the World Bank reports are often too abstract to do other than tease, titillate, and disappoint; nor do they sufficiently recognize the often-conclusive influence of idiosyncratic personalities. Inevitably, the urge to perfect the methodology of comparison—to quantify, to be significant, tends to dominate. The formidable mission weaponry is always aimed at the poor countries; missions never take their own agency actions or the actions of other donors to be part of the problem.

NGOs Follow the World Bank Example

The World Bank has managed to co-opt a few NGOs, turning them into the lowest rung on their bureaucratic ladder. NGOs that have become dependent on Bank contracts and funding, open offices in Washington gradually lose touch with what happens on the ground. They become an underclass, advertising for new staff by offering competitive packages and talking a good deal about visions and strategy. At this point the vitality and idealism of their young personnel, which is the NGOs' great strength, can all too easily go out the window. Unfortunately, it is not clear that NGOs that are getting closer to the World Bank do any better with recruitment and training. More and more of these NGOs seem to be developing the same presentation skills as the World Bank in order to generate funds and support. Too few international NGOs provide a worldwide career with an emphasis on service at the community level and too few have local hands-on community experience and local language capacity other than French, Spanish, and Arabic.[16]

Anomie

The World Bank has provided the perfect growing conditions for Max Weber's ideal-type bureaucracy, which students of bureaucracy have assumed would not be found in empirical reality.[17] The dominant tendency has been to define bureaucracy in terms of an organization's basic structural characteristics. The most compact formulation is that of Victor Thompson, who characterized Weber's bureaucratic organization as comprising a highly elaborated hierarchy of authority superimposed on a highly elaborated division of labor.[18] Several characteristics are frequently mentioned that fit the World Bank very well: (1) a well-defined hierarchy of authority, (2) a division of labor based on functional specialization, (3) a system of rules covering the rights and duties of positional incumbents, (4) a system of procedures for dealing with work situations, (5) impersonality of interpersonal relationships, and (6) selection for employment and promotion based on technical competence. Robert Merton saw the drawbacks to the Weberian bureaucracy very clearly: "The very elements which conduce toward efficiency in general produce inefficiency in specific instances and also lead to an over-concern with strict adherence to regulations which induces timidity, conservatism, and technicism. Stress on depersonalisation of relationships leads to conflict in relationships with bureaucratic personnel. Specific behavioural orientations often mentioned are 'buck passing,' 'red tape,' rigidity and inflexibility, excessive impersonality, oversecretiveness, unwillingness to delegate and reluctance to exercise discretion."[19]

A major problem with the Weberian heritage is that it has quite wrongly left an impression that the purpose of a public organization is control. That is certainly the purpose of a *bad* system of administration. Public organizations in developing countries need to produce social change as well as social control in order to achieve substantial public purposes. The work of government in a developing country can, broadly speaking, be divided into two categories—control and extension. Control can be seen with functions such as, obviously, law and order, finance, and revenue generation. However, an important part of the responsibilities of a civil servant is also to produce social change, such as change in public attitudes toward education and health. I remember asking a teacher at a school in Tanzania why the school had never had a head girl and he fell about laughing at the idea. That is a situation that needs to change. The same is true of health, where governments need to do all they can to get their citizens to take preventive medicine more seriously. Improving the lot of the poor can be seen as an extension activity just like an activity that can be seen in relation to agriculture and health.[20]

The World Bank official has unique personality traits, ways of behaving, and styles of work that seem to become more and more pronounced with the passing years. This is a person who is always looking forward, is never quite happy with performance, is never impressed, is never the sort of person who roars with laughter or bellows with rage. This is a taker, not a person who looks after his secretary or the needs of colleagues before his own concerns. This is a person who suffers from a certain social constriction, a person whose facile and easy familiarity with other cultures and peoples does not quite disguise an inability to hold to principle. This is a person who seldom has strong opinions or convictions. This is a person for whom it is almost impossible to imagine a raison d'être for resignation. Nor are these traits confined to work. It is not hard to develop a suspicion that such individuals see all persons in more or less the same light.

Small tribal groups—Indian, British, Pakistani, Turkish, US, and so on—have established tiny national plots in the World Bank. The strongest and most effective are the Asian groups, the least effective seem to be the Latin American and the US. These small mutual-aid associations are organized on cultural lines and they afford their members a degree of protection against uncertainty. What is remarkable about this protection is that it is afforded regardless of competence or performance. Senior people, who will be quite hard on the performance of someone who is not from their country, are willing to abandon all pretense of professionalism when one of their own is involved. These emotional relationships are perhaps a reaction to the cultural insensitivity of the organization as a whole. However, these national groups, or mafias as they are called, remain at rudimentary levels of organization. There are no formal meetings with minutes, no formal memberships, office bearers, and so on. Usually there is a leader who occupies some apical position as a vice president or director. If the groups were to attempt to grow larger, more formal, and more influential, then there would be attempts to have them suppressed. Their subterranean existence serves as a reminder that things are not entirely as they are supposed to be in cultural no-man's-land.[21]

By some curious process that is hard to understand, these groups do not seem to want to expand at the expense of other groups; it is very much a live and let live situation where each simply wants to maintain market share.

Officials live alone with their families in alien communities that they never seem to join. What is one to do on a weekend? Not all foreigners follow US sports though many become converted as a result of the activities of their children at school. Their apartments and houses are usually so dispersed that even those with the same nationality have difficulty making frequent contact in their off-duty moments. Some try to create a normal home life by bringing servants and relatives from home. However, it is usually the case that families and friends are in the home country. Those with children face the choice of seeing the youngsters become American or sending them to the home country to school. This existence is more remote than a colonial society that also did not have grandparents, aunts, or family reunions. The absence of family contact is a heavy burden—missed funerals, marriages, sicknesses, and so on. Nor is there always a network to support the staff member in times of trouble. The existence is much less culturally supportive than diplomatic society. Indeed, much of the meager cultural nourishment individuals from the smaller nations receive comes from contact with fellow citizens employed at their embassies. Those from the larger countries—Britain, France and so on—will usually have minimal contact with their embassies, since the staff of those embassies tend to ignore their own nationals unless they are frightfully important. At the end of their period of service, individuals decide to go home or stay in the US. Indians, Koreans, and Pakistanis tend to stay, and British, French, and Germans tend to return home to Europe.[22]

World Bank officials are alone. So many familiar cultural cues and signals are absent: Civil servants in most parts of the world listen to their music and read their papers on their way to work or at work. At work they drink mint tea or really good coffee. They eat food they have known all their lives, hot spicy food, bad greasy food, English sausages or kippers, strange vegetables, and meats and fish and their accompanying condiments and sauces. They tell jokes about local politicians, their families, and their neighbors. They celebrate national holidays, national events, and national victories in sports. They walk around in the middle of the day and meet fellow citizens who enforce their sense of working with the public. All day civil servants are reminded of this or hear a joke about that. Their grandmothers, their wife's relatives, or their school friends call them at the office. They are constantly reminded of educational reunions, family gatherings, political events, art shows, new films, and so on.

The World Bank official who comes from a developing country and lives in Washington is under constant strain because the social niceties that provide support for the individual in what the official knows as a normal civil service are absent. The presentation of self in the office in any society requires the invocation of culture in such a way as to confirm the common possession of core values and beliefs. Social cohesiveness comes from ritualized and stylized exchanges that have the effect of importing society into the office, an importation that reassures: inhabitants of offices are delighted to be reminded that a coworker or a boss has similar thoughts about children and their progress or lack of it, has similar feelings about relatives both useful and ungrateful, and has a similar sense of humor when a coworker tells jokes that show culturally normal instincts and feelings.

Bad Behavior

Behavior of a kind that would probably be discouraged in a national organization with a strong common cultural endowment or that would likely subject the perpetrator to internal organizational or even public criticism of a career-damaging nature is more common than might be supposed. Of course, all bureaucracies spawn reprehensible behavior, but the World Bank seems to produce staff who set a bad example in an institution that should exemplify the highest standards of personal behavior. When, as is the case with the World Bank, staff are chosen on the basis of their intellectual qualifications and experience, it should not be surprising to find that their behavior often leaves a good deal to be desired. As the World Bank's lending expansion accelerated, recruitment became more and more dependent on human resources specialists. Because these personnel specialists lacked substantial hands-on overseas experience when making appointment recommendations, more weight was given to academic qualifications than personal qualities.

Looked at from the perspective of a client country, World Bank vice presidents, when overseas, might well behave as if they were heads of state. A small Pacific Island nation received a communication saying that a World Bank regional vice president wanted to visit. Puzzled, because the proposed trip was supposed to be during Easter, the island's ministry of finance queried the dates. Back came an icy reply saying that the vice president would visit when the country was prepared to receive him. The ministry of finance thought it best to reply that the prime minister would be in his office ready to receive the visitor when he arrived on Easter Sunday. The finance minister then asked if the vice president would like to hire a plane but was told by the World Bank in Washington that simple travel was all that was wanted. The finance minister went ahead and hired a plane at high expense for trips, figuring that anyone who was so demanding probably wanted to be treated as important. Later, an ambitious Bank economist decided that when he visited the country he would like to visit the ministers of finance and agriculture. Despite having been told that the appointments could not be arranged, he persisted. The secretary for finance, who was also very busy on the annual budget, told the economist that if he came he would not be able to see him. The economist came, and the secretary of finance declined to cancel his other appointments. The vice president complained to the minister of finance that the secretary of finance was wasting the time of his staff. The government decided that it would be best to replace the secretary. A few months later, a chief planner came from Washington and stamped up and down like a five-year-old because no minister had met him at the airport. When the deputy prime minister and his colleagues met with the man, he sketched out some ideas for the improvement of economic management. When asked if he could help further the chief planner said he was already very busy with China.

Let us look briefly inside the Washington bubble. Peter, who identified himself as a British political scientist, had been a journalist. His university career had been going nowhere when one of his more distinguished colleagues, who had friends in Washington, offered to write a letter stressing Peter's understanding of economics. After he arrived, he had written a few papers from a political science perspective, but he soon saw that that kind of thing was going nowhere. He reserved his best efforts for work that would show up to good advantage; he joined work groups or task forces working on issues that would hit the press; he shone in large meetings. He wrote, as he was at pains to point out to potential sponsors, quite beautifully; he could take the most complicated argument and translate it into nice simple English. He was very good at doing away with anyone he saw as a potential competitor. He could raise his eyebrows and look as if it really hurt him to say anything that could even remotely be construed as criticism. He would imply that he knew that senior management thought this or that or that someone might have been doing very well in the eyes of senior people he knew, but of course if they used someone like this. . . . Sometimes a regretful, "Well, I think he is a very nice person but I've heard" or "Well, I'm not sure her writing is as good as it ought to be." In an institution that lived by paper, that was the end.

Mr. W. was working on an important policy document when he noticed that the draft made no mention of the contribution of secretaries, and suggested to his boss that it might be nice to acknowledge their contribution. His boss, claiming credit for the idea of thanking the secretaries, arranged to have their names inserted, while at the same time deleting all mention of Mr. W., who had been a member of his core team.

Mr. X. was in charge of a research team. He told members of the team that funds that had been granted to the project by a private foundation could not meet the cost of business class travel. He proposed that they all travel economy class. The consultants spent several uncomfortable overnight flights reaching various research locations. Months later they discovered that the staff member had gone first class to all his destinations, charging the cost of the trips to the foundation funds.

Mr. Z. advanced his career considerably as a result of a publication that was almost entirely the work of his assistant. After a highly successful release of the publication, he arranged for the nonrenewal of his assistant's contract. Subsequently he published another well-regarded piece that was almost entirely taken from the work of consultants that he had hired, though this fact was in no way acknowledged. Despite the fact that these maneuvers were common knowledge, Mr. Z's career prospered. So did the career of his colleague, who had himself listed as the principal author of a major policy paper for which he had not written more than two paragraphs.

One manager whose career had been greatly helped by consultants said they were like lice and would eat the hair off your head! There was an inexhaustible supply of bright young men and women who would do anything to get a chance of a permanent appointment. They knew that if you blotted your copy book that was it—the offender was out for good. Overseas, World Bank consultants were embedded in advisory positions in key ministries. Once in place they were expected to help ensure that their ministry followed Bank advice and always had loans in the pipeline. The civil service in many client countries is riddled with little clusters of World Bank–financed experts and advisers in finance, and planning ministries being paid much higher salaries than ordinary civil servants. When World Bank staff visit they ensure that they gain access to the right people in government. They are expected to brief the visitors so that they can put any pressure that is necessary on the ministry. It is the existence of these advisers, a sort of fifth column, that makes it unnecessary for World Bank staff to spend time meeting local people.

The best and the brightest in client governments do their best to get jobs at the World Bank and this ambition is used by Bank staff members to get what they need. None of this is likely to strengthen those areas not favored by the World Bank, such as local government. The World Bank bureaucracy now exhibits patterns of behavior identified by Max Weber a long time ago:

> It is still more horrible to think that the world could one day be filled with nothing but those little cogs, little men clinging to little jobs and striving toward bigger ones—a state of affairs which is to be seen once more, as in the Egyptian records, playing an ever-increasing part in the spirit of our administrative system, and especially of its offspring, the students. This passion for bureaucracy, as we have heard it expressed here is enough to drive one to despair. . . . What can we oppose to this machinery in order to keep a portion of mankind free from this parceling-out of the soul, from this supreme mastery of the bureaucratic way of life.[23]

Sadly, given the many fine public servants who have worked for the World Bank in the past, the result of money-moving and management by seclusion is that World Bank poverty alleviation does not now appear to offer a career to young people that combines intellectual challenge with moral purpose. It does, however, by way of compensation, offer the best terms and conditions of employment to be found in Washington, DC.[24]

Notes

1. For the past half century, the international civil service has observed the *Standards of Conduct in the International Civil Service* prepared in 1954 by the International Civil Service Advisory Board. I began to doubt that these UN organs had the attributes of an international civil service in the accepted understanding of what that term means after a bizarre experience with the UNDP. In 1990 when I was working in Sri Lanka, the UNDP resident representative told me that his agency was looking for a new (D1 or D2 level) director for their Management Development Division in New York (formerly known as the Development Administration Division) and that he would like to recommend me for the job. I put in an application and, after a while, I ended up at UNDP's UN Plaza office in New York with five other short-listed finalists. Three days later, after numerous board, panel, and one-on-one interviews, I was told I was the agency's choice for the position. Later that same day I was sent to see the administrator of UNDP, Mr. Draper. He started the meeting by telling me that my nationality was against me. Then he spent the rest of the meeting talking to his staff about an interesting little model that Jeffrey Sachs had given him. After the meeting I asked Dennis Halliday, UNDP's director of personnel (later well-known for running the UN operation in Iraq), if I should worry. He said not. After all, he said, UNDP had to follow International Civil Service rules that had just been updated—he expected the administrator to follow the selection panel recommendation with respect to my appointment. I was a bit worried because from time to time there were reports that such and such country had offered large sums of money if one of their nationals could have this or that senior job. On the other hand, in a civil service, appointments boards decided, and not political appointees like Mr. Draper. Anyway, Halliday said that given a little time it would all work out. Weeks later, back in Sri Lanka, I received a letter sent to all unsuccessful candidates thanking me for applying for the job but providing no explanation of what had happened to me. A new director had been appointed by UNDP, an out-of-office politician who had not been part of the selection process.

2. Goffman, *The Presentation of Self*, 59.

3. On bureaucracies, see Bauer, Krill, Eckhard, *International Bureaucracy*; Cochrane, *Max Weber's Vision*.

4. There has always been some contradiction between commercial conduct and public service behavior in the World Bank Group. It is made up of the IBRD; the IDA, which lends concessional finance to the very poorest countries; and the IFC, which has its own separate staff and organization but is responsible for making investments in the private sector. Forty years ago the IFC was seen as the junior partner and one with limited economic analysis capacity. As time has passed, the differences between IBRD and IFC have become less obvious.

5. Overseasmanship is a term coined by Harlan Cleveland; it points to the fact that working in the poor countries requires a special set of skills and knowledge. Cleveland and Mangone, *The Art of Overseasmanship*.

6. Presidential Circular SHC/C.230/8, Appendix 2, State House, Dar-es-Salaam, 21 October 1963.

7. House of Commons, Treasury and Civil Service Committee, xvii.

8. The economics profession does seem to turn out graduates with little enthusiasm for teamwork; indeed, economics seems to provide a useful training for those who want to create a pliant bureaucracy. On teamwork and economists, see Frank, Gilovich, and Regan, "Does Studying Economics."

9. Bob Geldof might have been able to make better use of the Band Aid money donated for the Horn of Africa if he had lived and worked in poor countries. The same is true of a number of economists.

10. Simon, *Administrative Behavior*, 180, 181; Redford, *Ideal and Practice*, 31–34.

11. Waldo, "Development in the West."

12. Gupta, *Red Tape*.

13. Jenkins, "Modernization of Tax Administrations."

14. Israel, "The Changing Role," 32–34.

15. A politician I knew in Papua New Guinea used to address the crowd as "my fellow citizens" when he was running for election. After he won he addressed those coming to listen as "my constituents."

16. Edwards, NGO Rights and Responsibilities.

17. Cochrane, *Max Weber's Vision for Bureaucracy*.

18. Thompson, *Modern Organization*, 3–4.

19. Merton, "Bureaucratic Structure," 12.

20. Discussed in Cochrane, *Max Weber's Vision for Bureaucracy*.

21. The term "cultural no-man's land" was used by Malinowski. See Malinowski, "Practical Anthropology."

22. British staff wore suede shoes, checked shirts, and plum red trousers; Americans dressed like the managers of supermarkets with white short-sleeved shirts and pockets holding glasses in big cases and lots of pens. They wore shoes with big fat soles and trousers that gave the wearer no behind, a waistband just under the armpits, and inches of visible sock. Spanish and Arabic staff, Italians, Japanese, French, and Turks wore beautiful highly polished slip-on shoes with little tassels. Very senior Indians had the most style: well-cut suits in vivid tropical colors, shirts that were perhaps a bit loud, and a little too much breast pocket handkerchief. Rumpled Italian silk suits—well, rumpled enough so you knew what it was—were universally popular.

23. Max Weber quoted in Mayer, *Max Weber*, 70, 71.

24. In 2018 when the World Bank asked major shareholders for a $15 billion capital increase, the US wanted to tie approval to greater salary restraint for senior World Bank staff.

Chapter 5

SOCIAL SOUNDNESS ANALYSIS

Poverty projects have challenges that separate them from the run-of-the-mill development project; meeting these challenges needs its own analysis. Development assistance that enables project participants to add small amounts of income or produce more crops, frequently involves changes that can be adopted and accommodated without local difficulty. These project calculations may not require a great deal of local knowledge. However, when social development projects touch on core cultural values and beliefs, as do projects that aim to alter diet and food preferences, adopt new habits of personal hygiene, decrease family size, or adjust relationships between men and women and their respect roles in agricultural production, then the difficulties experienced during implementation are likely to increase substantially. Project designers will need to know if changes or adjustments to core cultural values and beliefs could be involved, since experience has shown that this is where great resistance to change may originate and be sustained. Since poverty projects are, in effect, experiments in social change, the precise and detailed nature of the behavior change that a project needs to make in order to be successful should be identified and clearly stated.[1] The designer's aim should be to secure a permanent change in the behavior of project participants rather than a change that fails to survive the three- or five-year life of the project.[2]

It follows that the amount of local knowledge required for these social projects is of a much higher level than for projects whose participants can be assumed to be average. Those who are malnourished or unwell and who may never have been able to earn money on a regular basis cannot be expected to make the same kinds of buoyant and confident entrepreneurial decisions as the well-to-do.[3] They need a relationship that provides them with a helping hand. While a few extremely poor individuals can be helped by direct action, many cannot. To provide help to the difficult-to-reach individuals, governments have to rely on relationships that will also involve and affect ordinary well-off people. They may hope that the consequences of this contact will reach the very poorest, but they cannot be sure because this would depend on factors beyond the control of any government, such as social and political attitudes, religious beliefs, ethnicity, and so many other influences.

The skills and experience that had been developed for infrastructural and ordinary development were not necessarily those appropriate to poverty projects. Two adjustments were needed: First, targeted guidance had to be developed and made part of the required steps in the project preparation process. Second, project personnel needed training to help them to take on board what they had learned about the social dimensions of poverty projects. By working with Bob Berg and Dan Creedon, I helped to implement social soundness analysis in 1974.[4] This was guidance aimed at the social dimensions of these poverty projects. It became, and still is, a mandated part of USAID project procedures.[5] The behavioral assumptions of projects were intended to be written down clearly and succinctly as part of the project analysis. In 1974 I recommended that USAID start its own interdisciplinary Development Studies Program.[6] USAID designed and delivered training designed to familiarize overseas personnel with social soundness analysis and the requirements of the 1973 New Directions in Foreign Aid. The Development Studies Program was put in place by Dan Creedon, who was in charge of USAID manpower development.[7] Over a ten-year period four hundred Foreign Service personnel passed through this program.[8]

Any assumption that poor people will take advantage of economic development projects needs to be ground-truthed; this verification and discovery process offers considerable scope for anthropologists to make an important contribution. The poorest are fragile people who often live in fragile states whose institutions, governance and levels of corruption are more likely to constrain rather than assist poverty alleviation.[9] Without some on-the-ground idea of what the poorest are like, we have what Evans-Pritchard called, "If I were a horse thinking." "Because we are not horses, have never been horses, and cannot know what it is like to be a horse, our speculations about horse-sense probably have little or no connection to horse-reality."[10] To get beyond anecdotal understanding of grassroots situations, hands-on experience and relationship knowledge was required but social factors were still being treated as extrinsic variables in the work of development agencies or big NGOs. In their day-to-day work, recent entrants were exposed to an office life surrounded by and immersed in the sorts of data that economists collected. These statistical snapshots could capture dimensions of health, education, and poverty, but they could not capture the relationships between people in communities. This was an important omission because incomes might be rising while local society was being fragmented. The assumption that benefits might trickle down to those at the bottom of local society might be no more accurate than when it was made at the national level.

Projects

The benefits of centrally designed aid projects tend to be overestimated, and disadvantages underestimated, when designers put themselves in the shoes of people they do not know and then decide what would be best for them. To ensure that relationships with local people reflect social and cultural expectations, the ensemble of beliefs, values, and attitudes that animate local behavior must be understood in something more than an anecdotal way. A cost-benefit rate of return calculation on the funds invested does not routinely address the issue of whether a project could produce the behavior change required for success and cannot be assumed to take place automatically. What soundness analysis encouraged was for project designers to state quite clearly and explicitly what sorts of changed behavior their project was intended to produce and what means would be used to make sure that these changes happened.

The justification for a project is usually assumed to be the contribution that it can make to the broader situation of the poor in a country or region. If this contribution was to be made to poverty alleviation, then several things had to be demonstrated. First, whether the project was addressing a core behavioral constraint on poverty elimination that was acknowledged by local people as important. A project could be a success in economic terms and yet be a failure in terms of its contribution to poverty alleviation. Second, whether the innovation or adaptation represented by the project had the potential to spread to other areas.[11]

Since government resources may be too limited to allow for every poor person to become the direct recipient of project aid, achieving spread effects beyond the initial population is a critical issue in project design. The levels of Bank investment for individual participants in agricultural projects were often high, much higher than could be afforded by those living close to a project who might want to follow the new practices, approaches, and techniques used in the project. For a project to produce palm oil in New Britain, farmer incomes were projected at about A$1,000 per annum. Actual incomes turned out to be A$2,000. People living outside the project area had annual incomes of less than A$100 per annum; not surprisingly, they became antagonistic toward the project participants. Logic suggested that if project recipients were given unusual project resources in order to be able to participate productively in a project, then others would not to be able to do the same thing without the same level of resourcing. Experience suggested that the spread or diffusion effects of aid projects and programs were extremely limited. There was little evidence to show that those who did not have project or program resources—and they were the poorest— could repeat project or program activities on their own. There were not enough resources for all to become direct recipients of aid. Therefore, the only way that innovations could spread would be if the projects and programs had, as an explicit task, the determination of how these things could be done at a lower cost.[12]

In order to target the needs of the poor more efficiently and effectively, the traditional project needed adjustment in order to maximize the possibility of investment benefits reaching the poorest since following the engineering-inspired project model was not always helpful to social projects. Each stage of the project cycle—identification, preparation, and so on— saw the arrival of new personnel. This meant that contact with local project participants was lost at a time when local concerns arose and needed to be quickly resolved by consultation with known and trusted people. If we use the analogy of a railway station, when carriages reached the station, identification personnel disembarked and were replaced by preparation personnel, who at the next station disembarked and were replaced by appraisal personnel. What communities and local people need is a constant presence, people who stay with them all the way. Communities need to have a continuing presence from their helpers to provide reassurance and continuity. Introducing people who can be expected to stay with a project all the way should start at the earliest possible opportunity.[13]

Country Social Mapping

Remote areas and remote people are often missing from the data held by development assistance agencies.[14] USAID did not implement the country social mapping that I had recommended and that I thought was an essential part of the approach. Without country mapping, planners would not know how many projects of which type and magnitude would be needed to eliminate poverty in this or that part of the country. Country mapping would have allowed the agency to determine which project, among a number of alternatives, represented the best chance of implementing the country strategy and where it should be located.

Aid agencies have sometimes alluded to political obstacles to mapping poverty, but this hardly seems to justify the neglect or exclusion of this useful information source. There is no inevitable evil in social mapping; rather, it is an attempt to produce better outcomes in order to avoid wasting resources. It can be shown that in most countries where strong intergroup antagonisms exist, failure to allow for such situations in project planning leads to poor results. Social mapping is not judgmental: it merely seeks to describe the existing situation as it is.

Distinctive Social Groups

The social geography of poverty is one where anthropological skills and experience could be put to good use. Because of the different social meanings and measurements that poverty has within different societies, and that are essential for the design of poverty alleviation, global poverty statistics can be quite misleading. Since social cleavages are in many instances stronger than the ties, it is never sufficient to give aggregate data, such as that x thousand people live in the northeast region. Delineation of social groups should also indicate the size of the population involved. Poor people derive cultural identity from membership in ethnic, religious, or political groupings; within these groups the understandings about and the meanings associated with poverty may vary widely. Social groups in a country should be identified and mapped out if they appear to be distinctive groups with mutually unintelligible languages, opposing political parties or tribal groups, or different ethnic identities—peoples that for some reason act on the basis of a perception of their difference from others. Statistics need to be tied to settlement patterns or distinctive social groups. Global statistics do not usually have any information on the strength of the social units, or whether leadership is still intact and functioning. During times of famine and national emergency, it is important to have traditional discipline in place.[15]

Group delineation is also necessary to identify potential spread and replication effects of attempts to help the poor. Unless group delineation takes place, claims about the possible impact and spread effects may be highly inaccurate. The best way to uncover differences among groups that are significant enough for recording is to visit widely, interacting with the broadest possible range of people. The problem does not lend itself to questionnaire survey methods; rather, participant observation by one or more persons (depending on country size) is preferred. Three sets of questions will uncover most differences. The first seeks information about different ethnic groups and how they usually interact. Is there tension, fighting, or cooperation? A second refers to modernization and the progress of various groups or geographical regions. Which groups are thought to be advanced, which backward? In many nations where tensions between ethnic groups are high, discussion of ethnic differences is strongly discouraged. National unity and the need to project a national consensus discourage attempts to identify ethnic separateness. Another objection sometimes raised against social mapping is that mapping can be thought colonialist in ideology. Those who make this charge suspect mappers of wishing to preserve archaic social distinctions whereas they, the critics, seek extraordinary or revolutionary social change.

During project identification in North Africa, Berber, Tuareg, or Maghreb populations may need to be distinguished from the descendants of Islamic expansion of the sixth and seventh centuries. In Nigeria, notice may need to be taken of tension between the Islamic north and the Christian south of the country. In Sierra Leone there has been tension between the Mende and Temne people. In Fiji there has been tension between Indian descendants of immigrant plantation laborers and native Fijians. In Myanmar there has been tension between the majority Buddhist population and the Muslim Rohingya. Some groups can be unpopular because of their aptitude for business and economic development, such as the Chagga in Tanzania or Chinese merchants in the South Pacific. There are obvious differences between plains people and hill people in Myanmar and other Southeast Asian countries, such as Thailand, Laos, and Cambodia. In Peru there are several well-defined social classes: at the top are the descendants of Spanish colonists and at the bottom of the social pyramid are the aboriginal Indian inhabitants, or Choke. In India, there were traditionally four well-defined classes: priests, warriors, merchants, and untouchables. Although the passage of time has lessened the impact of some of these divisions in Indian society, there are those that must still be considered.

Faith Groups

Anthropology's view of belief systems on a national level has obvious utility. The form and content of ideological systems determine the nature of the types of opportunities that can be offered by development projects. Muslim, Hindu, and Christian belief systems, for example, correlate somewhat with attitudes toward projects. What must also be evaluated and mapped out at the national levels is the effect of various belief systems on the relationship between sexes, on modernization, on reproductive behavior, on health, and on food patterns. Each belief system presents different opportunities for change and adaptation. Ethnic and religious groups, living in different parts of the country, may have different attitudes and beliefs with respect to reproduction, health, or economic development.

E. F. Schumacher gave a good example of the importance of paying attention to beliefs:

> While the materialist is mainly interested in goods, the Buddhist is mainly interested in liberation. But Buddhism is "The Middle Way" and therefore in no way antagonistic to physical well-being. It is not wealth that stands in the way of liberation but the attachment to wealth; not the enjoyment of pleasurable things but the craving for them. The keynote of Buddhist economics, therefore, is simplicity and non-violence. From an economist's point of view, the marvel of the Buddhist way of life is the utter rationality of its pattern—amazingly small means leading to extraordinarily satisfactory results.
>
> For the modern economist this is very difficult to understand. He is used to measuring the "standard of living" by the amount of annual consumption, assuming all the time that a man who consumes more is "better off" than a man who consumes less. A Buddhist economist would consider this approach excessively irrational: since consumption is merely a means to human well-being, the aim should be to obtain the maximum of well-being with the minimum of consumption. Thus, if the purpose of clothing is a certain amount of temperature comfort and an attractive appearance, the task is to attain this purpose with the smallest possible effort—that is, with the smallest annual destruction of cloth and with the help of designs that involve the smallest possible input of toil.[16]

What are the significant beliefs related to women and where are they located? A national as well as a local view of the role of women is important. Development projects have frequently placed women in a less favorable position than was traditionally the case. Women in rural areas have, in effect, been bypassed by the development process. Women have not been able to earn money in a convenient manner. Industrialization has usually given work to men instead of women because women cannot always leave their children. Furthermore, industrialization has often been restricted to the educated, and women have not had the same educational opportunities as men.

Women have been underrepresented in agricultural extension services. Though women may perform a great deal of agricultural work, projects have tended to ignore their role and have concentrated on men. Such negative effects on the status of women are among the unintended consequences of social change.

Wealth Forms

Money income is measured in factative units of money—it can be added, multiplied, divided, etc.—whereas what might be thought of as a measure of cultural well-being among very poor people cannot always be dealt with in this way because well-being is often collective in nature. Cultural integrity and social or community solidarity, parent–child relationships, and religious attitudes are vital to the well-being of poor people. Income data do not usually show how income is distributed with respect to variables such as ethnicity, family or other social unity, social class, education, aptitude, geographical location, and so on. Each society has a set of rules—religious, political, ethical, formal, informal—that determine who gets what and why, but these have not been collected and kept up to date during the course of the past thirty years. Both the World Bank's *Economic Atlas* and the UNDP *Human Development Report* deal with national income data. They give average incomes, life expectancy, and so on. But this does not tell us about the poor who are below average, nor does it deal with the fact that the poorest in many traditional societies do not use money.

Economic anthropology could have helped to show how and when traditional wealth forms are often preferred to money. Geoffrey Masefield recalls that as a young and inexperienced agricultural officer in Uganda, newly posted to a remote district among an unfamiliar tribe, he was instructed by the government to open the first agricultural experiment station in the district. He was provided with money to purchase, among other things, the best local cattle he could find for a foundation herd with which to practice selective breeding. The agricultural officer bought some young bulls without difficulty, but then found that, such was the social prestige attached to owning numbers of cattle, no stockowner in the district would sell any female animals capable of producing offspring, much less the best ones. Eventually a herd was acquired of which half the female animals had to be bought outside the district and were therefore not climatized, and the remainder were stunted, maimed, or thought by their owners to be barren—hardly a good start for what was intended to be a model herd to be further improved by selected breeding![17]

Mobility Patterns

The analysis of mobility patterns at the national level has a number of uses. Public health and disease control depend greatly on this kind of knowledge. For the agricultural sector it can be helpful to consider not only human movement but also the distribution and siting of transport, credit, and marketing components. For a population project such considerations as allocation and overall geographic coverage of medical stations would be important in estimating the number of people likely to be affected by the project. Patterns of movement at the national level can be broken down by significant participant activity (agricultural, trade, religious, markets) so that the most frequented place of personal contact (with opinion leaders, especially) can be identified.

Fishing or harvesting activities are often seasonal; so, too, can be employment provided by tourism. In West Africa, for example, over large areas all farmers live in villages (or nucleated settlements) from which they travel on foot or by bicycle to work their farms, though by no means every day and often only for a short time. In East Africa, by contrast, there are large areas in which every farmer lives in an isolated house on his own holding far from villages. The effects of these two systems on agricultural extension work are very different. In the West African case, it is rare that an extension worker can find the occupant of a bad farm actually working the land when the worker happens to pass by, and the worker is therefore denied the opportunity to discuss soils, crops, and animals on the spot. The village system, however, makes it easy to gather together an audience of farmers for a talk or a demonstration. In East Africa, it is much easier to find the farmer on his farm because he lives there, but it is much more difficult to collect the scattered clients at a central point for a group session.

A similar obvious connection between social arrangements and extension work exists in the case of many grazing areas. Over most of Africa it is the custom that land not under crops or fenced is available to any local stockowner for grazing. It is impossible in these circumstances for the extension worker to advise any single individual to spend money or effort on the improvement of open pastures used by his stock by such measures as irrigation, drainage, or application of fertilizer. If the individual does so, his neighbors' animals will move in and take advantage of the improved growth of grass and he will get little reward for his effort. The extension worker therefore knows he has to affect group behavior or concentrate on getting pastures fenced before they will be improved.

Participation

With respect to participation, there are some who may, and others who may not, wish to join the mainstream economy. This may depend on whether they share the same social and political outlook, have a common ethnic background, or follow similar religious practices. Poverty may reflect discrimination, prejudice, or simply a wish to keep some people in what is seen to be "their place." Context may be a result of structural issues related to differing resource endowment in different regions of the country, the nature of economic activity, or an urban–rural divide.

Getting the participation of the relatively well-off is not particularly difficult. USAID has devoted, and still does devote, considerable effort to participation, but tends to think about it after project design has been settled rather than seeing participation as an initial and important test for feasibility.[18] That is a first-things-first requirement for projects that aim to have the poorest participate. What do poor people need in order to be able to participate? Social soundness analysis suggested that a profile of the potential participants should be constructed to specify the minimum requirements. For example, what sex, level of education, resources, skills, and attitude will make individual participation likely or even possible? For agricultural production projects, being able to read fertilizer labels may be important. For marketing projects, numeracy may be important. With all projects, some change is required. Is diligence, or patience, or perseverance required to an unusual degree? For example, growing tea requires regular and disciplined cultivation, which is why farmers in Papua New Guinea did not concentrate on that crop, preferring instead to grow coffee or coconut, which could tolerate a certain amount of neglect yet still produce a good income.

If the very poor already possessed the skills, attitudes, beliefs, and material resources that economic development requires, then many projects would not be necessary. When a project manager believes a project is necessary, a thorough description of what resources participants have or do not have is an important step in confirming the soundness of the design calculations. If a project is to be properly designed, then the minimum participant profile should be based on the attributes and resource requirements that characterize the poorest in the inventory of cultural resources and human needs. It is then possible to see who might be able to participate, considering the location and group with which a particular type of project could achieve maximum effect. It should then also be possible to identify those who cannot be expected to participate.

Motivation

Paying attention to motivation criteria can help tailor resources to project needs. Too often project designers assume that their appreciation of the benefits of project participation will be widespread. Yet each group of individuals expected to participate must be motivated—the actual motivation of the group, not that of a designer from outside that group, must be used. As in industrialized countries, some may be motivated by a desire for increased power and prestige, others may want to follow the example of opinion leaders, others may seek financial reward, and still others may be moved by patriotism due to the key role a project may play in the nation's economy. Careful assessment of motivation can avert wasting of project resources. Extension budgets need not be high when participants are highly motivated. It must not be assumed that all motivations are conducive to development as the planners perceive it. Motivation is twofold, comprehending both the incentive or perception needed to make a given population interested in a project and the population's perception of the probable gains from the project. In Turkey a printing press with modern machinery failed, even though there were many orders, due to motivation factors. The managers did not like to take large orders that would take up all their working time, since they then were unable to fulfil small orders from their friends for wedding invitations and so on.

An assessment of perceived need is important because it points to the kinds of extension work that may be necessary. A health project will usually require much more explanation than a road. If people perceive a need for innovation or change, then chances for adoption without significant resources being devoted to extension work are good. For example, when able-bodied males left their villages to work in Zambian copper mines, those who remained at home wanted to learn to write so that they could communicate with the migrants. Education projects succeeded.

By assessing the degree of risk from a potential participant's viewpoint, project managers can estimate the likelihood of participation. New seeds and plant types will often be adopted if they can first be tested, but most farmers are unwilling to commit all their resources to an unknown innovation. This is true of farmers all over the world, since failure threatens family security and well-being. Can the innovation or change be broken down into small or simple tasks? Can a small amount of a new crop be planted to see how well it does? One cannot assume a desire on the part of participants for profit maximization or cost minimization without supporting evidence: increased income might not be welcome if it obligates participants to support a whole new wave of relatives. Those who have increased incomes must be able to continue to discharge their traditional social obligations.

Social projects require a considerable amount of data and this preparation can be helped by up-to-date national-level social mapping. The project assumptions about affecting poverty needed to be compared to the national analysis to make sure that, first, the project was addressing common poverty issues, and that, second, the project was located in an area with a large number of poor people who were likely to become involved with, and benefit from, the investment.

Time

Fifty years ago planners and economists assumed that villagers in developing countries had lots of spare time. That was not the case, and these days project designers need to have knowledge of just how men and women allocate their time during the day and over the seasons. Most projects are supposed to last from three to five years, a life span of a project that has come from estimating how long it would take to complete the construction of buildings and bridges and to achieve certain levels of performance as a result of training. But a quite different set of calculations is needed for estimating how long it could take very poor people to be able to change or use their behavior on a sustainable basis. Sound project design requires an assessment, by anthropologists and others, of time required for new kinds of behavior to become so well-established that they will survive and spread after the withdrawal of externally provided project resources. If participants learn how to grow coffee from expatriate advisers teaching new methods and techniques, will they continue to care for the trees in the same manner after the advisers have left? In projects to train teachers of English as a second language, the same question arises: Will it continue after the experts have gone back home?

It can be useful to distinguish two dates: the date on which all project assistance will cease to be delivered and the date by which social change will have been achieved. For example, clinics to improve nutrition may be constructed and all personnel trained within two years, but the behavioral change in the population in response to the provision of these project inputs may take four to five years. Education projects may not achieve social change for five to ten years.

Projects frequently fail because they try to produce too much changed behavior in too short a period. Successful introduction of the kinds of social change represented by development projects calls for the least amount of social disruption consistent with the attainment of development objectives; an incremental approach is useful in this regard.[19] The use of incremental criteria can also enable project designers to calculate an appropriate scale of assistance for participants. Where do the project targets come from? It often seems that every small farmer is to have ten hectares in a resettlement project. Why ten? If too much assistance is given, then the project may succeed, though in other important respects, such as potential for spread or replication, the project may be unsuccessful.

Whether one is considering machinery, a systematic way of bookkeeping or accounting, or the use of fertilizer, it is necessary to examine the extent to which the kinds of social change the project calls for are incremental or considerably more than incremental. Income for project participants should also be incremental. It is not enough to simply assume adequate income levels; rather, one must understand the financial and cash flow needs of the poorest: What payments, social demands, ritual obligations, and so on are important? Levels of income should be adjusted to the financial needs of potential participants.

Accumulation of resources is only one side of the coin; distribution systems that meet local convention are equally important in project design. Can relatives benefit? What has to be avoided is the situation where successful entrepreneurs have to sever their social ties. This can happen if they have not fed, or lent money to, their poor relatives because they did not share what they had. Local people then see a pattern of social performance that is considered deviant.

Who Benefits, Who Does Not?

Increasing concern with benefiting poor groups that were largely bypassed by earlier development processes created a special need to identify the social impact of a project. The best opportunity to do this is at the initial stage of project conception and formulation, when it is still possible to reject a project if its social impact is regressive, to modify it to make it more compatible with equity objectives, or to consider appropriate compensatory measures to rectify the damage or losses to those who are likely to be adversely affected. It is important that the groups the project is intended to help, those who are likely to be adversely affected, and those who may be indirectly affected, either positively or negatively (e.g., ultimate consumers of a basic product, the price of which is reduced or increased), be identified at an early stage.

In assessing benefit incidence, one must bear in mind that the recipient of the goods or services provided under a project is not necessarily the person to whom the major benefits of the project accrue. A tenant farmer, for instance, may receive new seeds, fertilizer, and credit to pay for them, thus raising his yield, yet the landlord may raise the rent and so appropriate the lion's share of the incremental income flow. In order to continue to hire the land at the new, higher, rent the tenant farmer must continue his new practices, but doing so may involve much more labor on his part and perhaps greater risk. So how much benefit does he get?

Identifying the incidence of benefits is similar to identifying those who bear the burden of indirect taxes; both are affected by how much of the benefit or cost is passed on. Assessment of the distribution of benefits and costs uses data and insights obtained about the project population in connection with the study of the sociocultural feasibility of the plan. In considering equity and benefit incidence, a limited number of criteria—access to resources and opportunities; employment situation; rural displacement, migration, and urbanization; and changes in power and participation—are important in the calculation of the social costs and benefits of projects.

Notes

1. Those who are familiar with the Logical Framework (LogFrame) created by Leon Rosenberg and his colleagues at Practical Concepts Inc. that has achieved widespread use by aid agencies, including DfID in the UK and Australian Aid, will know that the purpose level of a LogFrame should reflect behavior change. A common mistake is made with the assumptions column. Assumptions are not supposed to be a fudge factor, a way of accounting for things not going as planned. Assumptions should be events over which the project designer has no control. For example, when constructing a road, it would be reasonable to assume the same weather pattern in future as have been experienced in the previous five or ten years (Practical Concepts, *The Logical Framework*).

2. What is suggested is that if aid agencies such as the World Bank and USAID want to target extreme poverty, then they need to do more to ensure that the quantitative data that is now collected as a result of country economic work, projects and household survey analysis is socially sound.

3. Foster, "Peasant Society."

4. Berg, "PA Comments." Social soundness analysis was described in Glynn Cochrane, *The Cultural Appraisal*.

5. Ingersoll, Sullivan, and Linkerd, *Social Analysis of Aid Projects*.

6. Creedon, "Introduction."

7. Dan Creedon had used faculty from the Maxwell School at Syracuse for a number of years to run project management training for USAID staff around the world. At the time Syracuse had a number of faculty and all-but-dissertation graduate students with an interest in project management and development administration: Bob Iverson, Dennis Rondinelli, John Nellis, George Honadle, Rudi Klauss, Bill Pooler, Jim Vedder, and Marcus Ingle.

8. See the first assessment of that course by Richard N. (Dick) Blue, who in 1976 was director of the Development Studies Program, Internal Assessment, at USAID. Instructional staff included on economics Albert Waterston, the World Bank planner; Jim Weaver from American University; political scientists Richard Gable and Dick Blue from California and Minnesota, respectively; Don Warwick on social psychology from Harvard; and anthropologist Michael Calavan from USAID.

9. Former UK prime minister David Cameron is the chairman of the LSE-Oxford Commission on State Fragility, Growth and Development that was launched in March 2017 to guide policy to address state fragility.

10. Evans-Pritchard, *Theories of Primitive Religion*, 24.

11. Geographers have looked at this question. See Hägerstrand, *The Propagation of Innovation Waves*.

12. In the Jenka triangle of Malaysia, the World Bank had a number of highly successful oil palm projects requiring an investment of $75,000 for each participating farmer. When this model was used in the Cape Hoskins oil palm project in Papua New Guinea, it produced incomes of several thousand dollars for participating farmers. Other farmers, living outside the project area, had incomes of less than $50 a year and were too poor to raise the initial investment oil palm required.

13. This has been practice in the mining industry; see Cochrane, *Anthropology in the Mining Industry*, 91.

14. "In an attempt to better understand the movements, decision-making patterns, and social structures of inaccessible communities across the country, the United Nations Children's Fund created a social map. [This is] A digital and printed map that combines topographic and geographic information with social institutions, which can be used to inform strategy, budgeting, partnerships, monitoring, and evaluation decisions. South Sudan's lack of infrastructure, road networks and access to information makes it exceptionally challenging to navigate— and access the country's most vulnerable and remote populations." Mednick, "Q&A: How UNICEF is mapping South Sudan's most remote states."

15. "Poverty analysis is often based on national-level indicators that are compared over time or across countries. The broad trends that can be identified using aggregate information are useful for evaluating and monitoring the overall performance of a country. For many policy and research applications, however, the information that can be extracted from aggregate indicators may not be sufficient, since they hide significant local variation in living conditions within countries. For example, poverty within a region can vary across districts." World Bank Institute, "Analysis of Poverty," 79.

16. Schumacher, *Buddhist Economics*, 54–60.

17. Masefield, "Anthropology and Agricultural"; see also Masefield, *A Short History*, 25–30.

18. Title XII of the US Foreign Assistance Act required USAID to pay specific attention to participation. Within the agency the issue was brilliantly handled by Jonathan Silverstone for many years. See Uphoff, *Social Capital*; Serageldin, *A Multifaceted Perspective*; Montgomery and Esman, "Popular Participation."

19. The classic discussion about choice of goals is in McClelland, *The Achieving Society*.

CONCLUSIONS

Not to put too fine a point on it, it looks as if the World Bank has used the circumstances of the poor to promote its own expansion. By relying on its universal quantitative approach to poverty, and eschewing direct engagement with the poor in favor of management by seclusion, the World Bank has promoted its own self-interest rather than public service benefitting the poorest. It is highly unlikely that the hands-on field skills and human attributes required for building relationships and rapport with the poorest, and the quantitative office skills required for lending and commercialized economic development, could ever prosper within a single institution like the World Bank—and they have not. Poverty alleviation that aims to reach the poorest needs leadership from an institution whose staff have grassroots social engagement skills and a sense of service, not a corporation with beliefs, values, and attitudes aligned with growing market share practicing management by seclusion. Addressing extreme poverty needs thousands of dedicated organizations whose main interest is extreme poverty and the building of local capacity to help poor people. Poverty relief requires hands-on community skills and the ability to work closely with local-level institutions, particularly at local government level. The lead institution needs to have a repository of experience with hands-on engagement with the poorest—which is something the World Bank does not have.

Mass poverty alleviation has been oversold at the World Bank and so has what economists and financial engineering can reasonably be expected to contribute. Poverty alleviation will be best handled by organizations like the Salvation Army and the faith organizations, NGOs, and bilateral aid agencies that have a community focus and grassroots skills. Given the reality of poverty in both rich and poor countries, a continuation of World Bank alleviation promises may well begin to look like bait and switch.[1]

With the increasing size of the World Bank has come increasing and unavoidable bureaucratization that inevitably erodes the possibilities for public service. Large organizations such as the Bank inevitably produce bureaucratic rigidities that inhibit the inventiveness and nimbleness required: Organizations with a headquarters staff of many thousands cannot do without an emphasis on authority and obedience—which are principles directly opposed to the free movement of intelligence. Providing staff with the freedom to do their own thing is likely to undermine the ability to provide a predictable and uniform performance as well as discipline, but installing a habit of unconditional obedience will destroy the independence of judgment without which intellectual progress is impossible.

A few bilateral aid agencies have or could have the requirements for poverty work but many, mainly those too close to the World Bank, will continue to rely on management by seclusion. What poverty alleviation needed, and still needs, was a small fit-for-purpose organization, a *force de frappe*, to reach and help the poorest, individual by individual.[2] The lesson of the Salvation Army and other faith organizations, and a lesson that the World Bank has not taken learned, has been that poverty alleviation is not just another add-on to the institutional agenda but is a root and branch challenge. Mass poverty alleviation needs more than top-down solutions: it needs administrative legs at the grassroots level, and a committed and not too expensive staff when engaging with the poor.

Helping the poorest is not a business activity. Personal effort that will not be seen or recorded is the very substance of duty and public service, and is the bedrock of volunteer service. The small anonymous acts of public service that are essential for this kind of poverty alleviation, and perhaps all the more so if they do not come naturally from the government or civil society, are the things that come from within; they are the product of self-discipline and a sense of service. The most important activity of the officer or public servant might well be the one where there was nobody to watch, no paper trail, no residue for purposes of accountability. For instance, an official visits a distant town or village, spending time with those who need help; a teacher goes out of her way to help a pupil who is not in her class; an examiner who is reviewing an exam paper changes the marking; an accountant who is reviewing tax receipts increases a refund because the taxpayer has made an arithmetical error, though no superior will know what she or he has done.

When a sense of calling is strong and is tied to the achievement of a compelling moral purpose, the result will tend to discourage individuals from putting their own self-interest first. A sense of service is a cultural florescence that cannot be assumed as a consequence of employment. It is not produced by a pay rise or productivity agreement, and is not ordinarily an outcome or reorganization or rationalization or downsizing. A calling or a sense of service comes from known and unwavering commitment to the pursuit of important public purposes. It comes from selecting the right people, those who have sensitivity and feeling for society and its works. It comes from a process of long organizational maturation, a process where those involved have repeatedly seen good work and how good work is done. And it comes from the imposition and acceptance of strict discipline. In essence, it comes from doing the public's business because the public is seen to be the ultimate superior.

The ability to account for culture is critical; because of this, the leadership in any future fight against extreme poverty should come from NGOs and faith organizations and others with a solid cultural infrastructure. The cultural constitution of UN agencies and the assumption that poverty (and culture) is all about income is an impediment to performance.[3] When one World Bank or UN official succeeds another, a client country cannot necessarily expect the successor to have the same work habits, the same way of doing things, the same instruction pedagogy, the same view of discipline, the same view of effort, the same view of incentives, the same way of managing.[4] Swedish officials will succeed Filipinos, and so on. A poor country must accommodate itself to the view of management and procedures held by Chinese, Indians, Mexicans, Nigerians, and so on. What constitutes effort or discipline or reward varies from society to society and from one official to another. Helping, assisting, serving, advising, and so on have meaning to only the extent that they are viewed within an existing horizon of experience by the representatives of a particular culture. World Bank officials may not possess any common view of assistance, kindness, or consideration. They may have no shared empathy, no shared values, beliefs and attitudes. Brazilians, Chinese, Germans, Marshall Islanders, and Zambians who work for the Bank will view project management ideas differently because they come from different cultural backgrounds. Public service behavior is hard to realize in an institution with 180 member countries, and the characteristics of a cultural no-man's-land. Had the World Bank made more of an imaginary effort to use anthropology it would have done better with poverty, and extreme poverty, using anthropology's hallmark fieldwork tradition and experience.

BRIC lending should be straightened out because this will result in a more right-size bank with right-size ambitions and objectives. The World Bank should stop growing, and stop lending to China and Russia. It should have fit-for-purpose leadership and fewer visions.[5] World Bank lending for economic development will not eliminate global poverty but it can have some impact on poverty, one that many countries will continue to value. Doubtless there is also useful work to be done with the world's increasing refugee problem and in the reconstruction of war-torn countries such as Syria.

Organizations addressing poverty and extreme poverty will need to re-cruit and train their own cadre and it cannot be assumed that these are people who are already in the market. The importance of unusual skills and commitment, as well as a facility for engagement with the poorest, is a les-son to be drawn from anthropology and the way faith organizations, social workers, and the Salvation Army now address extreme poverty. Salvation Army personnel have discovered that they had to do the hard yards on the ground and that they had to be close to those they were trying to help. Very poor people in both rich and poor countries will not put their welfare in the hands of helpers they do not know, or in the hands of proxy helpers, or help-ers with a different faith. Those who do not speak their language or know their customs or have the ability to speak a kind word cannot be expected to succeed. A few years ago, the failure of much of the aid donated to help victims of the Asian tsunami underlined the fact that poor people who have never had any help from rich people or government will not entrust their family's welfare to helpers they do not know. Poor people are often too shy or too frightened to accept assistance. Even in rich countries, indigent peo-ple lead solitary lives and do not want to have contact with officialdom.

Poverty alleviation needs hands-on skills rather than drip-down global money. The journey to help a billion starts with one person. Instead of starting with billions it is often necessary to start with an individual and to rely on building and using relationships between helpers and that person to create a partnership and common ground.[6] Helping an individual to rise out of poverty also takes a very large amount of time and effort. I was reminded just how hard it is to help one person by story from a mining company in Canada. The miners had realized that they needed to try to help a small number of poor people rather than assuming they could help thousands or millions to escape from poverty. In 2001 the Labrador West Employment Corporation in Canada had a program that aimed to help poor individuals to get jobs in the mining industry. The company, which believed in focusing on ability rather than disability, wanted every disabled person to have the opportunity to do useful work. The program began its work in the living room of one of the founding members. Seven years later it had managed to place eight individuals with various emotional and physical disabilities in jobs in Iron Ore of Canada, a local company. Each disabled individual had to be carefully assessed to see what potential he or she possessed. Then, working closely with the mining company, jobs had to be designed to fit that individual. The results have been very good. Families got help. Instead of having to carry the entire task of caring for their loved ones, they were able to share the care. The individuals who were employed as a result of the scheme were delighted to earn money for the first time in their lives.

This is not to dismiss global poverty alleviation ambition: it is to dismiss the idea that poverty can be eliminated and that scaling-up can be built on anything other than demonstrated success with individuals with differing circumstances and in diverse cultural settings. Success will never be achieved where a worker sitting behind a desk expounds and a worker digging a trench is expected to listen. Different poor people have different aptitudes and different needs and these need to be assessed by those with hands-on skills. Some may need jobs and training, some may need help from families and relatives. Top-down global nostrums and one-size-fits-all approaches have limited usefulness.

Reaching the poorest is a local challenge. What is missing from the World Bank's homogenous approach is a commitment to local development that could provide a useful countervailing influence to excessive emphasis on globalism that is distorting development assistance. We have known that poverty should be seen as a local government issue since a 1598 resolution by justices of the peace in Elizabethan England meeting at Speenhamland. Throughout history the lesson has been that the organization and delivery of assistance to the poor should be located as closely as possible to the poor.[7] Local government officials occupy the turning or tipping point between central government concerns and community concerns. Above local government level civil servants look upward for their future preferment to their nation's capital; at local government level civil servants look down to those citizens whose interests they wish to serve. Administrative integrity often depends on an assumption that those looking downward will represent and fight for these local interests; the bargain is made between what the center views as parochialism and the man on the ground sees as public service.

Rather than money-raising global visions, it would make sense to conclude, as the great faiths have done, that poverty will always be with us and that each society will have to decide for itself what constitutes poverty and what external help should be welcomed for its alleviation. In these materialistic times it seems reasonable to assume that the gap between wants and the means of their satisfaction will increase rather than decrease and that no matter what statistical sleight of hand the World Bank engages in, there will be more and more people who believe that they are poor. When it comes to poverty in either the rich or the poor countries, it may in the future make more sense to measure progress by how little things have slipped rather than how far they have advanced.

Accounting to the Poorest

When a business makes extravagant but doubtful claims about its products and services, those claims are likely to be challenged by consumer interest groups. This does not happen with the promises that the World Bank makes about ending poverty. It cannot be in the public interest, or in the interest of the poor, that the Bank is able to advertise globally—one of the very few aid agencies that does—and is free to put its actions and intentions in the most positive light and without any effective challenge since there is no effective countervailing force or regulation at a global level. Given the resources at the disposal of the World Bank, and the supportive attitude of a majority of member governments, this is not surprising and it is why the criticism of a few small well-informed NGOs has little chance of having an effective international hearing. Yet there is a strong case for a countervailing point of view, one that would also give the poor a voice.

Poor people have found that what was planned for their futures has been chosen by others whom they have not met and never will meet. It must be difficult to go through life, as the global poor do, without achieving best practice in any aspect of life. Others know better than you about your health and how it should be managed, how much water and electricity you consume, the sort of education you should aspire to, your employment prospects, your expenditure and that of your family, as well as their consumption, how many bedrooms you have in your house and who sleeps in them, the way you treat your wife and daughters, the amount of food you can produce for yourself, and the symbols, monuments, and statues that the community regards as important. The only thing they do not know is what you look like or what makes you a unique individual.

In principle, it is reasonable to hold public organizations to account for their behavior toward those very poor people into whose societies they intrude, including local society.[8] NGO concern over dams, resettlement and indigenous peoples made a case for the World Bank and other aid agencies needing to pay more attention to accounting for their social responsibilities to local people. That lesson needs to be taken on board because the Bank's Board of Governors has shown little evidence that self-regulation works. Any organization dealing with poverty alleviation cannot in all good conscience rely on its legal and fiduciary relationship with the government of the borrower while ignoring the need to acknowledge its responsibility to account for its performance to local people. The homogenization, secularization, and globalization of poverty alleviation encouraged and enabled the World Bank and other aid agencies to believe that they occupied the moral high ground, making it unnecessary to canvas the opinions of the poor whom they claim to be helping. Despite claims that the World Bank listens to the poor, and numerous publications saying that this is what it does, the global poor are George Orwell's unpersons.[9]

When so much information is given about what the poor do not have, and so little on what they do have, they become unrecognizable as people. Low incomes, unsanitary conditions, illiteracy, and so on, and a whole series of not so subtle suggestions all indicate that those being described are not a part of society. Like Orwell's unpersons, the poverty descriptions and statistics have deprived the poorest of culture, community, voice, and a human face.[10] The poorest are represented in aid agency documents as being abnormal in that they have incredibly low annual incomes; hopeless future prospects in that they often have absolutely no education or land; immoral, in that children who do not receive proper nourishment may not develop their intellectual potential. Distended stomachs, round eyes, food bowls, and pictures of urban squalor have become the norm. Descriptions of poverty emphasize with figures and graphs the degradation, squalor, ignorance, and hopelessness of the lives of the poor. The poorest of the world are lumped together. Pictures of kwashiorkor, barrios, favelas, and poor lands give vivid testimony to these conditions. What these descriptions of the poor often suggest is distasteful de-anthropomorphization used to try to secure funding from the public.

Description should not concentrate on what the poor do not have while ignoring their assets. Nobody can escape from poverty unless they can do something for themselves. Even a soup kitchen cannot be useful if people cannot walk to it. Of course, the poor need medicines, money, education, and food, but the material deprivation, degradation, and squalor of their existence is not all that those wishing to help need to appreciate. It is necessary to know the extent to which groups and communities in dire need can help themselves. Knowing what they can bring to any improvement attempt is essential if assistance is to succeed.[11]

The recent revelations about Oxfam's sexual misconduct in Haiti confirm what anyone who has worked overseas knows: there have been sinners and there are potential sinners in all the big organizations, including the faith organizations. These organizations and the bilateral aid agencies that have been happy to endorse the importance of corporate social responsibility for the private sector could be encouraged to acknowledge that they also need what the mining industry has called "a social license to operate."[12] Explaining the idea, Jim Cooney suggested, "As with political risk management at the national level, a mining company needed to maintain an ongoing positive relationship with local communities and their allies by demonstrating that they were acting in a manner consistent with local expectations and demands."[13] Failure to maintain government support could lead to the suspension of the mining permit. Similarly, failure to maintain community support could lead to the suspension of the social license. The metaphor highlights the equivalence of the social and cultural challenges at the community level with those at the governmental level.

The idea of a social contract or social license does not necessarily need to be reduced to writing, but both aid agencies and very poor people should be clear about their respective roles: Who should do what? And what should both parties be entitled to expect in return? The neat and useful social license idea can be seen as part of a long history of social contract thinking going back to Thomas Hobbes, John Locke, and Jean-Jacques Rousseau, and, more recently, to John Rawls.[14] Boiled down to its essentials, a social contract depends on consensus ad idem, the notion that both parties agree on what it is that they have agreed to do and what the other party to the contract has agreed to do. The hypothetical notion of a social contract was useful for citizens who had to endure bad monarchs. They could, with the idea of a social contract, be thought responsible for providing good government and reasonable laws and fairness. If the king did his job, then citizens would be responsible for willingly paying taxes, obeying laws, and defending the realm.

One of the useful things about the corporate social responsibility movement that has built on social license and social contract thinking is that it makes private sector investors adopt a local lens through which to view how their actions appear to local people. Corporate social responsibility's socially responsible corporate citizen is modelled on the legal fiction of the corporation that allows a company to be seen as an individual person in the eyes of the law.[15] The legal fiction facilitates commercial relationships in society because of the way it mimics functioning social relationships. Social responsibilities are defined by custom and convention established over a long period. Reciprocity is a key component of these social relationships and is fundamentally important for aid agencies who are trying to help poor people. What do aid agencies expect in return for their assistance?

There would be no point in an aid agency saying, "We are good people with good intentions with great skills who want to help you." When private sector assistance was explained to local people, they did not believe that the help was a consequence of companies being full of kind-hearted people. The existing horizon of experience within which poor people operate seldom includes organizations full of kind, generous people. To be believable, aid agencies have to provide a locally believable motive for what they are doing if they want to establish and maintain relationships characterized by mutual understanding and respect. Private sector companies have learned that they need to show that they can expect some value in return for helping communities and that might be improving the ability to recruit good workers or helping to gain access to new resources.

Despite the continuing use of the ideology of development assistance the skills that are thought to be useful overseas have increasingly become the same as those used in large corporations in the industrialized countries. (See appendix D "Culture and Development Assistance.") Something important has been lost when poverty alleviation and development assistance see no special need for an apprenticeship and special training to prepare for work overseas. New entrants don't spend years learning about other cultures and they don't make house calls on the poor. Generations of young men and women—and I know because I was one of them—benefited from living and working in other cultures and brought those benefits back to enrich their own societies. We were helped to grow up to be better people than we would have been if we had stayed at home. And, in turn, if there were enough of us, we affected our host communities in some small ways that they thought to be useful. By living overseas for some years, we gradually came to understand that ours was not the most important culture in the world—the one less-fortunate peoples did not possess. Instead, we learned to appreciate how other societies managed the business of living and dying and how others had designed rituals and customs that showed greater delicacy and sensitivity than we had grown up with. Moreover, it provided us with the much clearer idea of the strengths and weaknesses of our own upbringing. And anyway, we were not so expert, and we often made mistakes. Fortunately, we were often forgiven.

Notes

1. Bait and switch occurs when customers are attracted by the offer of a bargain and then find when they go to make a purchase that inferior goods have been substituted.

2. Wisbey, *Soldiers without Swords*; Hoover and Schofield-Clark, *Practicing Religion*.

3. Homogenized poverty has been treated as if it were a total social fact by those promoting global poverty alleviation: "These phenomena (total social facts) are at once legal, economic, religious, aesthetic, morphological and so on. They are legal in that they concern individual and collective rights, organised and diffuse morality; they may be entirely obligatory, or subject simply to praise or disapproval. They are at once political and domestic, being of interest both to classes and to clans and families. They are religious; they concern true religion, animism, magic and diffuse religious mentality. They are economic, for the notions of value, utility, interest, luxury, wealth, acquisition, accumulation, consumption and liberal and sumptuous expenditure are all present" Mauss, *The Gift*, 76–77.

4. The relationship between culture and administration is not usually dealt with in most assessments of the institution-building requirements of poor countries. See Cohen, "Building Sustainable."

5. "Stick to the knitting and the things you know about" was very sensible advice in Peters and Waterman, *In Search of Excellence*.

6. Simmel, "The Poor."

7. Elton, "An Early Tudor Poor Law"; Marshall, "The Old Poor Law."

8. Holme and Watts, *Corporate Social Responsibility*.

9. The concept of an unperson was created by George Orwell in his book *Nineteen Eighty-Four*.

10. ul Haq, *The Poverty Curtain*; Strathern, "The Nice Thing about Culture."

11. "Thus, poverty arises when people lack key capabilities, and so have inadequate income or education, or poor health, or insecurity, or low self-confidence, or a sense of powerlessness, or the absence of rights such as freedom of speech. Viewed in this way, poverty is a multi-dimensional phenomenon, and less amenable to simple solutions. So, for instance, while higher average incomes will certainly help reduce poverty, these may need to be accompanied by measures to empower the poor, or insure them against risks, or to address specific weaknesses (such as inadequate availability of schools or a corrupt health service)." World Bank Institute, "Analysis of Poverty," 66.

12. Cooney, "Reflections on the 20th Anniversary," 197. Jim Cooney's concept of social license is spelled out in chapter 7 of Cochrane, *Anthropology in the Mining Industry*.

13. Cooney, "Reflections on the 20th Anniversary," 199.

14. Curely, *Thomas Hobbes*; Locke, *The Second Treatise*, 283–446; Bertram, *Rousseau*; Rawls, "Justice as Fairness."

15. Maitland, "The Corporation Sole."

ENGAGEMENT ISSUES FOR ANTHROPOLOGY

Development assistance agencies, NGOs, and faith groups that aim to help the very poorest need young men and women who are, to an unusual degree, committed to the business of establishing and maintaining personal relationships with the poorest members of society. However, if the World Bank continues to pursue global poverty alleviation in the same manner as it has for the past fifty years, then the prospects for those who believe in the importance of personal engagement with the poorest, such as anthropologists, will not be good. A few may manage to get work with an overseas office of the Bank but, although they may secure interesting assignments, they will, in relation to the deskbound economists and, increasingly, the environmentalists, still be in the bottom bunk.

Of course, anthropologists may be involved with the civil society campaigns that can be expected, now or in the future, to address the waste and the limitations of the current World Bank approach to poverty. And for those who want to work in the international development field, but not in a large organization, there are excellent opportunities in the consulting industry and with small NGOs. Beginning professionals would be well advised to explore what is on offer rather than automatically considering the big aid agencies. When hiring consultants, I have had no difficulty in finding very competent and highly experienced anthropologists in consulting firms and in private practice who were available to provide a year-round service. The consulting companies are an excellent resource and fast becoming the major repository of implementation experience with hands-on engagement for bilateral and multilateral development assistance.[1] In fact, as already mentioned, it is now the case that the consulting companies have more experience, and more up-to-date experience, than either the aid agencies or commercial companies when it comes to grassroots engagement.

Paul Appleby made a useful contribution when he pointed to what a university cannot be expected to provide:

> A university cannot be expected to confer outright all of the qualities needed; it could best add to the equipment of persons already strongly formed to the de-sired patterns. Selection and training should identify those with skill in human relations, flexibility, diversified experience and varied acquaintance with peo-ple and activities of people in other cultures. They should select with the hope of finding persons peculiarly slanted toward the business of relating, apparently unlike things, persons already in exceptional degree devoted to the public in-terest, and persons temperamentally bent toward collegial action.[2]

The university training that is given to anthropologists still does not do enough to recognize that they will spend much of their working lives in teams rather than as individuals and they will usually report to a manager who has a different disciplinary background.[3] Working in a large or small bureaucracy is not easy. These large bureaucracies require professionals who can both grasp the big picture and do detailed work. They should be people who have a facility for getting on with those at the top, as well as those at the bottom, of society.[4] Those preparing for a career need to carefully consider whether they should acquire geographical skills and the ability to cover Asia, Africa, or Latin America or whether they should de-velop functional expertise in land tenure, nutrition, reproductive behavior, education, and health. Employers need practitioners who are familiar with development economics, environmental and social impact assessment, hu-man rights, and the UNDRIP.[5]

My sense is that the majority of practitioners are engaged in short-term temporary assignments with NGOs and the private sector lasting a matter of months or a couple of years. Those who want an active hands-on ca-reer will spend their professional lives working as advisers, though some may want a managerial role. An anthropologist can, of course, become a manager but then—vide the discussion about generalists and specialists earlier in this book—there would be fewer and fewer opportunities to use disciplinary skills as she or he rises in the organization.

Most anthropologists in large complex organizations occupy staff roles and as such are expected to assist line managers in the performance of their re-sponsibilities. That is the meaning of staff: something to lean on. Initially, advisers provide information that will be needed to frame line-management decisions. Then they provide advice and counsel related to what needs to be done and finally they provide supervisory advice. But it is the line manager who is accountable for what is done or not done, and sensible managers will take care to know the quality and experience of their advisers. In terms of the management process the adviser's suggestions move up to line managers who have the power to transform these suggestions into orders that, in turn, flow down through the line. A group of advisers is a thought organization in terms of planning and a will organization in terms of its supervisory and coordinating capacity rather than its authority or command.

Line managers will often try to dodge their responsibilities by saying they really do not understand anthropology. There may be a struggle to get them to understand that they, and not the anthropologist who is an adviser, are accountable for the performance or nonperformance of the discipline. In most instances the problems can be sorted out by discussion but, if not, then assistance must be sought from the most senior managers in the organization.

My sense is that a great deal of confusion and ongoing debate over whether to engage has been, and still is, created by the conflation of the rights of the citizen with the not always very clear, well-defined, or universally accepted and recognized obligations, conferred, or acquired by studying anthropology.[6] The decision to address or research this or that problem, whether population or land tenure, and to do this in Africa or Asia or in North America or Europe, is the responsibility of the individual. How that choice is handled is one for the anthropological professional who, when others may be affected, can be asked, as John Beattie has said, to show a degree of objectivity and dispassionate analysis.[7] It is hard to imagine law schools around the country engaging in a debate that pits the university against those who work in the courts or sit on the bench. Moreover, a legal professional is expected to use all his or her skill when seeking the acquittal of someone accused of a horrible crime even should that professional privately doubt that person's innocence. In the medical profession there are strict codes of conduct that are enforced, and professionals are struck off for misconduct. This happens because there are agreed and accepted surgical procedures and standards that can be audited and followed.[8]

Anyway, practitioners will make their own decisions about what sort of jobs they want and it seems clear that if anthropology does not turn out what employers want then employers will come up with their own solutions. What I have noticed is that more and more jobs that could have been filled by anthropology graduates have been filled by graduates from a range of other disciplines.[9] Many of these graduates have started with an economics or an environmental degree to which they have added some anthropology.

Few would argue with the use of anthropologists in disaster relief. Received wisdom in the aid business is that if and when an event can be seen as a disaster, then everything done is upside. Few will carp or criticize and good press can be expected. Unfortunately, the disasters in which anthropology can play a useful role are often small and limited in nature, though famine situations and health epidemics such as Ebola are obvious exceptions.[10]

Katy Gardner and David Lewis have supplied a more positive view of engagement and I agree with many of their conclusions.[11] I am sure that the developing countries are producing very good practitioners, but why do so many anthropologists assume, and quite wrongly in my view, that the major effort will be done by academic anthropologists?[12] Too many of the anthropologists teaching and preparing students for a practical career appear to have had limited work experience outside the academy. What specialists from other disciplines and professions complain about is what they see as a reluctance on the part of anthropologists to acquire sufficient technical literacy in other fields to enable effective communication of the thoughts, observations, and findings generated during fieldwork. The Oxford agricultural scientist Geoffrey Masefield highlighted some of these issues:

> Let us start with an irritant to agriculturalists in anthropological works . . . the way anthropologists refer to plant and animal organisms. An anthropologist of very high repute mentions five insects on one page. . . . The names of two are printed in italics and are presumably the local language: they are meaningless to anyone who does not know that rather obscure language. The third is printed between inverted commas and appears to be in some other non-English language, though one cannot guess what. A fourth, in italics with a Latin name of a genus of insects but does not give the species. The fifth name is "the common black fly" and one is left guessing as to which of many flies of black colour on a world scale, on the African scale, or in that region of Africa is meant.
>
> Several anthropologists who have described crop production by peoples in eastern Africa seem to have been unaware that some of the crops they were dealing with had been cultivated there for 1,000 years and others (originally of American origin) for only about 200. Thus, they missed the point that many ancient customs and ceremonies are attached to the former group, and hardly any to the latter. Again, an anthropologist who makes many references to the great outbreak of rinderpest in tropical Africa in the 1890s as if he did not know that it was so destructive because it was the first of its kind, and it was started by a movement of herds following the Italian invasion of Ethiopia in 1890.[13]

Duncan Derrett, who was professor of oriental laws at the University of London, raised many of these same issues:

> I have worked alongside anthropologists for a quarter of a century and no one (of them) ever wanted to learn from me, for more than five minutes, anything I could teach in Sanskrit law or modern Hindu law, though I was far from being a typical law teacher, and no human alternative has offered himself.
>
> It is not the *professional* aim of an anthropologist to prevent change in his society, nor to protect his "friends" from the ravages of "development." If he speaks as if it were it is the man speaking not the anthropologist. Similarly, it is the lawyer's aim to know the law and plot its course, to help it work in resolving disputes and anticipating them and to work in, with, and through it. It is not his task to change it, nor to protect it from change. The typical "conservatism"

of the lawyer is not a matter of his resisting change, so much as his insistence before students (if he is a teacher) and to new discoveries which work experimentally judges, that this is the law (as he would say "this is my life"). If the law is changed by the Supreme Court, or the house of Lords, he at once, without shame, hesitation or consciousness of any anomaly, tells the very same students and the very same judge, that the law has changed; and he is as strongly for it as he was for yesterday's law which was wrong: he has no attachment to any rule, only to his function. This is not intellectual flexibility, as men versed in literature, divinity or even history might suppose. It is the natural reaction of the practical man.[14]

Training in a large number of departments of anthropology still pays insufficient attention to interdisciplinary needs. The biggest gaps in the university curriculum are statistics, environmental science, organization theory, human rights, and economics.[15] Public health has become an outstanding exception to the lack of an interdisciplinary focus and the future seems bright for that specialty.[16] Practitioners who discover, as many do, that their university training has not prepared them well for an active career will have to do their best to find jobs that help them gain the experience needed. Some university departments will study what is happening, see where demand exists, and adjust their offerings; others will not. Meanwhile, the training for economists and environmentalists has, like engineering and accountancy, moved to reflect more exactly what employers are looking for; as a result, good students want the training and the universities are receiving valuable feedback on graduate performance.

Notes

1. Faas and Barrios, "Applied Anthropology"; Sillitoe, "Ethnobiology."
2. Appleby, "Address to the Institute."
3. Cochrane, "Policy Studies."
4. Cochrane, "The Non-Expert Side."
5. See Wilson, *Human Rights*. The ways UN human rights initiatives have affected the private sector is dealt with in Cochrane, *Anthropology in the Mining Industry*. For UNDRIP, see Haenn, "Citizens, Experts," 102.
6. Gardner and Lewis, *Anthropology, Development*; Eyben, "Review of Gardner and Lewis"; Gow, "Anthropology and Development"; Mosse and Lewis, *The Aid Effect*; Mosse, "Social Analysis."
7. Beattie, *Other Cultures*.
8. Some years ago, Joe Jorgensen reminded us that there is an ethics of intention but not of result (Jorgensen, "On Ethics and Anthropology"). See also Albro, "Anthropological Research Ethics."
9. Besteman, "In and Out of the Academy."
10. This is particularly the case where famine is concerned. See Raymond Firth's remarks on famine on Tikopia (Firth, *The Elements of Social Organisation*); and Horowitz and Salem-Murdock, "Development-induced Food Insecurity."

11. Gardner and Lewis, *Anthropology and Development*. Look at the capacity of the so-called Beltway bandits, the name for consulting firms in the vicinity of Washington, DC. What university has the capacity of development alternatives (DAI) in rural development? Academic anthropologists need to address their critical constraint: part-time involvement. Ironically, the academic side of the discipline faces the same problem as the World Bank and other development agencies where staff anthropologists spend most of their careers in an office far from the field and gradually become out of date. "To study details apart from their setting must inevitably stultify theory, field work and practical handling alike" (Malinowski, *The Dynamics of Culture Change*, 41).

12. Rylko-Bauer, Singer, and van Willigen, "Reclaiming Applied Anthropology."

13. Masefield, "Anthropology and Agricultural," 39.

14. Derrett, "The Roles of Anthropology," 50.

15. Little, "Environments and Environmentalisms," 253–260. Human rights reflected American and European experience, although the 1948 Declaration did not commit the US to eliminating racial segregation or Britain and France to liberating the subject populations in their colonies. Obviously, it would be reasonable to assume that a number of rights are universal—rights to life, property, and liberty—but when it comes to punishment or free speech, things may be different depending on the cultural context. Alison Renteln Dundes has drawn attention to the importance of considering the cross-cultural implication of human rights. See Dundes, *The Cultural Defense*. Economics is discussed in Grillo and Rew, *Social Anthropology*, 23; and Hyde, "Building a Subdiscipline."

16. Leach, "The Ebola Crisis"; Farmer, *Aids and Accusation*.

Appendix B

THE CULTURE OF POVERTY DEBATE

In 1965 a firestorm was unleashed following Daniel Patrick Moynihan's report, *The Negro Family: The Case For National Action*.[1] The idea that black families had tangled pathologies that resulted in poverty as learned behavior, supposed by some to have come out of Oscar Lewis's work in Mexico, was vigorously resisted by a number of anthropologists.[2] In fact Lewis's Mexican work was empirically unsound and it is doubtful that he really intended to father a full-fledged culture of poverty debate, since that would have required a degree of universalism few anthropologists would agree with. But the idea that there was such a thing as a culture of poverty, with ingrained values, beliefs, and attitudes, led to assumptions that the number of poor people in the US was the number of individuals on welfare.

Any assumption that there is a culture of poverty certainly does not accord with my experiences in different social and cultural contexts. My sense is that the local social context is all-important, as are the choices that people make. Of course, ability to make choices may be affected by upbringing or a lack of access to education or health care, but this does not alter the importance that I believe should be attached to the common perceptions that local people have about poverty and what can and should be done to make their lives better.

That poverty is real and that it has tragic human costs is unquestionable. To the extent possible it must be eliminated, but the idea that there is a silver bullet solution calculable in terms of income and consumption deserves to be questioned with the same energy and passion that was generated by the suggestion that there was a culture of poverty whose norms and values were transmitted from generation to generation.

Questioning the Nature of Poverty

The causes of poverty can vary widely because of differing political, ethnic, and faith groups; as a consequence, an emphasis is required on relationships and supporting data collection at national, subnational, local, and individual levels. Also required is an acceptance of the likelihood that poverty will always be with us. There may be a range of different attitudes toward modernization that vary significantly depending on their geographical location with respect to political or religious associations. What will people work hard to achieve? What are the desired symbols of modernization? Education for children, a white-collar job, material goods, money, access to better health, or opportunities to leave home and go to the city? If possible, people's desires should be ranked and recorded for the whole country, together with any significant variations. In this respect, it is important to see if women's wants, rights, and life choices are significantly different from those of men, and if age differences elicit different patterns.[3]

The poverty paradigm has equated material advance with development and thus it overlooks those areas where life in developing countries can appear to be ahead of the industrialized countries. For example, more and more citizens in the industrialized countries worry about what will happen to them when they get old because they cannot expect, as can many in the developing countries, that their family and neighbors will take care of them.

Learning about the Poorest

USAID began its drive to eliminate poverty in the early 1970s by assuming that it needed to learn more about the behavior of the poor and their relationships with each other and external agencies in order to design and deliver the right assistance. The need for individual freedom and opportunity for risk increases when the goals sought and the means of accomplishing them increase in ambiguity. For example, fairly specific norms of behavior and expectations can be applied to a clerical training program. It needs relatively little freedom. But when the mission is to seek improvement in the condition of poor communities, the ambiguity is very high. There is, if aid agencies are honest, relatively little agreement in client countries about what should be done, or the competence required in order to do it.

In order to design interventions whose benefits could reach the poorest, USAID wanted to know the behavioral reasons for poverty. Did the poor lack skills in agriculture? Were their organization and management capabilities weak? Was an absence of literacy the root cause of their condition in life? Was ignorance a problem? Was fatalism responsible for maintaining poverty? Were hunters and gatherers in tropical rain forests or desert pastoralists so attached to their way of life that they did not want to participate in wage labor or cash cropping? Alternatively, was it the behavior of the rich that was a constraint on improvement? In a country with great geographical and social diversity, it was unlikely that one quantitative definition of poverty would suffice or tell those who want to help a great deal about the challenges they faced.

When private-sector companies realized that local relationships had to be based on mutual understanding and mutual respect if they were to be credible they undertook to develop ethnographic profiles often referred to as a baseline. A baseline can identify contemporary preferences, perceptions, and aspirations concerning poverty, livelihoods, economic development, and engagement with the wider society. It should illustrate how life is affected by an increasing need for money, a burgeoning demand for jobs, health care, and education, and a growing number of time-consuming relationships with the outside world.

Important questions need to be answered in any baseline. USAID said that, "Just as a road's design must be suited to the physical terrain so must many activities be adjusted to the particular social terrain—some features of which will present major design questions while other features may not affect the activity or, indeed, may be counted upon to significantly boost the probability of activity success."[4] Are work and its rituals at the center of local lives? A first task is to describe the nature of ongoing social change. Care must be exercised to separate out those changes that would continue to proceed regardless of the presence or absence of outside interventions. This calculation and recording may be helpful because outsiders are often blamed for changes that would have taken place regardless of their activities.

There are also practical questions to be answered in a baseline. How should aid agencies provide the community with information? If the information is written, what language should it be in? Should the information be verbal or visual? How long should communities be given to make up their minds? Since Westminster-style democracy and focus groups may not work and listening to those who always tell visitors what they think they want to hear is not safe, an authoritative and accurate explanation of how decisions are made in the community is essential. It is useful to know how both agreement and disagreement are signified. Must all agree, or can there be minority dissent? Who can decide and who cannot? To what extent is there factionalism?

Operational issues that USAID wanted to be covered included information about "leaders—both modern and traditional—whose support or cooperation or lack of opposition will be essential to the success of particular activities." Leadership may not be of great importance in situations where individual choice is heavily circumscribed by social obligations or institutional regulations. In other situations, USAID thought it would be useful to know "how leaders exercise authority. The support of such people may ultimately be vital to the success of . . . technical or institutional innovation. These leaders may not by themselves be involved in the activities; instead, they may be political or religious leaders, high officials, or even the most senior citizens."[5]

How can consultation and negotiation be maintained? Little things going wrong can make a big difference. Those designing toilet facilities need to know if locals are squatters or sitters, if toilet facilities for men and women need to be kept separate because of religious or other beliefs. Water rights need special attention because wells are easily polluted when the community has no history of well use and disease can easily spread if the introduction of these well-meaning innovations is not accompanied by lots of hands-on assistance.

Notes

1. Lewis, "Culture of Poverty."
2. Bourgois, "Culture of Poverty"; Small, Harding, and Lamont, "Reconsidering Culture and Poverty"; Valentine, *The Culture of Poverty*; Whitten and Szwed, *Afro-American Anthropology*.
3. See, for example, Miller, *The Endangered Sex*.
4. USAID, "Social Soundness Analysis," 1.
5. Ibid., 8.

World Bank Social Development Group

Given the state of knowledge in the discipline, and the contributions already made in the field of economic anthropology, it was surprising to read the 1997 Social Development Task Group recommendations such as this:

> It was also agreed that we need to move rapidly to learn more in areas where less is known: for example, about the social relations that underpin economic behavior, the rationale and modalities for strengthening social institutions and social capital; and the changing roles of the state, market, and civil society. To achieve these objectives, multidisciplinary approaches will be required.
>
> Finally, there was widespread recognition in the Task Group that, given the complexity of both economic and social development, the Bank can have little impact acting on its own and simply adding to its agenda and capacity. In the future, it will need to put far more emphasis on partnerships: first, with borrowers and with the range of development actors in client countries; and second, with other agencies. . . .
>
> The word *social* has a number of meanings. It can refer to education and health (the social sectors) or to poverty reduction and policies to benefit the poor and disadvantaged (social welfare). It can also refer to the relationships and institutions within a society (social capital) or to the historical and institutional conditions that affect project and policy outcomes (the social context of development). Because people can use the language in various ways, there is some confusion. To date, the Bank has spent considerable time on the first two meanings; in this report more attention is paid to the third and fourth. This report focuses more on societies, somewhat less on individuals.

What Is Meant by Social Development?
There are many definitions of social development. But there also is a continuum that matters to practitioners and that figured prominently in the debates among Task Group members.

- *Positive Meaning.* At one end of the definitional continuum, social development simply refers to the condition of people—their level of education, quality of life, and the quality and sustainability of their relationships and institutions. It does not presuppose what ought to be, it simply describes what is.

- *Normative Meaning.* Seen through a normative lens, however, social development also connotes social goals and objectives. For example, at the 1995 World Summit for Social Development (WSSD), governments issued declarations supporting investments in poverty alleviation, human resource development, employment creation, and other objectives such as democracy, social justice, nonviolence, and equality. In this sense, social development entails objectives to be pursued in their own right.

This normative versus positive debate has been at the center of much of the discussion within the Task Group. All task group members agreed that social conditions provide the context for economic development. But some members took the position that the objectives of the WSSD reflect both an emerging international consensus and a testable set of hypotheses about the social correlates of sustainable economic and social development; factors that are therefore of crucial interest to the Bank's development efforts. Others, however, argued that the declarations of the WSSD include objectives and statements of conviction that go well beyond the development mandate of the Bank.[1]

Access

The Bank's anthropologists and sociologists did do useful work on the access that poor people have to opportunities and services. Assessing access is a process of showing the existing availability and use of the basic necessities required to sustain a minimum standard of living. Data should indicate the availability of income-earning opportunities, food and shelter, and services for education and health care, with particular reference to poor rural populations. Health care should not only include preventive and curative measures for characteristic diseases but also adequate supplies of potable water. Schools and hospitals are often sited near administrative centers whose locations were determined during the colonial period when concern was with the maintenance of law and order rather than with development. NGO capacity needs to be estimated.[2] Likewise, estimating health care in terms of hospital beds, while sometimes useful, is less useful in cultures that consider illness a consequence of fate or that place a high value on caring for sick persons at home through the use of traditional remedies.

Access to land, capital, credit, education, health, nutrition services, and markets, and the ways and extent to which such access is broadened or narrowed, was often nationally assessed. The issues to be identified and analyzed under this heading include, in the case of an agricultural loan, for example, trends in land tenure arrangements and how they would be affected: the availability to target farmers of improved input—seeds and fertilizers—tools, and the credit with which to finance them; access to technical information and to markets, including the existence and extent of farm-to-market roads; and how price policy, including taxes and subsidies, affects the target group. Such criteria measure the potential effort of the project on the distribution of wealth and income.

Measurement of access is more useful than measurement of money incomes alone, since the very poor do not always use money. Poor people with low money incomes might be quite satisfied with their lot and with the level of government services; those with high money incomes might be completely unsatisfied with government services, such as health and education. Country analysis needs to understand, record, and monitor the social barriers to enhanced participation for the very poorest living in these groups. Experience suggests that the very rich do not tend to become more kind or generous as they grow wealthier. There is no trickle-down of social attitudes and values: indeed, quite the opposite can be seen. Surely it is naïve to assume that in the absence of deliberately induced change, redistribution will gently and naturally result in the betterment of the lives of the poorest.[3]

Notes

1. Burki et. al, "Social Development and Results on the Ground," 2–10.

2. Uphoff, "Why NGOs Are Not a Third Sector"; Korten, *Getting to the 21st Century*.

3. The World Bank's independent evaluation group reporting on the World Bank's attempt to target the bottom 40 percent said in 2017, "This implies that continued attention will be needed to ensure success of the new shared prosperity agenda. To that end, a key factor identified in this evaluation will be the inclusion in World Bank Group strategies and projects of well-defined theories of change that explain how and under what conditions World Bank interventions are expected to lead to improved shared prosperity outcomes." World Bank, *Growth for the Bottom 40 Percent*, viii.

CULTURE AND DEVELOPMENT ASSISTANCE

Development assistance in the sense of addressing a special set of problems in a special set of countries requiring the attention of development specialists is beginning to make less sense. Management by seclusion has contributed to a situation where development assistance has become like any other corporate activity in the industrialized countries. Aid money is raised and accounted for in the rich countries, the goals and objectives of aid are increasingly those of the developed countries, and the skills used by the World Bank and other aid agencies are increasingly those used by big corporations in the US and Europe.

Poverty in rich countries has been in decline since the Industrial Revolution but it still exists. Easy-to-influence poverty in poor countries has also been successfully addressed by governments and the private sector and it would be wrong to say that this has been mainly as a result of aid. Nevertheless, aid agencies such as the World Bank tend to imply that they have a much larger role in lowering poverty than has actually been the case. Much of the poverty elimination that has taken place in rich and poor countries has had less to do with aid and more to do with economic and social change and the millions of individual acts of assistance made in many walks of life by ordinary people. Conscientious citizens do what they can to help eliminate or alleviate poverty when they come across a poor individual but, like Adam Smith's principle of the hiding hand, there is no visible master plan in which all citizens consciously participate.

This book has argued that the cultural context of poverty is important and that global agencies such as the World Bank are less well-equipped to deal with these issues than bilateral agencies. Traces of the idea that development assistance is first of all cultural assistance (or conquest) still survive. For example, bilateral development assistance agencies (involving an industrialized country and a developing nation) still try to establish a cultural bridgehead wherever they are working overseas.[1] The French have the Alliance Française, the Germans have the Goethe Institute, the British the British Council. Few successful multinational corporations avoid culture. International business is organized on a country basis: Americans work with Americans overseas, Japanese with Japanese. When an American or Japanese company expands its global operations by buying a local company, it leaves the running of the company to locals who possess the same culture. UN armies are not organized the way UN agencies are organized. When serving for the UN, each country keeps its own forces under its own control. They share a command structure. Why should the war on poverty be so different? Nor is that other considerable multinational, the Roman Catholic Church, organized like an international assistance agency; Holy Orders tend to have homes in particular countries. Those Holy Orders serve overseas on the same basis. NGOs are not organized along multicultural lines. Each industrialized country has its own NGOs staffed by its own nationals. Volunteer groups, such as the US Peace Corps, the British Voluntary Service Overseas, and the Japanese International Cooperation Agency, reflect the same principle of nationalism.

It is useful to remember that a very strong sense of public service emerged among local people in the course of the contest between the culture of the colonizers and the local culture. The locals sometimes had a chance to win. Sometimes the colonizers won and, as a result, locals tried to be like them; sometimes the locals won and succeeded in getting the colonizers to try to be like them. For example, as time passed, Indians serving in the Indian Administrative Service became more English than the public school–educated officials from England whose behavior they copied. In the twelfth and thirteenth centuries the descendants of the Norman conquerors of England tried to bring their culture to Ireland and ended up being *Hibernis Hiberniores*: more Irish than the Irish themselves. The contest was often brutal; colonizers examined local social landscape most carefully in order to see whether destruction or preservation would best serve their purpose. In some instances local leadership classes or cultural symbols were done away with, as was the case with Polynesian chiefs in Tahiti or the kilt in Scotland after the 1745 rebellion against the English. In other instances, such as the Ashanti in West Africa, traditional leadership structures were used as a conduit for colonial control.

The culture of the colonizer was distilled into simple unambiguous messages and signals shaping the social relationships of both colonizer and colonized. Role models provided by colonialists incorporated preferred behavior and values. The stuff and substance of the role models was real. It was seen to be just as important for local technicians that they acquired the behavior associated with the role models as it was that they acquired the new techniques and kept the books correctly. Colonialists had a common social identity; colonizers provided a trelliswork on which local institutions could grow.[2] The trelliswork was of value, whether it was the case that the colonized followed the pattern offered or whether it was the case that the trelliswork offered a coherent framework against which to rebel.[3]

Representatives of the colonial powers, British, French, and American (these last in the Philippines), did best when they lived for long periods in those societies, when they studied the people, and when they understood their cultural heritage, language, and customs. They brought with them a strong sense of their own societies and their own cultural heritage. If they aspired to a modicum of success the colonialists had to show that they understood that what the citizens of any country and the representatives of any culture are ultimately, even if unconsciously, interested in is self-assertion and self-expression. They may want some advantages of civilized technique, and some of the results of civilized knowledge, but they will inevitably want to make use of them in a rhythm of their life and in a society that they have inherited even if it is a modified society.[4] What this suggests is that bilateral assistance, aid that goes from an industrialized to a developing country, may have advantages denied to the World Bank and other multilateral institutions and that this national aid ought to be playing a very much more prominent role than nations simply giving their aid money to the Bank to spend.

Ending Poverty

Sorokin offered sensible advice that might well be listened to by those who want to eliminate global poverty:

> Since socio-cultural life changes incessantly, planning is unavoidable as an adaptive reaction to these changing conditions. In this sense it took place in the past, goes on at the present, and will continue in future. But from this unavoidable necessity it does not follow that any such scheming will be successful or that with the passage of time the percentage of successful planning (i.e. where the expected and actual results coincide) will increase, or that it has become so much more "scientific" that we have a right to boast of our ability to forecast and control socio-cultural phenomena. At the present, all such schemes remain as much guess-work and gambling as they were in the past. . . . but better underdo than overdo your gambling. Still better, if you can, study carefully the phenomena you are going to engineer before engineering them; still better if you can, try your plan experimentally, on a small scale before recklessly starting it on a large scale and in earnest. If you see that in the experimental setting it does not work, you will readily be able to abstain from its actual application to social life.[5]

Notes

1. The World Bank's social observatory provides an interesting example of how and why bilateral assistance has an advantage. Observatory staff who appear to be Indian nationals or Indians working in the World Bank and US universities obviously work closely with government officials.

2. Traces of the colonial idea that development assistance is first of all cultural assistance (or conquest) still survive. For example, bilateral development assistance agencies still try to establish a cultural bridgehead wherever they are working overseas.

3. See, for example, Minogue and Mollooy, *African Aims and Attitudes*.

4. Thurnwald, "Price of White Man's Peace."

5. Sorokin, "Is Accurate Social Planning Possible?," 25.

BIBLIOGRAPHY

Aghion, Philippe, and Patrick Bolton. 1997. "A Theory of Trickle-Down Growth and Development." *Review of Economic Studies* 64(2): 151–72.

Albro, Robert. 2015. "Anthropological Research Ethics." In Wright, *International Encyclopaedia*, 734–739.

Alm, Alvin. 1988. "NEPA: Past, Present, and Future." *EPA Journal* 14(1, Jan/Feb) 4988. Office of Public Affairs, US Environmental Protection Agency, Washington, DC.

Angrosino, Michael V., ed. 1976. *Do Applied Anthropologists Apply Anthropology?* Athens: University of Georgia Press.

Appleby, Paul. 1950. "Address to the Institute of Public Administration of Canada." Toronto, September 20. Appleby Papers, Syracuse University Archives Box 56.

Aronson, Dan R. 1995. "Participation in Country Economic and Sector Work." Social Development Notes No. 5. World Bank, Washington, DC.

Ascher R. E., and E. S. Mason. 1973. *The World Bank Since Bretton Woods.* Washington, DC: Brookings Institution.

Balogh, Thomas. 1978. "Failures in the Strategy against Poverty." *World Development* 6(1): 11–22.

Baster, Nancy. 1972. *Measuring Development: The Role and Adequacy of Development Indicators.* London: Frank Cass.

Bateman, Milford. 2010. *Why Doesn't Microfinance Work? The Destructive Rise of Local Neoliberalism.* London: Zed Books.

Batten, T. R. 1957. *Communities and Their Development.* London: Athlone Press.

Bauer, Michael W., Christopher Krill, and Steffen Eckhard, eds. 2017. *International Bureaucracy: Challenges and Lessons for Public Administration Research.* London: Palgrave MacMillan.

Bauer, Peter, and Barbara Ward. 1966. *Two Views of Aid.* Bombay: Vikas.

Baum, W., and S. Tolbert. 1985. *Investing in Development: Lessons of World Bank Experience.* Oxford, UK: Oxford University Press.

Beattie, John. 1964. *Other Cultures: Aims, Methods and Achievements in Social Anthropology.* London: Cohen & West.

Belshaw, Cyril. 1976. *The Sorcerer's Apprentice: An Anthropology of Public Policy*. New York: Pergamon.

Bendix, Reinhard. 1960. *From Max Weber: An Intellectual Portrait*. New York: Doubleday.

Benor David, and John Q. Harrison. 1977. *Agricultural Extension: The Training and Visit System*. Washington, DC: World Bank.

Berg, Alan (with Robert J. Muscat). 1973. *The Nutritional Factor: Its Role in International Development*. Washington, DC: Brookings Institution.

Berg, Robert. 1981. "PA Comments." *Practicing Anthropology* 3(4): 21–22.

Bertram, Christopher. 2003. *Rousseau and the "Social Contract."* London: Routledge.

Besteman, Catherine. 2010. "In and Out of the Academy: Policy and the Case for a Strategic Anthropology." *Human Organization* 69(4): 407–13.

Black, R., and H. White, eds. 2004. *Targeting Development: Critical Perspectives on the Millennium Development Goals*. New York: Routledge.

Bolton, Kerry. 2015. "BRICS Development Bank an Instrument for Globalization." *Foreign Policy Journal*, July 14.

Bouglé, Celestin. 1935. "Essay on the Regime of Castes." Paris: Les Presses Universitaires de France.

Bourgois, Phillipe. 2001. "Culture of Poverty." *International Encyclopedia of the Social & Behavioral Sciences*. Long Grove, IL: Waveland Press.

Boyer, William, and Mun Anh Byong. 1991. *Rural Development in South Korea: A Sociopolitical Analysis*. London: University of Delaware Press.

Brereton, D., et al. 2011. "Integrating Social and Economic Assessment into local Procurement Strategy." In Brereton, et al., *Proceedings of the First International Seminar*.

Brereton, D., et al., eds. 2011. *Proceedings of the First International Seminar on Social Responsibility in Mining*. Santiago, Chile, 19–21 October. Chile: Gecamin.

Brokensha, David. 1966. *Applied Anthropology in English-Speaking Africa*. Monograph 8. Ithaca, NY: Ithaca Society for Applied Anthropology.

Brosius, Peter J. 1999. "Analysis and Interventions: Anthropological Engagement with Environmentalism." *Current Anthropology* 40(3, June).

Brown, Lester R. 1971. *The Social Impact of the Green Revolution*. New York: Carnegie Endowment for International Peace.

Buck, Pearl S. 1984. *Tell the People*. Cavite, Philippines: International Institute for Rural Reconstruction.

Burdge, Rabel J., ed. 1998. *A Conceptual Approach to Social Impact Assessment: Collection of Writings by Rabel J. Burdge and Colleagues*, rev. ed. Middleton, WI: Social Ecology Press.

Burdge, Rabel J., and Robert A. Robertson. 1998. "Social Impact Assessment and The Public Involvement Process." In Burdge, *A Conceptual Approach to Social Impact Assessment*.

Burger, Julian. 2005. "Standard-Setting: Lessons Learned for the Future." International Commission of Jurists Workshop, Geneva, 13–14 February.

Burki, Shahid, et al. 1997. "Social Development and Results on the Ground." Social Development Paper 22, World Bank, Washington, DC. http://documents.worldbank.org/curated/en/830511468766247125/ Social-development-and-results-on-the-ground-task-group-report.

Caillods, F., ed. 2010. *The World Social Science Report: Knowledge Divides*. Paris: UN Educational, Scientific and Cultural Organization.

Callahan, Michael D. 1999. *Mandates and Empire: The League of Nations and Africa, 1914–1931*. Brighton, UK: Sussex Academic Press.

Camus, Albert. 1947. *La Peste*. Paris: Gallimard.

Castro, Peter, A. Hakansson, N. Thoma, David Brokensha. 1981. "Indicators of Rural Inequality." *World Development* 9(5, May): 401–27.

Cernea, Michael. 1984. *Operational Manual Statement on Project Appraisal*. OMS 2.20, Section F Sociological Aspects. Washington, DC: World Bank.

Cernea, Michael, ed. 1985. *Putting People First: Sociological Variables in Rural Development*. New York, NY: Oxford University Press for the World Bank.

Cernea, Michael. 1996. *Sociology, Anthropology, and Development: An Annotated Bibliography of World Bank Publications, 1975–1993*. Washington, DC: World Bank.

Chambers, E. 1985. *Applied Anthropology, A Practical Guide*. Englewood Cliffs, NJ: Prentice-Hall.

Chambers, Robert. 1980. "Rural Poverty Unperceived: Problems and Remedies." World Bank Staff Working Paper No. 400, Washington, DC.

Chambers, Robert. 1981. "Rapid Rural Appraisal: Rationale and Repertoire." *Public Administration and Development* 1: 95–106.

Chambers, Robert. 1997. *Whose Reality Counts? Putting the Last First*. London: Intermediate Technology Group.

Chambers, Robert, and Gordon R. Conway. 1991. "Sustainable Rural Livelihoods: Practical Concepts for the 21st Century." IDS Discussion Paper, 296, Brighton, East Sussex.

Chandy, Laurence, and Cory Smith. 2014. *How Poor Are America's Poorest: Poverty in a Global Context?* Washington, DC: Brookings Institution.

Chandy, Laurence, and Homi Kharas. 2012. "The Contradictions in Global Poverty Numbers." Brookings Institution blog, 6 March. https://www .brookings.edu/opinions/the-contradictions-in-global-poverty-numbers/.

Chenery, Hollis, Montek S. Ahluwalia, C. L. G. Bell, John H. Duloy, and Richard Jolly. 1974. *Redistribution with Growth*. Oxford: Oxford University Press.

Christen, Robert Peck, Richard Rosenberg, and Veena Jayadeva. 2004. "Financial Institutions with a Double Bottom Line: Implications for the Future of Microfinance." CGAP Occasional Paper, World Bank, Washington, DC.

Clark, William. 1967. *Number 10*. New York: Houghton Mifflin.

Clemens, Michael, and Gabriel Demonbynas. 2010. "When Does Rigorous Impact Evaluation Make a Difference? The Case of the Millennium Villages." Working Paper 225, Center for Global Development, Washington, DC.

Cleveland, Harlan, and Gerard Mangone, eds. 1957. *The Art of Overseasmanship: Americans at Work Abroad*. Syracuse: Syracuse University Press.

Cobo, José Martinez. 1986. *Study of the Problem of Discrimination Against Indigenous Populations*. UN Document E/CN.4/Sub.2/1986/7.

Cochrane, Glynn. 1968. "Review of J. S. G. Wilson: An Economic Survey of the New Hebrides." *Economica* (May 25): 217–18.

Cochrane, Glynn. 1969. "The Administration of Wagina Resettlement Scheme." *Human Organization* 29 (Summer).

Cochrane, Glynn. 1970. *Big Men and Cargo Cults*. Oxford: Clarendon Press.

Cochrane, Glynn. 1971. *Development Anthropology*. New York: Oxford University Press.

Cochrane, Glynn. 1974. "What Can Anthropology Do for Development?" *Finance and Development* 11(2, June): 20–25.

Cochrane, Glynn, ed. 1976. *What We Can Do for Each Other: An Interdisciplinary Approach to Development Anthropology*. Amsterdam: B. R. Grüner Publishing.

Cochrane, Glynn. 1976. "The Perils of Unconventional Anthropology." In Pitt, *Development from Below*.

Cochrane, Glynn. 1979. *The Cultural Appraisal of Development Projects*. New York: Praeger.

Cochrane, Glynn. 1980. "Policy Studies and Anthropology." *Current Anthropology* 21(4): 445–58.

Cochrane, Glynn. 1980. "Review of David Brokensha, Michael Warren, and Oswald Werner, *Indigenous Knowledge Systems and Development*." *American Anthropologist* 84(2).

Cochrane, Glynn. 1983. "Policies for Strengthening Third World Local Government." World Bank Staff Working Paper No. 582, World Bank, Washington, DC.

Cochrane, Glynn. 1984. *Issues in Budgeting*. Washington, DC: Economic Development Institute, World Bank.

Cochrane, Glynn. 1986. *Reforming National Institutions for Economic Development*. Boulder, CO: Westview for the World Bank.

Cochrane, Glynn. 2008. *Festival Elephants and the Myth of Global Poverty*. New York: Pearson.

Cochrane, Glynn. 2017. "Resettlement." In Cochrane, *Anthropology in the Mining Industry*, 181–94.

Cochrane, Glynn. 2017. *Anthropology in the Mining Industry: Community Relations after the Bougainville Civil War*. London: Palgrave.

Cochrane, Glynn. 2018. *Max Weber's Vision for Bureaucracy: A Casualty of World War I*. London: Palgrave.

Cochrane, Glynn. 1971. 'The Non-Expert side of the Expert." In Cochrane, *Development Anthropology*, 65–79.

Cochrane, Glynn, and Raymond Noronha. 1973. "Recommendations on the Use of Anthropology in Project Operations of the World Bank Group." Central Projects, World Bank, Washington, DC.

Cochrane, Glynn, and Raymond Noronha. 1973. *The Use of Anthropology in Project Operations of the World Bank Group*. Washington DC: Central Projects Department, World Bank.

Cohen, John. 1993. "Building Sustainable Public-Sector Management Capacity: A framework for Analysis and Intervention." Harvard Institute for International Development, Discussion Paper no. 473, Harvard University, Cambridge, MA.

Cooney, Jim. 2017. "Reflections on the 20th Anniversary of the Term 'Social Licence.'" *Journal of Energy & Natural Resources Law* 35(2): 197–200. DOI: 10.1080/02646811.2016.1269472.

Cooper, Frederick, and Randall Packard, eds. 1998. *International Development and the Social Sciences: Essays on the History and Politics of Knowledge.* Berkeley: University of California Press.

Creedon, Daniel F. 1974. "Introduction to Glynn Cochrane, Social Science Training and Manpower Development." US Agency for International Development, Washington, DC.

Crystal, David. 2000. *Language Death.* Cambridge: Cambridge University Press.

Curely, Edward, ed. 1994. *Thomas Hobbes, Leviathan.* Indianapolis: University of Indiana Press.

Daily Telegraph. 2000. "Obituary for David Brower." November 8.

das Gupta, Monica (with Mayra Buvinic and Ursula Casabonne). 2009. "Gender, Poverty, and Demography: An Overview." *World Bank Economic Review* 23(3): 347–69.

das Gupta, Monica, T. N. Krishnan, and Lincoln C. Chen, eds. 1996. *Health, Poverty and Development in India.* Oxford: Oxford University Press (paperback edition 1998).

das Gupta, Monica (with Manju Rani). 2005. "How Well Does India's Federal Government Perform Its Essential Public Health Functions?" World Bank Policy Research Working Paper 3447, World Bank, Washington, DC.

Dasgupta, Partha, and Ismail Serageldin, eds. 2000. *Social Capital: A Multifaceted Perspective.* Washington, DC: World Bank.

Davis, Gloria. 2004. "A History of the Social Development Network in the World Bank, 1973–2002." Social Development Paper 56, World Bank, Washington, DC. http://documents.worldbank.org/curated/en/806361468779696310/A-history-of-the-social-development-network-in-The-World-Bank-1973-2002.

Davis, Gloria, and Garrison, H. 1988. *Indonesia: The Transmigration Program in Perspective.* Washington, DC: World Bank.

Davis, Gloria, et al. 1997. "Social Development Update: Making Development More Inclusive and Effective." Social Development Paper 27, World Bank, Washington, DC. http://documents.worldbank.org/curated/en/1474514687 66811314/Social-development-update-making-development-more-inclusive-and-effective.

Davis, Gloria, et al. 1996. *Social Assessment: Incorporating Participation and Social Analysis into the World Bank's Operational Work. Informal Guidelines.* Social Policy Division. Washington, DC: World Bank.

Davis, R., and D. Franks. "The Cost of Conflict with Local Communities in Extractive Industry." In Brereton et al., *Proceedings of the First International Seminar.*

Davis, S. 1999. "Bringing Culture into the Development Paradigm: The View from the World Bank." *Development Anthropologist* 16(1–2): 25–31.

Davis, Shelton. 1993. "The World Bank and Indigenous Peoples." Denver Initiative Conference on Human Rights, University of Denver Law School, Denver, CO, 16–17 April.

Dennis, Norman. 1998. *The Invention of Permanent Poverty*. London: Institute for Economic Affairs.

Denoon, Donald. 2000. *Getting under the Skin: The Bougainville Copper Agreement and the Creation of the Panguna Mine*. Melbourne: Melbourne University Press.

Derrett, J., and M. Duncan. 1976. "The Roles of Anthropology and Law in Development." In Cochrane, *What We Can Do*.

Dowla, Asif, and Dipal Barua. 2006. *The Poor Always Pay Back: The Grameen II Story*. Bloomfield, CT: Kumarian Press.

Drèze, Jean, and Amartya Sen. 1992. *Hunger and Public Action*. Oxford: Oxford University Press.

Drewnowski, Jan. 1977. "Poverty: Its Meaning and Measurement." *Development and Change* 8(2, April).

Dundes, Alison Renteln. 2004. *The Cultural Defense*. New York: Oxford University Press.

Easterly, William. 2006. *The White Man's Burden: Why the West's Efforts to Aid the Rest Have Done So Much Ill and So Little Good*. New York: Penguin Press.

Edwards, Michael. 2000. *NGO Rights and Responsibilities: A New Deal for Global Governance*. London: Foreign Policy Centre.

Elkington, J. 1997. *Cannibals with Forks: The Triple Bottom Line of 21st Century Business*. Oxford: Capston.

Elton, G. R. 1948. "An Early Tudor Poor Law." *Economic History Review* 7(1).

Epstein, A. L. 1969. *Matupit: Land, Politics and Change among the Tolai of New Britain*. Berkeley: University of California Press.

Epstein, Scarlett. 1962. *Economic Development and Social Change in South India*. Manchester, UK: Manchester University Press.

Epstein, Scarlett. 1963. *Capitalism, Primitive and Modern—Some Aspects of Tolai Economic Growth*. Canberra: Australian National University Press.

Epstein, Scarlett. 1976. "The Ideal Marriage between the Micro View of the Anthropologist and the Macro View of the Economist." In Cochrane, *What We Can Do*, 9–24.

Escobar, A. 1991. "Anthropology and the Development Encounter: The Making and Marketing of Development Anthropology." *American Ethnologist* 18:16–40.

Escobar, A. 1995. *Encountering Development: The Making and Unmaking of the Third World*, 1st ed. Princeton, NJ: Princeton University Press.

Escobar, A. 2012. *Encountering Development: The Making and Unmaking of the Third World*, 2nd ed. Princeton: Princeton University Press.

Evans-Pritchard, E. E. 1965. *Theories of Primitive Religion*. Oxford, UK: Clarendon Press.

Extractive Industries Transparency Initiative (EITI) International Secretariat. 2017. "Upholding the Standard Internationally: Validation." Extractive Industries Transparency Initiative, 17 July, Oslo, Norway.

Eyben, Rosalind. 1995. *A Guide to Social Analysis for Projects in Developing Countries*. London: Overseas Development Administration, Her Majesty's Stationery Office.

Eyben, Rosalind. 1997. "Review of Gardner and Lewis." *Social Development Newsletter*, Institute for Development Studies, Brighton, East Sussex.

Eyben, R, ed. 2006. *Relationships for Aid*. London: Earthscan.

Faas, A. J., and Barrios, Roberto E. 2015. "Applied Anthropology of Risk, Hazards, and Disasters." *Human Organization* 74(4): 287–95.

Fanon, Franz. 1961. *The Wretched of the Earth*. With a preface by Jean-Paul Sartre. Paris: Éditions Maspero.

Farmer, Paul. 1999. *Infections and Inequalities: The Modern Plagues*. Berkeley: University of California Press.

Farmer, Paul. 2003. *Pathologies of Power: Health, Human Rights, and the New War on the Poor*. Berkeley: University of California Press.

Farmer, Paul. 2006. *Aids and Accusation: Haiti and the Geography of Blame*. Updated with a new preface. Berkeley: University of California Press.

Ferguson, James. 1998. "Anthropology and Its Evil Twin: Development in the Constitution of a Discipline." In Cooper and Packard, *International Development and the Social Sciences*.

Firth, Raymond. 1963. *We the Tikopia*. Boston: Beacon Press.

Firth, Raymond. 1964. *The Elements of Social Organisation*. Boston: Beacon Press.

Firth, Raymond. 1982. "Methodological Issues in Economic Anthropology." *Man, New Series* 7(3, September): 467–75.

Foster, George M. 1965. "Peasant Society and the Image of Limited Good." *American Anthropologist* 67(2, April): 293–315.

Foster, George M. 1969. *Applied Anthropology*. Boston: Little Brown.

Frank, Robert, Gilovich, Thomas, and Regan Dennis. 1993. "Does Studying Economics Inhibit Co-operation." *Journal of Economic Perspectives* Spring.

Franks, Daniel, Courtney Fidler, David Brereton, Frank Vanclay, and Phil Clark. 2009. *Leading Practice Strategies for Addressing the Social Impacts of Resource Developments*. Brisbane, Australia: Centre for Social Responsibility in Mining, Sustainable Minerals Institute, The University of Queensland & Department of Employment, Economic Development and Innovation, Queensland Government.

Frazer, Sir James. 1995. *The Golden Bough*. New York: Touchstone Edition.

Freeman, Samuel, ed. 1999. *John Rawls, Collected Papers*. Cambridge: Harvard University Press.

Freudenburg, William R. 1986. "Social Impact Assessment." *Annual Review of Sociology* 12(1986): 451–478. https://www.jstor.org/stable/2083211.

Furse, Ralph. 1962. *Ancuparius: Memoirs of a Colonial Recruiting Officer*. London: Routledge.

Galbraith, J. K. 1979. *The Nature of Mass Poverty*. Cambridge: Harvard University Press.

Gardner Katy, and David Lewis. 1997. *Anthropology, Development and the Postmodern Challenge*. London: Pluto Press.

Gardner, Katy, and David Lewis. 2015. *Anthropology and Development: Challenges for the 21st Century*. Chicago: Chicago University Press.

Gjording, C. 1981. "The Cerro Colorado Copper Project and the Guaymi Indians of Panama." Cultural Survival, Occasional Papers, No. 3, 1–50, Cambridge, MA.

Glasson J. 1999. "Environmental Impact Assessment: Impact on Decisions." In Petts, *Handbook of Environmental Impact*.

Glewwe, Paul, and Jacques van der Gagg. 1988. "Confronting Poverty in Developing Countries: Definitions, Interventions, Policies." Living Standards Measurement Study Working Paper No. 48, World Bank, Washington, DC.

Goffman, Erving. 1959. *The Presentation of Self in Everyday Society*. New York, Harper & Row.

Goldman, Michael. 2006. *Imperial Nature: The World Bank and Struggles for Social Justice in the Age of Globalization*. New Haven: Yale University Press.

Goodenough, Ward H. 2002. "Anthropology in the 20th Century and Beyond." *American Anthropologist* 104(2): 423–30.

Goodland, Robert. 1999. "Social & Environmental Assessment to Promote Sustainability: An informal view from the World Bank." International Association of Impact Assessment, Glasgow.

Goodland, Robert, David Maybury-Lewis, Raymond Noronha, and Francis Lethem. 1983. *Economic Development and Tribal Peoples: Human Ecologic Considerations*. Washington, DC: World Bank.

Gow, D. D. 1988. "Development Anthropology in Search of a Practical Vision." *Development Anthropology Network* 6(2): 13–17.

Gow, D. D. 1993. "Doubly Damned: Dealing with Power and Praxis in Development Anthropology." *Human Organization* 52(4): 380–397.

Gow, David D. 2002. "Anthropology and Development: Evil Twin or Moral Narrative?" *Human Organization* 61(4): 299–313.

Grillo, Ralph, and Alan Rew, eds. 1985. *Social Anthropology and Development Policy*. ASA Monograph no.23. London: Tavistock Publications.

Gupta, Akhil. 2010. "The Construction of the Global Poor: An Anthropological Critique." In Caillods, *The World Social Science Report*, 13–16.

Gupta, Akhil. 2012. *Red Tape: Bureaucracy, Structural Violence, and Poverty in India*. Durham, NC: Duke University Press, 2012.

Guggenheim, Scott. 1990. "Resettlement in Colombia: The Case of El Guavio." *Practicing Anthropology* 12(3): 14–20.

Hackenberg, Robert A., and Beverly H. Hackenberg. 2004. "Notes Toward a New Future: Applied Anthropology in Century XXII." *Human Organization* 63(4): 385–98.

Haenn N. 2007. "Citizens, Experts, and Anthropologists: Finding Paths in Environmental Policy." *Human Organization: Journal of the Society for Applied Anthropology* 66(2): 102.

Hageboeck, Molly, Glynn Cochrane, Lawrence Cooley, and Gerald Hursh-Cēsar. 1979. *The Manager's Guide to Data Collection*. Washington DC: US Agency for International Development.

Hägerstrand, T. 1952. *The Propagation of Innovation Waves*. Lund Studies in Geography, vol. 4. Lund: Royal University of Lund, Department of Geography.

Halberstam, David. 1972. *The Best and the Brightest*. New York: Random House.

Hamilton, Judith Ann. 1993. *Pages from Paradise*. Unpublished mss.

Hancock, Graham. 1989. *The Lords of Poverty*. New York: Atlantic Monthly Press.

Heap, Simon. 2000. *NGOs Engaging with Business: A World of Difference and a Difference to the World*. Oxford: The International Non-governmental Organisation Training and Research Centre.

Held, David, and Charles Roger, eds. 2013. *Global Governance at Risk*. Oxford: Blackwell.

Herskovits, Melville. 1941. "Economics and Anthropology: A Rejoinder." *Journal of Political Economy* 49(2): 269–78.

Heyman, Josiah McC. 2004. "The Anthropology of Power-Wielding Bureaucracies." *Human Organization* 63(4): 487–95.

Hickel, Jason. 2017. "Aid in Reverse: How Poor Countries Develop Rich Countries." *The Guardian*, January 14.

Hicks, Ursula. 1961. *Development from Below*. Oxford: Clarendon Press.

Hoben, Alan. 1982. "Anthropologists and Development." *Annual Review of Anthropology* 11: 349–375.

Hogbin, Ian. 1958. *Social Change*. London: Watts.

Holland, Jeremy. 1998. *Whose Voice?* London: Intermediate Technology Group.

Holme, Richard, and Phil Watts. 2000. *Corporate Social Responsibility: Making Good Business Sense*. London: World Business Council for Sustainable Development.

Hood, C. 1990. "Beyond the Public Bureaucracy State?" Public Administration in the 1990s, inaugural lecture, London School of Economics, London.

Hoover, Stewart M., and Lynn Schofield-Clark. 2002. *Practicing Religion in the Age of the Media: Explorations in Media, Religion, and Culture*. New York: Columbia University Press.

House of Commons. 1993. *Fifth Report: The Role of the Civil Service*, vol. I. Treasury and Civil Service Committee. London: Her Majesty's Stationery Office.

Hyde, Janice. 1991. "Building a Subdiscipline of Development Anthropology." *Reviews in Anthropology* 18(1–4): 183–91.

Ingersoll, Jasper, Mark Sullivan, and Barbara Linkerd. 1981. "Social Analysis of Aid Projects: A Review of the Evidence." US Agency for International Development, Washington, DC.

International Federation of Chemical Engineering and Mine Workers. 1997. *Rio Tinto: Tainted Titan, The Stakeholders Report*. Brussels.

International Rivers. 2008. *The World Commission on Dams Framework: A Brief Introduction*. Oakland, CA.

Israel, Arturo. 1990. "The Changing Role of the State: Institutional Dimensions." Country Economics Department, World Bank, Washington, DC. http://documents.worldbank.org/curated/en/375321468764732804/The-changing-role-of-the-state-institutional-dimensions.

Izquierdo, Silvio. 2014. "BRICS Nations to Form Bank to Rival World Bank, IMF." *Huffington Post*, July 16.

Jacobs, Sue, et al. 1994. *Methods and Tools for Social Assessment*. Washington, DC: World Bank.

Jenkins, Glenn P. 1994. "Modernization of Tax Administrations: Revenue Boards and Privatization as Instruments for Change." *Bulletin of the International Bureau of Fiscal Documentation*, Washington, DC.

Jorgensen, Joseph G. 1971. "On Ethics and Anthropology." *Current Anthropology* 12(3): 321–34.

Jung, C. G. 2002. *Flying Saucers: A Modern Myth of Things Seen in the Sky*, 2nd ed. London: Routledge, Psychology Press.

Kamarck, Andrew. 1983. *Economics and the Real World*. Philadelphia: University of Pennsylvania Press.

Kay, Cristobal. 1982. "Achievements and Contradictions of the Peruvian Agrarian Reform." *Journal of Development Studies* 18(2): 141–170.

Kemp, Deanna, and John Owen. 2018, May. "Social Performance Gaps in the Global Mining Industry. A Position Paper for Executives." Centre for Social Responsibility in Mining, University of Queensland, St. Lucia.

King, John A. 1967. *Economic Development Projects and their Appraisal*. Baltimore, MD: Johns Hopkins University Press.

Kirsch, Stuart. 2001. "Lost Worlds: Environmental Disaster, 'Culture Loss,' and the Law." *Current Anthropology* 42(2): 167–98.

Knight, F. H. 1941. "Anthropology and Economics." *Journal of Political Economy* 49(2): 247–68.

Knox, Ronald. 1950. *Enthusiasm: A Chapter in the History of Religion*. Oxford University Press.

Korten, David C. 1990. *Getting to the 21st Century: Voluntary Action and the Global Agenda*. West Hartford, CT: Kumarian Press.

Kravis, Irving B., A. Heston, and R. Summers. 1978. *International Comparison of Real Product and Purchasing Power*. Baltimore and London: Johns Hopkins University Press.

Kücher, Suzanne, and Andrea Eimke. 2009. *Tivaivai: The Social Fabric of the Cook Islands*. London: British Museum.

Lamphere, Louise. 2004. "The Convergence of Applied, Practicing, and Public Anthropology in the 21st Century." Social Science Database. *Human Organization* 63(4): 431–42.

Laslett, Peter, ed. 1960 [1689]. *Two Treatises of Government*. Cambridge: Cambridge University Press.

Leach, M. 2015. "The Ebola Crisis and Post-2015 Development." *Journal of International Development* 27(6): 816–34.

Leonard, David. 1974. *Reaching the Peasant Farmer*. Chicago: Chicago University Press.

Lewis, David. 2010. "Political Ideologies and Non-Governmental Organizations: An Anthropological Perspective." *Journal of Political Ideologies* 15(3): 333–45.

Lewis, D., and S. Madon. 2004. "Information Systems and Nongovernmental Development Organizations: Advocacy, Organizational Learning, and Accountability." *Information Society* 20: 117–26.

Lewis, D., and D. Mosse, eds. 2006. *Development Brokers and Translators: The Ethnography of Aid and Agencies*. Bloomfield, CT: Kumarian.

Lewis, Oscar. "Culture of Poverty." In Moynihan, *On Understanding Poverty*, 187–220.

Lienhardt, Godfrey. 1993. "Frazer's Anthropology: Science and Sensibility." *Journal of the Anthropological Society of Oxford* 24(1): 1–12.

Liese, Bernhard H., Paramjit S. Sachdeva, and D. Glynn Cochrane. 1991. "Organizing and Managing Tropical Disease Programs." Technical Paper no. 159, World Bank, Washington, DC.

Lipton Michael. 1977. *Why Poor People Stay Poor: Urban Bias in World Development*. Cambridge: Harvard University Press.

Little, Paul E. 1999. "Environments and Environmentalisms in Anthropological Research: Facing a New Millennium." *Annual Review of Anthropology* 28: 253–60.

Locke, John. 1960 [1689]. "The Second Treatise of Government." In Laslett, *Two Treatises of Government*.

Lofstedt, Ragnar E., and Ortwin Renn. 1997. "The Brent Spar Controversy: An Example of Risk Communication Gone Wrong." *Risk Analysis* 17(2).

Luther, Linda. 2005. "The National Environmental Policy Act: Background and Implementation." Congressional Research Office, Washington, DC..

Lutzenberger, J. 1985. "The World Bank's Polonoroeste Project: A Social and Environmental Catastrophe." *Ecologist* 15(1985) 69–72.

Maimbo, Samuel Munzele, and Dilip Ratha, eds. 2005. *Remittances Development Impact and Future Prospects*. Washington, DC: World Bank.

Maitland, Frederic Sumner. 1900. "The Corporation Sole." *Law Quarterly Review* 16.

Malinowski, Bronislav. 1929. "Practical Anthropology." *Africa* 2: 22–38.

Malinowski, Bronislav. 1934. *Introduction to Ian Hogbin, Law and Order in Polynesia*. New York: Harcourt Brace & Co..

Malinowski, Bronislav. 1945. *The Dynamics of Culture Change*. New Haven, CT: Yale University Press.

Mangin, William, ed. 1970. *Peasants in Cities. Readings in the Anthropology of Urbanization*. Boston: Houghton Mifflin.

Marshall, D. 1927. "The Old Poor Law R." *Economic History Review* 8(1).

Masefield, B. 1950. *A Short History of Agriculture in the British Colonies*. Oxford: Oxford University Press.

Masefield, G. B. 1976. "Anthropology and Agricultural Extension Work." In Cochrane, *What We Can Do for Each Other*.

Mauss, Marcel. 1967. *The Gift*. Translated by Ian Cunnison. New York: Norton.

Mawhood, P., ed. 1983. *Local Government in the Third World*, 2nd ed. Pretoria: Africa Institute.

Mawhood, P., ed. 1993. "The Search for Participation in Tanzania." In Mawhood, *Local Government*.

Mayer, J. P. 1955. *Max Weber and German Politics*. London: Faber & Faber.

Mayfield, James B. 1986. *Go to The People*. West Hartford, CT: Kumarian.

McClelland, David. 1961. *The Achieving Society*. New York, Van Nostrand.

McIntosh, Malcolm, Deborah Leipziger, Keith Jones, and Gill Coleman. 1998. *Successful Strategies for Responsible Companies*. London: Financial Times Management.

Mednick, Sam. 2018. "Q&A: How UNICEF is mapping South Sudan's most remote states." Devex, 8 May. https://www.devex.com/news/q-a-how-unicef-is-mapping-south-sudan-s-most-remote-states-92666.

Mehta, Lyla. 2000. "The World Bank and Its Emerging Knowledge Empire." *Human Organisation* 60(2): 189–96.

Meier, Gerald, and Joseph E. Stiglitz. 2001. *Frontiers of Development Economics: The Future in Perspective*. Washington, DC: World Bank.

Meltzer, Allan H. et al. 2000. *Report of the International Financial Institution Advisory Commission*. Senate Committee on Banking, Housing, and Urban Affairs. Washington, DC.

Mencher, Samuel. 1967. "The Problem of Measuring Poverty." *British Journal of Sociology* 19.

Meren, Michael. 2002. *The Road to Hell: The Ravaging Effects of Foreign Aid and International Charity*. New York: Free Press.

Merkle, R. 2003. "Ningxia's Third Road to Rural Development: Resettlement Schemes as a Last Means to Poverty Reduction? *Journal of Peasant Studies* 30(3/4).

Merton, Robert. 1949. "Bureaucratic Structure and Personality." In Merton, *Social Theory and Social Structure*.

Merton, Robert. 1949. *Social Theory and Social Structure*. New York: Free Press.

Miller, Barbara D. 1981. *The Endangered Sex: Neglect of Female Children in Rural North India*. Ithaca, NY: Cornell University Press.

Minogue, Martin, and Judith Molloy, eds. 1974. *African Aims and Attitudes, Selected Documents*. London: Cambridge University Press.

Montgomery, John D., and Milton Esman. 1971. "Popular Participation in Development Administration." *Administration in Society* 3(3): 358–83.

Morse, Bradford, and Thomas R. Berger. 1992. *Sardar Sarovar: Report of the Independent Review*. Ottawa: Resource Futures International.

Mosse, David, ed. 2013. *Adventures in Aidland: The Anthropology of Professionals in International Development*. Oxford: Berghahn Books.

Mosse, David. 2013. "The Anthropology of International Development." *Annual Review of Anthropology* 42(October): 227–246.

Mosse, David. 2013. "Social Analysis as Corporate Product: Non-Economists/Anthropologists at Work at the World Bank in Washington DC." In Mosse, *Adventures in Aidland*.

Mosse, David. 2014. "Knowledge as Relational: Reflections on Knowledge in International Development." *Forum for Development Studies* 41(3): 513–523. DOI:10.1080/08039410. 20.14 959379.

Mosse, David. 2006. "SOAS, Localized Cosmopolitans: Anthropologists at the World Bank." Paper prepared for "Cosmopolitanism and Development," Panel 4, ASA Conference, Keele, Staffordshire.

Mosse, David. 2013. "Social Analysis as Corporate Product, Non-Economists/Anthropologists at Work at the World Bank in Washington, DC." In Mosse, *Adventures in Aidland*.

Mosse, David, and David Lewis. 2005. *The Aid Effect: Giving and Governing in International Development.* London: Pluto Press.

Moynihan, Daniel P. 1969. *On Understanding Poverty: Perspectives from the Social Sciences.* New York: Basic Books.

Noronha, Raymond. 1979. "Social and Cultural Dimensions of Tourism." Staff Working Paper no. 326, World Bank, Washington, Washington, DC.

Noronha, Raymond. 1985. "A Review of the Literature on Land Tenure Systems in Sub-Saharan Africa (English)." Agricultural Research Unit, Discussion Paper no. 43, World Bank, Washington, DC.

Nunberg, Barbara. 1990. *Public Sector Management Issues in Structural Adjustment Lending.* Washington, DC: World Bank.

O'Reilly, John Boyle. 1915. "In Bohemia." In *The Cry for Justice: An Anthology of the Literature of Social Protest*, edited by Upton Sinclair. Philadelphia: The John C. Winston Co. www.bartleby.com/71/.

O'Rourke, P. J. 1998. *Eat the Rich: A Treatise on Economics.* London: Picador.

Orwell, George. 1949. *Nineteen Eighty-four.* London: Secker and Warburgh.

Palmier, Leslie. 1985. *The Control of Bureaucratic Corruption: Case Studies in Asia.* New Delhi: Allied Publishers Private.

Perry, Richard. 1996. *From Time Immemorial: Indigenous Peoples and State Systems.* Austin: University of Texas Press.

Peters, Tom, and Robert H. Waterman Jr. 1982. *In Search of Excellence.* New York: Harper-Collins.

Petts J., ed. 1999. *Handbook of Environmental Impact Assessment*, vol. 1. Oxford: Blackwell.

Pfiffner, John M., and Frank P. Sherwood. 1960. *Administrative Organization.* Englewood Cliffs, NJ: Prentice Hall.

Pitt, David C., ed.. 1976. *Development from Below: Anthropologist and Development Situations.* The Hague: Mouton.

Please, Stanley. 1984. *The Hobbled Giant.* Boulder, CO: Westview Press, 1984.

Poverty: A Violation of Human Rights. 1999. Report of the Civil/Global Conference for Poverty Eradication, October 14–16, Council of Europe, Strasbourg.

Practical Concepts Inc. 1979. "The Logical Framework: A Managers Guide to A Scientific Approach to Design and Evaluation." Practical Concepts, Washington DC.

Purcell, Trevor W. 1998. "Indigenous Knowledge and Applied Anthropology: Questions of Definition and Direction." *Human Organization* 57(3): 258–72.

Quodling, Paul. 1991. *Bougainville: The Mine and the People*. Sydney, Australia: Centre for Independent Studies.

Radelet, Steve. 2005. *Grants for the World's Poorest: How the World Bank Should Distribute Its Funds*. Washington, DC: Center for Global Development (CGD).

Rawls, John. 1999 [1958]. "Justice as Fairness." *Philosophical Review* 67(2): 164–94. Reprinted in Freeman, *John Rawls*.

Redford, E. S. 1958. *Ideal and Practice in Public Administration*. Birmingham: University of Alabama Press.

Rich, Bruce. 1998. *Mortgaging the Earth: The World Bank, Environment and the Crisis of Development*. Boston: Beacon Press.

Rigg, Jonathan. 1991. "Land Settlement in Southeast Asia: The Indonesian Transmigration Program." In Rigg, *Southeast Asia*, 80–108, 160–191.

Rigg, Jonathan. 1991. *Southeast Asia: A Region in Transition*. London: Unwin Hyman.

Robertson, A. F. 1984. "People and the State: An Anthropology of Planned Development." *Cambridge Studies in Social Anthropology*, vol. 52. Cambridge University Press, 1984.

Robertson, Robert A. 1998. "Social Impact Assessment and the Public Involvement Process." In Burdge, *A Conceptual Approach*.

Rogger, Daniel. 2018. "How Does Anthropology Help Us Understand Bureaucracy?" [blog], January 4. World Bank, Washington, DC.

Rondinelli, D. A., J. R. Nellis, and G. S. Cheema. 1983. "Decentralization in Developing Countries: A Review of Recent Experience." Staff Working Paper No. 581, World Bank, Washington, DC.

Rowntree, Seebohm B., and G. Lavers. 1991. *Poverty and the Welfare State: A Third Social Survey of Youth Dealing Only with Economic Questions*. London: Longmans, Green and Company.

Rylko-Bauer, Barbara, Merrill Singer, and John van Willigen. 2006. "Reclaiming Applied Anthropology: Its Past, Present, and Future." *American Anthropologist* 108(1): 178–98.

Sainsbury, C., C. Wilkins, D. Haddad, G. Sweeney, et al. 2011. *Generation Next: A Look at Future Greenfield Growth Projects, Citi Investment Analysis*. New York: Citibank.

Salisbury, Richard S. 1976. "The Anthropologist as Societal Ombudsman." In Pitt, *Development from Below*.

Salmen, Lawrence F. 1987. *Listen to the People: Participant Observation Evaluation of Development Projects*. Oxford: Oxford University Press for the World Bank.

Santayana, George. 1968. *Santayana on America: Essays, Notes, and Letters on American Life, Literature, and Philosophy*. New York: Harcourt, Brace & World.

Schumacher, E. F. 1966. *Buddhist Economics*. London: New Economics Institute.

Schumpeter, E. F. 2010. "Principle before Profit." *The Economist*, November 25.

Scott, Dick. 1991. *Years of the Pooh-Bah: A Cook Island History*. Auckland: Hodder and Stoughton.

Scudder, T. 1987. "Opportunities, Issues and Achievement in Development Anthropology since the Mid-1960s: A Personal View." *Anthropology UCLA* Winter.

Sharma, Patrick Allan. 2017. *Robert McNamara's Other War: The World Bank and International Development*. Philadelphia: University of Pennsylvania Press.

Shaw, George Bernard. 1949. *Back to Methuselah*. In *Selected Plays with Prefaces*, vol. 2. New York: Dodd Mead & Co.

Shell Oil Company. 1998. *Business and Human Rights: A Management Primer*. London.

Shokeid, Moshe. 2007. "From the Tikopia to Polymorphous Engagements: Ethnographic Writing under Changing Fieldwork Circumstances." *Social Anthropology/Anthropologie Sociale* 15(3): 305–19.

Short, Clare. 1997. *Eliminating World Poverty: A Challenge for the 21st Century*. Presented to Parliament by the Secretary of State for International Development [Clare Short] by Command of Her Majesty. November 1997. http://webarchive.nationalarchives.gov.uk/20050404190659/http:/www.dfid.gov.uk/Pubs/files/whitepaper1997.pdf.

Sierra Club. 1987. *Bankrolling Disasters: International Development Banks and the Global Environment*. San Francisco: Sierra Club.

Sillitoe, Paul. 2006. "Ethnobiology and Applied Anthropology: Rapprochement of the Academic with the Practical." *Journal of the Royal Anthropological Institute*, suppl. Ethnobiology and the Science of Humankind, London, S119–S142.

Simmel, George. 1965. "The Poor." *Social Problems* 13(2, Fall).

Simon, Herbert A. 1961. *Administrative Behavior*. New York: Macmillan.

Skyrms, Brian. 1996. *Evolution of the Social Contract*. Cambridge: Cambridge University Press.

Small, M. L., D. J. Harding, and M. Lamont. 2010. "Reconsidering Culture and Poverty." *Annals of the American Academy of Political and Social Science* 629(1): 6–27.

Smillie, Ian. 1995. *The Alms Bazaar, Altruism under Fire: Non-Profit Organizations and International Development*. London: Intermediate Technology Publications.

Sorokin, Pitrikim. 1936. "Is Accurate Social Planning Possible?" *American Sociological Review* 1(1, February).

Spicer, Edward H. 1952. *Human Problems in Technological Change: A Casebook*. New York: Russell Sage Foundation.

Stern, Ernest. 1991. "Beyond the Transition." 20th World Conference of the Society for International Development. Amsterdam, May.

Stocking, George W. Jr. 1996. *After Tylor: British Social Anthropology 1888–1951*. London: Athlone Press.

Strathern, Andrew. 1971. *The Rope of Moka: Big Men and Ceremonial Exchange in the Mount Hagen Area of Papua New Guinea*. Cambridge: Cambridge University Press.

Strathern, Marilyn. 1995. *The Relation: Issues in Complexity and Scale*. Cambridge: Prickly Pear Press.

Strathern, Marilyn, M. 1996. "The Nice Thing about Culture Is That Everyone Has It." In Strathern, *Shifting Contexts*, 153–76.

Strathern, M., ed. 1996. *Shifting Contexts: Transformations in Anthropological Knowledge*. London: Routledge.

Streeten, Paul. 1976. "Why Interdisciplinary Studies." In Cochrane, *What We Can Do.*

Streeten, Paul, Shahid Javed Burki, Mahbub Ul Haq, Norman Hicks, and Frances Stewart. 1981. *First Things First: Meeting Basic Human Needs in Developing Countries.* New York: Oxford University Press.

Swithern, Sophia, et al. 2015. *Global Humanitarian Assistance Report.* London: Development Initiatives, 2015.

Tendler, Judith. 1975. *Inside Foreign Aid.* Baltimore: Johns Hopkins University Press.

Teskey, Graham, and Richard Hooper. 1999. "Tanzania Civil Service Reform Programme Case Study." UN African Training and Research Centre in Administration for Development, Addis Ababa. http://unpan1.un.org/ intradoc/groups/public/documents/CAFRAD/UNPAN010583.pdf.

Therkildsen, Ole. 1988. *Watering White Elephants? Lessons from Donor Funded Planning and Implementation of Rural Water Supplies in Tanzania.* Uppsala, Sweden: Scandinavian Institute of African Studies.

Thompson, Victor. 1961. *Modern Organization.* New York: Knopf.

Thurnwald, Richard. 1929. "Price of White Man's Peace." *Pacific Affairs* 9(3): 32–40.

Tolstoy, Leo. 2017 [1873–1877]. *Anna Karenina.* In *The Complete Works of Leo Tolstoy.* Translated by Louise Maude et. al. Musaicum Books.

ul Haq, Mahbub. 1976. *The Poverty Curtain: Choices for the Third World.* New York: Columbia University Press.

United Nations Development Programme (UNDP). 1991. "Poverty Alleviation in Asia and the Pacific: Report of a Regional Workshop." Kuala Lumpur, May.

United Nations Development Programme (UNDP). 1993. *Human Development Report.* New York: Oxford University Press.

United Nations Development Programme (UNDP). 1994. *Human Development Report.* New York: Oxford University Press.

United Nations Development Programme (UNDP). 1995. *Human Development Report.* New York: Oxford University Press.

Uphoff, Norman. 1994. "Why NGOs Are Not a Third Sector." Paper presented at Manchester University Workshop on NGOs and development: performance and accountability in the new world order. Manchester, June.

Uphoff, Norman. 2000. "Social Capital: Learning from the Analysis and Experience of Participation." In Dasgupta and Serageldin, *A Multifaceted Perspective.*

USAID. N.d. "Social Soundness Analysis." ADS Supplementary Reference: 200. http://www.usaidgems.org/Documents/ADS200HelpDoc_ SocialSoundnessAnalysis.doc.

Valdez, Joseph, and Michael Bamberger. 1994. "Monitoring and Evaluating Social Programs in Developing Countries." EDI Development Studies, World Bank, Washington, DC.

Valentine, Charles A. 1968. *The Culture of Poverty.* Chicago: University of Chicago Press.

Van Willigen, J. 1993. *Applied Anthropology: An Introduction.* London: Westport.

Vetterlein, Antje. 2012. "Seeing Like the World Bank on Poverty." *New Political Economy* 17(1): 35–58.

Wade, R. H. 2013. "Protecting Power: Western States in Global Organizations." In Held and Roger, *Global Governance.*

Waldo, Dwight. 1961. "Organization Theory: An Elephantine Problem." *Public Administration Review* 21: 210–25.

Waldo, Dwight. 1968. "Development in the West: The Administrative Framework." Paper delivered at the State University of New York at Albany.

Walsh, J. A. 1988. "Selectivity Within Primary Health Care." *Social Science and Medicine* 26(9): 899–902.

Walsh J. A., and K. S. Warren. 1980. "Selective Primary Health Care: An Interim Strategy for Disease Control in Developing Countries." *Social Science and Medicine* 14C: 145–64.

Walton, Michael. 2000. "Do the World Bank, IMF and WTO Help the Poor?" *The Ecologist* 30(6): 1.

Warde, F. 1961. "Mills and Marx." *International Socialist Review* 22(1, 1/61): 11–16.

Weber, Marianne. 1988. *Max Weber.* Translated by N. Zohn. New Brunswick, NJ: Transition.

Weber, Max. 1968. *Economy and Society,* vols. 1, 2, 3. Edited by Guenther Roth and Claus Wittich. New York: Bedminster Press.

Weber, Max. 1958. *The Protestant Ethic and the Spirit of Capitalism.* Translated by Talcott Parsons. New York: Scribners.

Weber, Max. 1947. *The Theory of Economic and Social Organization.* Translated by A. M. Henderson and Talcott Parsons. New York, Oxford University Press.

Whitten, Norman E., and John F. Szwed, eds. 1970. *Afro-American Anthropology: Contemporary Perspectives.* Foreword by Sidney W. Mintz. New York: Free Press.

Wilbur, Charles K. 1984. *The Political Economy of Underdevelopment.* New York: Random House.

Williams, Oliver F. 2004. "The UN Global Compact: The Challenge and the Promise." *Business Ethics Quarterly* 14(4, October): 755–74.

Wilmsen, Brooke. 2011. "Development for Whom? Rural to Urban Resettlement at the Three Gorges Dam, China." *Asian Studies Review* 35(1): 160–91.

Wilson, Richard A., ed. 1997. *Human Rights and Cultural Context: Anthropological Perspectives.* London: Pluto Press.

Wisbey, Herbert A. Jr. 1955. *Soldiers without Swords: A History of the Salvation Army in the United States.* New York: Macmillan.

Wolfensohn, James D. 1999. "Address to the Board of Governors." World Bank, Washington, DC, September 28.

Wolfensohn, James D. 1999. "A Proposal for a Comprehensive Development Framework, Discussion Draft." World Bank, Washington, DC.

Wolfensohn, James D. 2005. *Voices for the World's Poor: Selected Speeches of the World Bank President James D. Wolfensohn, 1995–2005.* Washington, DC: World Bank.

Woo, Wing Thye. 1990. "The Art of Economic Development: Markets, Politics, and Externalities." *International Organization* 44(3, Summer): 403–29.

World Bank. 1971. Press release, September 27. World Bank, Washington, DC.

World Bank. 1974. *Environmental, Health, and Human Ecologic Considerations in Economic Development Projects.* Washington, DC: World Bank.

World Bank. 1974. Press release, September 30. World Bank, Washington, DC.

World Bank. 1981. *Annual Report 1981.* Washington, DC: World Bank.

World Bank. 1980. *World Development Report 1980.* Washington, DC: World Bank.

World Bank. 1989. *World Development Report 1989: Financial Systems and Development.* New York: Oxford University Press.

World Bank. 1990. *World Development Report 1990: Poverty.* New York: Oxford University Press.

World Bank. 1993. *World Development Report 1993: Investing in Health.* New York: Oxford University Press.

World Bank. 1994. *World Development Report 1994: Infrastructure for Development.* New York: Oxford University Press.

World Bank. 1995. *World Development Report 1995: Workers in an Integrating World.* New York: Oxford University Press.

World Bank. 1999. *Poverty Trends and Voices of the Poor 1999.* New York: Oxford University Press.

World Bank. 1999. *World Development Report 1999/2000: Entering the 21st Century.* New York: Oxford University Press.

World Bank. 2000. "IBRD Articles of Agreement." As amended February 16, 1989. World Bank, Washington, DC. http://siteresources.worldbank.org/ EXTABOUTUS/Resources/ibrd-articlesofagreement.pdf.

World Bank. 2001. *World Development Report 2000/2001: Attacking Poverty.* New York: Oxford University Press.

World Bank. 2015. "World Bank Forecasts Global Poverty to Fall Below 10% for First Time; Major Hurdles Remain in Goal to End Poverty by 2030." Press release, 4 October. World Bank, Washington, DC

World Bank. 2017. Press release, April 5. World Bank, Washington, DC

World Bank. **2017**. *World Development Report 2017: Governance and the Law.* Washington, DC: World Bank.

World Bank. n.d. "Open Knowledge Repository." https://openknowledge.world bank.org/.

World Bank Independent Evaluation Group. 2010. *Cost Benefit Analysis in World Bank Projects.* Washington, DC: World Bank.

World Bank Independent Evaluation Group. 2017. *Growth for the Bottom 40 Percent: The World Bank Group's Support for Shared Prosperity.* Washington, DC: World Bank.

World Bank Institute. 2005. "Introduction to Poverty Analysis." World Bank, Washington, DC.

World Bank Institute. 2017. "Analysis of Poverty." World Bank, Washington, DC.

World Health Organization (WHO) and Cook Islands Ministry of Health. 2012. *Health Sector Delivery Performance.* Rarotonga, Cook Islands.

Worsley, Peter. 1968. *The Trumpet Shall Sound*. New York: Schoken.

Worsley, Peter. 1973. *Two Blades of Grass: Rural Cooperatives in Agricultural Modernization*. New York: Wiley.

Wright, Graham A. N. 2000. *Microfinance Systems: Designing Quality Financial Services for the Poor*. London: Zed Books.

Wright, James D., ed. 2015. *International Encyclopaedia of the Social and Behavioral Sciences*. Amsterdam: Elsevier.

Yekutiel, P. 1981. "Lessons from the Big Eradication Campaigns." *World Health Forum* 2: 465–90.

Yen, Y. C. James. 1975. *The Ting Hsien Experiment in 1934*. Cavite, Philippines: International Institute for Rural Reconstruction.

Yoshida, Nobuo, Hiroki Uematsu, and Carlos E. Sobrado, 2014. "Is Extreme Poverty Going to End? An Analytical Framework to Evaluate Progress in Ending Extreme Poverty." Policy Research Working Paper, No. 6740. Washington, DC, World Bank. SSRN: https://ssrn.com/abstract=2375459.

Young, Crawford. 1976. *The Politics of Cultural Pluralism*. Madison: University of Wisconsin Press.

Zadek, Simon. 2001. *The Civil Corporation: The New Economy of Corporate Citizenship*. London: Earthscan.

Zhang, T. F., and Y. F. Zhang. 1999. The Practice of Accepting Rural Resettlers into Factories in the City of Yima. *Memorandums of Hydraulics, Poverty Relief, and Development of Reservoir Areas* 2: 28–31.

INDEX